THE
SALMON RIVERS
OF THE NORTH HIGHLANDS AND
THE OUTER HEBRIDES

THE
SALMON RIVERS
OF THE NORTH HIGHLANDS AND
THE OUTER HEBRIDES

Andrew Graham-Stewart

ROBERT HALE · LONDON

ISBN 0 7090 7589 8

Robert Hale Limited
Clerkenwell House
Clerkenwell Green
London EC1R 0HT

A catalogue record for this book is available from the British Library

2 4 6 8 10 9 7 5 3 1

Typeset by e-type, Liverpool
Printed by
Kyodo Printing Co (S'pore) Pte Limited, Singapore

CONTENTS

NORTH HIGHLANDS

OUTER HEBRIDES

Dedicated to the memory of my father Colin Graham-Stewart, who introduced me to the wild parts of the Highlands and Islands and instilled in me a lifelong love of fishing.

ACKNOWLEDGEMENTS

I am indebted to a great many people who have assisted with my research for this volume. They include current and previous owners of fishings and estates, river managers, factors and gillies. Some have worked on particular beats or rivers for decades (in some cases for the best part of half a century), acquiring that special depth of insight which only a close association with a river throughout the year can bring. These individuals, both on the riverbank and elsewhere, have given freely of their time and allowed full access to their records and other material. I am immensely grateful to them all.

In addition, I wish particularly to thank the following: Sandy Leventon, editor of *Trout and Salmon*, who has been most encouraging as this project developed and has published some of the material in article form; George MacDonald, David S.D. Jones and Tony Scherr, who were invaluable sources for the history and background to many of the Outer Hebridean systems; Mark Farrer, who was especially helpful with detail on the systems of the far north-west of the mainland; Niall Graham-Campbell, who contributed much detail on the Carron, Oykel and Naver; Iain McMyn (Kyle of Sutherland DSFB), Dr Mark Bilsby (Western Isles Fisheries Trust), Peter Cunningham (Wester Ross Fisheries Trust), and Dr Shona Marshall (West Sutherland Fisheries Trust), who provided pertinent advice on a scientific level and reviewed the draft chapters relevant to their areas; Mrs Olive Geddes of the National Library of Scotland, who helped me steer a course through the seemingly endless archive of Sutherland Estate papers.

Michael Wigan, whose understanding of the sporting estates of the north is unparalleled, read the manuscript and made innumerable suggestions to the considerable benefit of the final text. And finally my wife Annette also read the draft, bringing much objective clarity of vision.

FOREWORD

BY JEREMY PAXMAN

For anyone who loves salmon fishing, the rivers of the northern Highlands are a sort of heaven. Tumbling through untamed hills, splattered by cascading water-falls and punctuated with deep resting pools, they are places to dream about.

By comparison with the more plutocratic rivers – the Spey, Dee, Tay and Tweed – these are smaller, more sensitive and unpredictable watercourses, in which guile is more important than firepower. Their banks are not mown, there are very few places indeed where you need a boat, and very many where you can wade across the stream. In places, on some of them, you will have to walk long distances and scramble up and down gorges, just to be able to flick a fly down a few yards of water, or to dibble at the head of a run. When times are hard and there has been no decent rain, you may trudge for a mile for the sake of no more than a few casts. But for the sheer pleasure of a day spent walking, wading and fishing rivers as you sense they ought to be fished, they can't be beaten.

They are just about all spate rivers, of course. Which means that in summer, everyone spends the week before their arrival scanning the forecasts and praying for some decent rain. I suspect I am not alone in saying to friends that if the condi-tions are bad we simply won't go. But then we always go anyway, whatever the weather. And it's always worth it, even if there's nothing much to be caught.

Famously, no fisherman can ever cross a bridge without looking down and wondering what's in the water below. When I was younger, these rivers seemed the preserve of tweedy old gents with strange stains on their breeks and the sort of voices which, a foreigner once observed, 'the English reserve for their women and their dogs'. The chances of getting to cast a fly oneself seemed vanishingly remote. It's probably still true that the surest way to get out onto the best of the northern rivers is to have a generous friend or a relative who dies conveniently. But, as Andrew Graham-Stewart shows in an appendix, almost all of them have owners and agents who want a steady stream of tenants.

Most salmon rivers seem to have pools named after ancient fisherfolk. Almost all have one called 'The Major's' or 'The Colonel's', where in the dim recesses of time titanic struggles took place between a monster fish and a man with a luxuriant moustache, or others where vast numbers of salmon were caught on a fly tied up from a few strands of tweed plucked from a gillie's deerstalker. Those days were long ago, and may never return (although we all refuse to give up hope). But the stories of enormous fish and the colourful characters who took them will sustain all of us on long winter evenings.

Sometimes the origins of the names of these pools are obvious. There is, for example, one on the upper Brora called 'Plank' for the entirely understandable reason that there is no plank across it. Others, like the many Nordic-sounding pools on the Naver, are endlessly mysterious. The names of pools tell the history of these rivers, and sometimes, late at night, over a glass or six of whisky, one can dimly recall the explanation a gillie once offered.... But the precise details are opaque.

No one has attempted a comprehensive survey of these wonderful rivers for a century. Their history is fascinating, and here you have a chance to wander along their banks without ever leaving your armchair.

ILLUSTRATIONS

NORTH UIST

SOUTH UIST

All illustrations by Andrew Graham-Stewart

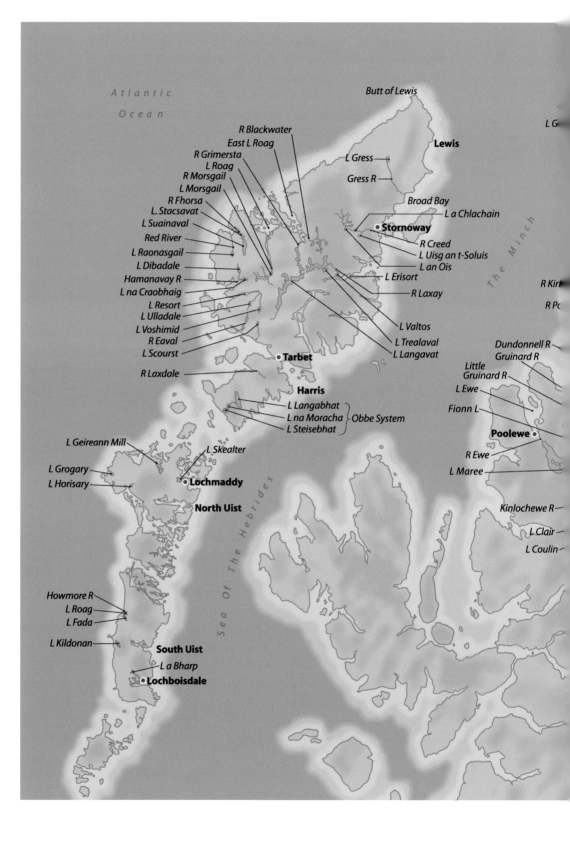

Atlantic

Ocean

Butt of Lewis

R Blackwater

East L Roag

R Grimersta

L Roag

R Morsgail

L Morsgail

R Fhorsa

L. Stacsavat

L Suainaval

Red River

L Raonasgail

L Dibadale

Hamanavay R

L na Craobhaig

L Resort

L Ulladale

L Voshimid

R Eaval

L Scourst

R Laxdale

Lewis

L Gress

Gress R

Broad Bay

L a Chlachain

● **Stornoway**

R Creed

L Uisg an t-Soluis

L an Ois

L Erisort

R Laxay

L Valtos

L Trealaval

L Langavat

● **Tarbet**

Harris

L Langabhat

L na Moracha } Obbe System

L Steisebhat

L Geireann Mill

L Skealter

L Grogary

L Horisary

● **Lochmaddy**

North Uist

Sea Of The Hebrides

The Minch

L G

R Kir

R Po

Dundonnell R

Gruinard R

Little

Gruinard R

L Ewe

Fionn L

● **Poolewe**

R Ewe

L Maree

Kinlochewe R

L Clair

L Coulin

Howmore R

L Roag

L Fada

L Kildonan

South Uist

L a Bharp

● **Lochboisdale**

Cape Wrath

R Dionard
L Dionard
R Grudie
Durness
Kyle of Tongue
L Eriboll
R Borgie
Strathy Point
R Dyke
L Shurrery
R Forss
Thurso
R Thurso
R Hope
R Polla
Melvich
R Halladale
L Watten
R Wick
L Hope
Tongue
Bettyhill
Strathy R
L Strathy
L Loyal
L Choire
R Naver
L. More
Wick
Laxford Bridge
R Strathmore
L Naver
Badanloch
Little River
L More
R Mudale
Altnaharra
R Mallart
Bannock Burn
Dunbeath R
L Assynt
R Blackwater
Dunbeath
R Berriedale
R Tirry
R Langwell
Berriedale
R Loanan
L Shin
R Skinsdale
Helmsdale
Fionn L.
R Cassley
R Brora
R Helmsdale
scaig
L Ailsh
Lairg
R Shin
L Brora
R Brora
Kanaird
R Oykel
R Fleet
Brora
R Einig
Rosehall
R Carnaig
Golspie
pool R
L Achall
Kyle of Sutherland
L Fleet
Ullapool
R Blackwater
Bonar Bridge
R Evelix
R Douchary
R Carron
Dornoch
Dornoch Firth
R Broom
R Blackwater
Moray Firth
L Morie
R Alness
Alness
Cromarty Firth
L Luichart
R Blackwater
Inner Moray Firth
R. Bran
Dingwall
Nairn
Forres
L Meig
R Conon
R Meig
Orrin Reservoir
R Orrin
Beauly
Inverness
R Farrar
R Ness
R Nairn
R Beauly
R Findhorn
R Cannich
R Glass
L Duntelchaig
R Affric
Tomatin
L Affric
R Findhorn
Loch Ness
R Moriston
Fort Augustus
R Garry
R Oich
L Garry
L Oich

INTRODUCTION

In the 1980s and early 1990s I spent an inordinate amount of time spring fishing for salmon in the North Highlands. This included one or two weeks each February on the River Helmsdale. In this context 'spring' is something of a misnomer for a month that readily produces some of the most extreme winter weather. These sojourns were the perfect antidote to a frenetic business life, in particular several years based in New York City.

Early spring fishing is not prolific – just the occasional salmon. Each one is truly memorable, though; indeed no one could forget a springer landed in the teeth of a horizontal blizzard. Such fishing also involves long periods when one is simply going through the motions. Fish rarely show, and, aside from brief encounters with kelts, there is little to interrupt one's thoughts. Mine often drifted to the history of the river in terms of salmon and salmon angling. Inevitably, this soon broadened to encompass the other northern rivers that I knew.

As I began to delve and research further, I was struck by the dearth of literature in this field. Augustus Grimble (*The Salmon Rivers of Scotland*, 1899) wrote from Brighton and clearly had, as I have identified, little first-hand knowledge of some of the northern systems. William Calderwood (*The Salmon Rivers and Lochs of Scotland*, 1909) was much better informed and distinctly unimpressed by some of Grimble's inaccuracies (he was after all the Edinburgh-based Inspector of Salmon Fisheries for Scotland), although himself by no means infallible. Both these volumes, whilst immensely useful, are nonetheless in essence snapshots of their time.

In recent years I have found myself ideally placed to explore the history and traditions of the northern rivers. Whilst I have known the North Highlands and Outer Isles, and the area's rivers and lochs, from boyhood and have been resident in Sutherland since 1995, my understanding has increased immeasurably since 1998, when I took on the responsibility for writing the monthly reports on most of the significant mainland northern systems for *Trout and Salmon* magazine. To produce these I have frequent contact with an extensive network of gillies, bailiffs, angling clubs, estate factors and river owners. Inevitably, their detailed expertise has furthered my own knowledge.

In this volume I have set out to chronicle the development of each river system, where possible going back to around 1800 (i.e. before the growth of angling) and then right through the nineteenth and twentieth centuries to the present day. On the mainland the geographical limits – from the Findhorn in the east to the Ewe in the west – mirror those of my reports for *Trout and Salmon*. By and large the criterion for a river's inclusion is the existence of a tradition of organized salmon angling; sea trout are also covered, so long as salmon run the system in question. Where possible I have used original manuscript sources in my research: for instance, the vast uncatalogued archive of Sutherland Estate papers in the National Library of Scotland, most of which have clearly lain unexamined for the best part of a century, and in some instances much longer.

Of all the significant natural resources of the North Highlands and the Outer Hebrides (an area that includes much of Scotland's most inhospitable terrain), salmon was for centuries the most consistently reliable. Although the life cycle of salmon was not fully understood until the latter part of the nineteenth century, there had long been a rudimentary appreciation that, providing sufficient adult fish survived to spawn, then somehow multitudes of gleaming silver fish would emerge from the sea and run up the rivers each year. It is no coincidence that some river names in the most barren areas incorporate the old Norse word for salmon (*lax*).

The sustainable nature of the resource, plus the facts that it required virtually no husbandry and could be harvested without even venturing out into the open sea, ensured that the rights to its exploitation were always jealously guarded. It is no accident that Scotland's salmon fishings, both within river systems and in coastal waters, have been protected by legislation since the twelfth century. Originally, all salmon fishing rights emanated from the Crown, and almost universally in the north they were granted along with ownership of the adjacent land. Salmon fishing is in fact a separate heritable right; however it is only in recent years, with the further fragmentation of many of the great estates, that its severance from land ownership has developed, although this is still far from common.

Two centuries ago land (and river) ownership was highly concentrated in the hands of the few. The rise and fall of the estates of the Sutherland family is worth examining, particularly as their gradual dispersal was paralleled elsewhere. In 1816, 63 per cent of the total rents in Sutherland were payable to Sutherland Estates. This was prior to their acquisition of further great tracts of land, including 'Reay Country' (the parishes of Edrachilles, Durness and Tongue) in 1829 for £300,000, and Bighouse in 1830 for £52,000. By the latter part of the nineteenth century Sutherland Estates' empire included a dozen complete rivers (as well as 50 per cent of the Shin) and 'many minor streams'; in addition, they had exclusive coastal netting rights over 113 miles (excluding sea lochs) on the east, north and west coasts.

By the 1890s Sutherland Estates had debts of almost £300,000, whilst rental income amounted to some £50,000 per annum. The fourth Duke of Sutherland decided to reduce the estate's landholdings. In 1896 he sought Parliament's 'authority to disentail'. (Entails were commonly used by the major landowning dynasties as legal instruments to retain land in the family for generations. Once an entail was in place, the heir in possession could only sell the land, or part thereof, once a private Act of Parliament had been passed to remove the restriction of the entail; this would then permit sales of land – for instance to pay off debts.) Later that year various parts of the estate on the north and west coasts were advertised for sale, but interest was muted. In 1900 the parishes of Durness and Edrachilles were sold to William Ewing Gilmour for just £100,000, representing a massive loss on the original purchase price. This sale, together with much of the River Shin and associated land to Andrew Carnegie in 1898, did at least buy time.

A more determined effort to market numerous properties on the north coast was made in 1914. The fifth Duke wrote to the local press, explaining that large tracts were being sold because of 'excessive death duties and other taxation'. The auction catalogue was produced, but the sale was called off at the eleventh hour due to the outbreak of war. It was later rescheduled for October 1918, by which time the demand for sporting properties had plummeted, not least because many potential purchasers had not survived the war. All the same, the great dispersal proceeded, although the auction and private treaty sales realized much less than would have been the case before the war.

It is noteworthy that the Sutherland Estate landholdings were neatly parcelled up and marketed as *sporting estates*, when just a hundred years earlier such a concept had not even existed. Whilst the roots of Highland salmon angling date from about 1820, it was another forty years or so before sporting estates became sought-after entities in their own right. The early part of the nineteenth century had been a period of massive social upheaval in the northern counties.

This is not the forum for discussing the Highland Clearances – which began in the 1760s and continued through the first half of the nineteenth century – in any detail. The manner in which some inhabitants were driven from their homes was indefensible; however, such episodes were few and far between, a reality ignored by many commentators. The peasant Highlanders' way of life could not have been sustained in the long term, and the potato blights of 1846–8 underlined the fragility of their existence. As food shortages escalated, the second Duke of Sutherland, whose father had earlier sanctioned some of the most notorious evictions, distributed large sums to prevent starvation and to assist with emigration; thus, in the parish of Assynt alone, 1,000 inhabitants were helped with their passage to Canada and Cape Breton at a cost of £7,000.

It is worth emphasizing that in only a minority of cases were the inhabitants driven out, although the latter image suits the purposes of some historians and politicians with their own agendas. Particularly in the first wave of migration, the majority of emigrants departed voluntarily. They mainly went to Novia Scotia and Cape Breton with the purpose of acquiring land, for which they were able to pay. They included many who were quite well-to-do, and indeed they travelled in some of the best ships of the time. This migration, in search of greater freedom and prosperity, has been well documented by Lucille H. Campey, herself a descendant of such migrants, in her challenging book *After the Hector: The Scottish Pioneers of Nova Scotia and Cape Breton, 1773–1852*.

One should stress that the driving force behind the actual Clearances (as opposed to the economic migrations) had been the creation of massive sheep farms. The collapse in the price of wool and sheep meat from the 1870s undermined the viability of these farms, and this coincided with an increase in demand for sporting tenancies, pushing up sporting rents. To meet this demand the North Highlands were developed as sporting estates, offering a mix of shooting, stalking and fishing; hitherto this area had been largely unexploited for sporting purposes. In the forty years leading up to World War I there was a widespread programme of sporting lodge construction. The 'deer forests' with their lodges were let on an annual basis, providing a significant source of income for the major hereditary landowners. This was the pattern until 1914; between the wars the majority of these sporting units were sold off, often to the existing tenants. These units have survived, albeit with some fragmentation, and in much of the north they still retain the associated salmon fishing rights.

This structure of ownership is by no means perfect but it has served salmon well, at least compared to public or highly fragmented ownership. It has on the whole maintained the vital freshwater environment and, by limiting the number of rods, prevented overexploitation. Today's politicians who call for more public access to salmon rivers fail to appreciate that such a move would only put further pressure on stocks; the same politicians are also apparently unaware that there is already a plethora of easily accessible water either owned or controlled by angling clubs, whose members and visitors enjoy fishing at minimal cost.

Indeed it is important to expose the myth that salmon fishing remains the exclusive preserve of the wealthy. Angling club members (membership is usually restricted to local residents) can generally fish their own water throughout the season on payment of an annual subscription, the cost of which in the Highlands varies between £20 and £80. The clubs also offer day tickets to visitors for between £10 and £25 per day. Some angling club waters are extremely productive; there are four clubs within the area covered by this volume, where an annual *declared* catch of over 500 salmon is by no means exceptional. (Throughout Scotland club returns tend to underestimate the actual catch, because traditionally a significant percentage of members and visitors underdeclare their catches, partly out of concern that rents and/or subscriptions could rise if actual catches were known. It is also relevant that the declared catch determines the amount of rates payable to the fishery board.)

In the last twenty years or so salmon numbers have declined in the North Highlands and Outer Hebrides, and this fall has been almost universal across the species' range. All the available studies confirm that, for the majority of rivers covered here, there is no problem with juvenile production. Indeed, helped to some extent by the growth of catch and release in recent years, more than enough adult salmon have survived to spawn, and electro-fishing surveys consistently show excellent counts of juvenile salmon. The number of smolts going to sea has also remained high. In other words, with few exceptions, the northern rivers have been well managed; district salmon fishery boards may appear archaic but for the most part they approach their duties – the protection and improvement of the fisheries within the district, for the increase of salmon – with due diligence.

The declining trend in salmon numbers over recent years is clearly attributable to a marked increase in marine mortality: whereas in the 1960s and early 1970s the number of smolts surviving to return as adults was usually between five and ten per cent, by the 1990s this had slumped to between one and three per cent. The main reason for the decline in marine survival is understood to be changing climatic conditions in the North Atlantic; these in turn affect the availability of krill and other small organisms, which are important prey species for salmon, especially in their first months at sea. Climatic conditions would seem to be subject to great volatility, though as I write this, at the start of October 2004, it is clear that, with the current season over or drawing to a close, most systems in the north (indeed throughout most of Scotland) have seen some of the best salmon runs for many years. Some catch records are being broken; this suggests much improved availability of food, and hence better marine survival.

Climatic shifts are beyond man's control, but there are other factors affecting marine survival, which *can* be addressed – so long as there is the political will. These include halting, or at least severely limiting, the industrial sand-eel fishery (sand-eels are vital food for smolts in their first weeks at sea); tackling the problem of post-smolts being taken as a by-catch in near-surface pelagic fisheries; confronting illegal high-seas netting of adult salmon as well as illegal coastal netting (mainly in the Outer Hebrides and the north coast of the mainland); and permitting meaningful control of the burgeoning seal population. The record of pussyfooting inertia on these matters by the Scottish Executive and the Westminster Government is a source of constant frustration to all managers of salmon rivers.

The last time that the authorities took decisive action in response to a significant threat to the health of salmon fisheries north of the border was in 1971, when they moved to ban drift netting off the Scottish coast. The use of miles of monofil-ament nets (virtually invisible to fish) can have a devastating impact on salmon stocks. This reprehensible method of taking salmon in the open sea was first employed off Scotland in around 1960. Over the next decade it spiralled out of control, posing a major threat to both coastal and river interests, both of which joined forces in campaigning for the practice to be outlawed.

I have charted the history of nineteenth-century salmon netting in the north in an appendix (see p.245). There has always been a tension between angling and netting interests. Even though coastal netting was greatly reduced by buy-outs in the latter part of the twentieth century, the declining stocks have exacerbated these tensions, particularly in the context of poor marine survival of salmon and a growing appreciation that mixed-stock interceptory netting makes a mockery of attempts to manage fish on an individual-river basis. Most of the remaining coastal netting in the Highlands is centred on the north coast – notably the noto-rious Strathy Point operation (owned by the Scottish Executive). To most anglers, salmon netting is now an anachronism, a hangover from a bygone age; the contrast between today's practice of catch and release, widespread within rivers, and the efforts of netsmen to kill as many as possible could hardly be more extreme.

There is an additional, insidious and deadly pressure on migratory fish stocks in the west Highlands and Islands. The west Highlands in particular has seen the greatest crash in numbers in the last two decades; here so many of us remember wonderful sport in the 1960s and 1970s, with summer and autumn salmon, and of course sea trout. However, as we know too well, the unchecked and inexorable growth of salmon-farming has decimated the runs. All the while, the salmon-farming industry has publicly denied that it was in any way responsible. (In the 1990s the top management of one of the multinational companies used to take a week's angling on a west-coast river. Its members would readily admit to the gillie that their industry was destroying wild-fish runs, but, cynically, they signalled that they would always deny it in public.)

Migrating west-coast salmon smolts must run the gauntlet of the sea-lice concentrations of the farms before they reach open water, but sea trout, which do not venture any further than coastal waters, are especially vulnerable to infesta-tion with sea-lice; consequently many of the truly great sea-trout fisheries have been decimated. Although in recent years dialogue between wild-fish interests and the fish-farmers has improved, through the Tripartite Working Group and the development of Area Management Agreements, there has been little effective progress. Despite countless scientific studies that indicate otherwise, the industry is locked in a blanket denial mode, aided and abetted by the Scottish Executive, to whom salmon-farming is a sacred cow. (The Executive and its predecessors have been heavily subsidizing the industry for over thirty years.)

Wild-fish interests in the north of Scotland are not natural allies of the Scottish Executive. This was perhaps most apparent in the lead-up to the passing of the 2003 Land Reform Act. The latter gave crofting communities the right to buy those sections of salmon rivers that adjoin crofting land by means of compulsory purchase aided by public money. There was virtually no meaningful consultation on this despite the potential implications for employment on salmon rivers as well as investment by the existing owners. No consideration was given to where the communities would find the money to run rivers in such a way as to maintain salmon numbers for the future. The perception of riparian owners and river workers was that the legislation was based on ignorance, spite and prejudice – and this was fuelled by the admission by some politicians and activists promoting land reform that it somehow represented just revenge for historic wrongs, notably the Clearances. It remains to be seen how often the compulsory purchase provision of the Act will be used. The threat that it *could* be inevitably undermines the confidence of owners.

The importance of angling to the economy of the Highlands and the Outer Hebrides was underlined by research published in 2004 by Glasgow Caledonian University and funded by the Scottish Executive. This estimated that in this particular region (the area actually includes the Spey, which is outside the scope of this book) salmon and sea-trout anglers spend over £36 million annually, almost half of the total for Scotland as a whole. Time will tell whether the findings will help them appreciate that, particularly in the far north, the salmon is far more than just another fish.

ANDREW GRAHAM-STEWART   October 2004
Bonar Bridge
Sutherland

NOTES

1. Catch statistics, for both rods and nets, appear in every entry – for which I make no apology. However, it should be stressed that the relationship between salmon catches and stocks of fish is a complex one. Catch figures are most valuable when it comes to assessing long-term trends. Historically, there was obviously no alternative to catch data. Fish counters are a recent phenomenon, although in due course they will allow far more accurate monitoring of stocks.
2. Generally, the spelling of lochs and rivers is in accordance with the Ordnance Survey maps. I have made some exceptions to avoid confusion. For instance I have not incorporated the latest spelling of Loch Voshimid, the well-known loch in North Harris; in the 2002 Landranger edition this has evolved into an unrecognizable Loch Bhoisimid.

North Highlands

FINDHORN

The country close to the lower Findhorn has suffered a catalogue of episodes demonstrating nature's overwhelming power. But, despite the river's awesome reputation for floods, the natural phenomena that have had the most enduring legacy relate not to water but to sand.

The Culbin Sands, stretching for eight miles to the west of the Findhorn estuary, were always notoriously menacing. Time and time again over the centuries the dunes would shift, in great sandstorms more akin to the Sahara than the inner Moray Firth, engulfing all that lay in their path. The best-documented movement occurred in 1694, when quite literally waves of drifting sand overwhelmed thousands of fertile acres of the estate of Culbin, including its mansion. It remains buried, although the sands are now largely stabilized through the judicious planting of conifers, and this vast area is still bereft of any dwellings. Two villages of 'Findhorn' were lost to either the sand or the sea, and the present village stands on the opposite side of Findhorn Bay, in recognition of the fact that some forces are irresistible.

The River Findhorn rises high in the Monadhliath Mountains between the watersheds of the Spey and the Nairn. Its catchment is 346 square miles, and its course runs for 62 miles through very varied terrain. A fan of rivulets, all rising between 2,500 and 3,000 feet, combine above Coignafearn Lodge to form the head of the river. Thereafter the strath (known as Strathdearn) gradually opens up, whilst the Findhorn maintains its pace, absorbing a steady succession of tributaries. Below Tomatin it takes a meandering path for five miles, before it enters a narrow and enchanting ravine section (the Streens), where the hills often seem to be extensions of the river's banks. It then broadens out briefly until just above Dulsie Bridge, which sees the start of the gorge: a place of awe, and at times dread, amidst infinite vistas. For over twenty miles the Findhorn cuts a tortuous trail, alternating between rapids and dark sullen pools, largely hemmed in by steep, often sheer cliffs (up to 200 ft high) crowned by swathes of fine mature woodland. The river itself flows over a bed of boulder-strewn rock. At certain points it funnels dramatically into narrow chasms – just 7 ft wide at Randolph's Leap, for instance.

Inevitably, given its spectacular natural character, the gorge abounds in legend. Perhaps the most poignant tale relates to the Princess Stone at Glenferness. In Celtic times a Danish nobleman, held hostage by the local chief, eloped with the latter's daughter. They were pursued and took refuge by the river. To avoid capture they plunged into the swollen torrent and certain death, and when their bodies were eventually recovered, they were still locked in a final embrace. The Stone marks their burial site.

Below the gorge the river tracks across the plain of Forres to its mouth in virtually land-locked Findhorn Bay. The splendour of the Findhorn with all its diverse habitats has long been extolled in print, and commentators have never compromised with their superlatives. The great sportsman Charles St John, who knew the river intimately, wrote in 1847: 'surely there is no other river in the world so beautiful.'

As mentioned above, the Findhorn is subject to spates of epic proportions, and their power is obviously most pronounced within the confines of the gorge. The great flood of August 1829 raised the level at Dulsie Bridge by 40 ft, and at Randolph's Leap by 50 ft; at the latter the torrent spilled over the top of the gorge, where an under-gardener is reported to have caught a fine salmon in an umbrella. The devastation was widespread, with 20 square miles of the Forres plain covered by the turbulent waters and sea-faring boats venturing inland to conduct rescue operations; it is remarkable that the final death toll was only two. There have been other great floods since, though not on the same scale, and salmon have often perished as a consequence. In 1914 farmers were able to fill their carts with fish washed up in the fields, and as recently as July 1997 hundreds of grilse were choked to death by shifting gravel.

In the mid-sixteenth century the vast Earldom of Moray, of which the Findhorn was a very small constituent part, was granted to the Stuart family, which holds the title to this day, although the land-holdings are greatly reduced. However the family still retains considerable lengths of the Findhorn, most notably Darnaway in the lower part of the gorge. It is remarkable how most of the most productive sections of the river have remained in the same ownership for a century or more, among them Glenferness (held by Lord Leven and Melville and heirs since 1869), Lethen (held by the Brodies since 1634), and Cawdor. One stretch of river changed hands in somewhat exceptional circumstances. In 1891 Sir William Gordon-Cumming, laird of Altyre and owner of fishings in the lower gorge, was the central figure in the notorious Tranby Croft baccarat scandal. Sir William, who had been accused of cheating at cards, brought an action to clear

Lethen Estate water upstream of Dulsie Bridge near the top of the gorge

his name, and Edward VII, then heir apparent to the throne, gave evidence against him. Many believed at the time that Sir William had been unjustly treated and furthermore that Edward himself should also have been in the dock, given that baccarat was illegal in Britain at the time. Sir William lost his case, and as a consequence was obliged to raise a considerable sum – which, it is understood, was achieved by selling the Altyre fishings to Lord Moray. Since then the Gordon-Cummings have leased the Altyre fishings from Moray Estate.

The Poolie Falls on the Darnaway water constitute a typical temperature barrier, with salmon unlikely to ascend before the water temperature reaches 42°F. With adequate reserves of snow in the high corries, this temperature seldom used to be seen before May. Below this threshold all fish are held back downstream – particularly in the legendary Sluie pool, ten miles up from the mouth. The netting activities here were an important source of revenue, and so were exercised with unrelenting intensity. The catches were indeed prodigious: in 1648 the Earl of Moray wrote: 'in one night on the pool of Sluie alone 1,300 salmon were taken, and 26 scores at one draught'. Grimble recorded the figure as 13,000 – surely inconceivable – and both Calderwood and Henderson (*The Findhorn*, 1932) quote the more modest number.

Over the centuries the in-river netting effort was maintained, and in the nineteenth century, according to Grimble, netting by boat and coble was 'carried on

The Suspension Bridge Pool on the Forres AA water of the lower Findhorn

with the greatest energy' right down to the mouth. In 1800 Sluie produced 360 fish in one day, but by 1842 all the in-river nets landed less than 700 for the season. As elsewhere, the reason for the decline was the proliferation of coastal nets: by 1882 21 miles of the immediate coastline was festooned with 137 fixed nets – or one every 270 yards. Grimble put it succinctly: 'the whole coast bristles with stake and bag nets.' By the turn of the century the fixed nets on the Moray coast were taking between 13,600 and 18,600 salmon/grilse, and the in-river nets between 3,600 and 6,060. The rod catch (before the explosion in coastal nets, individuals could occasionally catch between five and ten per day) was reduced to between 150 and 200 off the whole river for the season – and most of those were landed after the closure of the nets on 26 August! As salmon angling had become more fashionable, and indeed a significant source of income for the estates above the Poolie Falls, this imbalance was the source of ever-increasing tension between them and Lord Moray, who held the in-river netting rights.

In 1898 the lease to net Sluie, held by Hogarth & Co of Aberdeen, expired. Hogarth was unwilling to renew it, as the netsmen's houses were in need of expensive repairs. Lord Leven together with Brodie of Lethen seized the opportunity and approached Lord Moray, offering to pay him an annual sum (£100) not to net Sluie, which equated to that which he received from Hogarth in rent. The negotiations were protracted, with Lord Moray (described by Lord Leven as the 'most impracticable man I have ever met') insisting for some time that he would net one day per week in June, July and August.

At one point the negotiations stalled, and in April 1899 Lord Leven wrote to Lord Moray in the most forceful terms. It is worth quoting this letter at some length, as it encapsulates the great sense of frustration felt by angling proprietors:

> The Findhorn is naturally, and indeed used to be, one of the most important and finest salmon rivers in Scotland. From its mouth to the spawning beds it has an almost unbroken succession of beautiful pools, made for angling.... To prevent excessive destruction of the fish and to protect their breeding, the law has provided that for 24 hours in every week (every Sabbath) no nets shall be used at the mouth or in the estuaries, so that fish may during that interval have free passage to the spawning beds. Unhappily, your nets at Sluie have made this wise provision practically inoperative. Sluie is at such a distance from the sea ... that the vast majority of the fish which, under the law's protection, enter the river on Sunday are killed at Sluie on Monday and the following days.... Do you think that it is right or expedient that one proprietor should practically defeat the intention of the law which provides free passage for fish during a certain period in each week?

At last, in early 1900, agreement was reached, and the netting of Sluie ceased. This arrangement is still in force, and the proprietors above continue to pay £100 a year.

In 1912 there was further correspondence with the new Lord Moray with a view to buying out his nets in the river mouth and lower reaches. The upper proprietors were prepared to pay up to £20,000, but only on condition that the Poolie Falls was blasted – enabling spring fish to move upstream before May. Initially Lord Moray was amenable, but in the end the proposed deal came to nothing, and Poolie remained intact.

Netting in the lower river (including the bottom seven pools) persisted for most of the twentieth century. In low water this operation was devastatingly efficient. These nets were finally bought out in 1989 by the Atlantic Salmon Conservation Trust, under the chairmanship of the late Sir William Gordon-Cumming (proprietor of Altyre Estate), who was also chairman of the River Board. The Trust had already, between 1985 and 1987, bought up the great majority of the Moray Firth coastal nets, at last allowing fish a relatively free run into the river. The pinnacle of their achievement was their purchase in 1987 of the Moray Firth Salmon Fishing Company, which in the previous ten years had accounted for over 11,000 salmon/grilse per annum.

It is worth noting that Darnaway's Home beat, which includes the Poolie Falls and the Sluie Pool, was first let to tenants in 1983. Before that it was fished, mainly in the spring months, by estate staff, with rod and line, the fish being sold. As winters become milder, so salmon are surmounting Poolie much earlier, even in March.

Findhorn springers are very short and deep. What has been most noticeable in recent years, though, is the decline in the number of heavy spring fish, in the 15 lb to 30 lb class; UDN is thought to have been responsible. When the Home beat was fished commercially, springers between 20 lb and 30 lb were common (though, as they were destined for the dealer, they were not weighed accurately). But, even if the average weight of salmon was impressive, the Findhorn cannot claim to be a 'big-fish river'. Fish over 40 lb are almost unheard of. It is believed that the record is a salmon of 42 lb, taken by Mrs C. W. Wise after a battle lasting two hours in the White Stream at Glenferness in July 1962.

Whilst salmon numbers have suffered in recent years, grilse can still be very abundant, and in favourable conditions catches are prolific. Below are catch figures for the whole river for the past six seasons; those for 2003 suffered from the summer-long drought.

| | Salmon | | Grilse | | Total |
	retained	released	retained	released	
1998	1,166	194	1,199	98	2,657
1999	753	203	429	49	1,434*
2000	655	443	970	278	2,346
2001	919	736	1,098	368	3,121
2002	574	338	939	313	2,164
2003	456	437	452	215	1,560

* Five proprietors failed to submit catch numbers.

Rod catches before 1990 are to a great extent immaterial, because of the considerable in-river netting pressure.

The river's tendency to rise with astonishing speed, especially in the gorge, has led to many anxious moments. Very occasionally what is known as the 'Findhorn bore' surges downstream; this wave of water up to six feet high is by all accounts a terrifying phenomenon, as there is little if any warning. Charles St John was on the receiving end whilst fishing below the gorge, and ended up stranded on an island. Later he reflected that, 'had we been in any one of several spots [within the gorge], where we fished every day, nothing would have saved our lives'. In some vulnerable locations escape paths have been created. That fatalities are rare is due largely to the fact that there is very little wading in the gorge.

High summer on Sonnie's Pool (Forres AA water)

Indeed much of the fishing in this section is carried on from positions high above the water level, requiring considerable flexibility in casting.

The lower Findhorn is host to Forres Angling Association, arguably northern Scotland's most prosperous angling club, judged by the annual catch in relation to the size of the membership. Founded in the 1930s, it benefited from a major bequest to the people of Forres in 1962, which facilitated the purchase of the fishings from the Red Craig down to the footbridge at the Broom of Moy, as well as two pools below. During the 1960s, 3,000 to 4,000 sea trout were taken each year, and in the mid-1980s the annual catch of salmon/grilse was 600 to 700. Now it is a little more modest, at 300 to 400 per season. Recently the club has increased its fishings by leasing the old 'Netting Water' upstream from the mouth.

NAIRN

The River Nairn follows a north-easterly course, parallel to that of the Findhorn, down to its mouth in the Moray Firth at the ancient town of Nairn. Like those of its more illustrious neighbour, its lower reaches flow through the rich farmland of the coastal strip. Further inland their headwaters interlock extensively on the north side of the Monadliath Mountains. The major difference between the two systems is that the Nairn's catchment of 122 square miles is little over a third of that of the Findhorn. The Nairn drains a comparatively narrow strip, and hence is far more of a spate river.

As industry developed in the nineteenth century the Nairn was heavily exploited as a source of water, and particularly of water power, with the free passage of migratory fish given little priority. According to Grimble, up until 1881 the weir at Nairn Mills, not far above the mouth, 'almost entirely barred the ascent of fish'. Then in a rare example of co-operation the upper proprietors clubbed together and purchased the mill and weir. They breached the latter, and that season rods landed over 300 salmon/grilse above the obstacle, when previously they had struggled to catch 20.

Despite this episode, the fragmentation of ownership (by the late 1800s there were a dozen or so riparian owners) on a comparatively small system was a major disadvantage when it came to ensuring that upstream migration was unimpeded. Calderwood noted that there were no fish passes on the river (in contravention of the Salmon Acts), but evidently there was little concerted effort to remedy the situation. It is perhaps relevant that one of the main owners, Cawdor Estate, also had prime angling beats on the Findhorn.

There was another serious disincentive to improving the river from an angling

The Old Hut Pool in a September spate

point of view: the nets had a virtual stranglehold. Between Findhorn Bay and Fort George (twenty miles of coastline) there were some 150 stake nets at the end of the nineteenth century, including a great concentration on the 'Bar' to the north-east. There was also an intense netting effort by Brodie of Brodie very close to and within the mouth of the Nairn. His nets (within two miles of the estuary) averaged 6,000 salmon/grilse per annum between 1893 and 1896, whereas rods on the river averaged a little over 200 per annum in the same period. The benefits of opening up the Nairn Mills weir had been short-lived.

The fact that the salmon runs remained viable (at least for the nets) is testimony to what Calderwood termed the river's 'splendid spawning'. But, although smolt runs remained healthy, the interests of salmon angling were never likely to prosper because of the fragmentation of ownership. However, from small beginnings in 1923 a structure of management has evolved which is almost unique in the north of Scotland. This date marks the formation of the Nairn Angling Association.

Initially the club was restricted to a limited clique of well-to-do residents of the town of Nairn. It leased rights to the sea-trout fishing from the harbour up to Howford Bridge (some two-and-a-half miles). In the early 1930s membership (five shillings for adults and two shillings and sixpence for juniors) was widened to 70 members, and soon afterwards fishing rights were extended to include salmon. In around 1950 the club entered into leases with both Cawdor and Kilravock estates. Since then the extent of the club's fishings has steadily developed, so that it now has access to all but a mile of the bottom ten miles of river – from the harbour up to Cantray Bridge. In addition it has a mile-and-a-half stretch up at Clava (by the railway viaduct). Basically the club has the fishings (from seven different proprietors) on almost all of the most productive water, with the notable exception of Nairnside (upstream of Clava). Nairnside, with a five-year average of close to 100 salmon/grilse, is the only other significant beat that is readily accessible; the north bank is syndicated, whilst lets are available on the south bank.

For most of the twentieth century the proliferation of nets remained a major problem. Great numbers of fish being transported by horse and cart from the estuary nets to the town's railway station were a daily spectacle up until the 1930s. The nets always fished hard from opening day (11 February), and catches were often prodigious; thus, in about 1950 a single stake net at Whiteness Head was found to contain 365 salmon/grilse when emptied one morning. Matters were finally resolved with the ground-breaking buy-outs of the great majority of the Moray Firth nets by the Atlantic Salmon Conservation Trust between 1985 and 1987; the pinnacle of achievement was the purchase of the Moray Firth Salmon Fishing Company, whose ten-year average at the time was 3,536 salmon and 8,023 grilse. All nets, both coastal and estuary, in the vicinity of Nairn were closed. According to regular Nairn anglers this made a significant difference to the

The Jubilee Pool on the lower river close to the town of Nairn

numbers of fish running the river. This has not necessarily been reflected in catches – or at least reported catches – as, in many clubs, there is reticence or reluctance amongst members to submit returns. Consequently the average annual catches for Nairn AA, as set out below, tell only part of the story.

	Salmon	Grilse	Sea trout*
1980–84	25	43	60
1985–89	107	96	151
1990–94	38	82	137
1995–99	45	134	129
2000–03	58	185	128

* Only sea trout over 1 lb are recorded; the river has tremendous runs of finnock.

As the Nairn AA's stature has increased over the decades, so its role as regards the fishery as a whole has developed. It is worth noting that, whilst the major players in terms of riparian ownership have altered little in the past century, the total number of owners has increased dramatically to over 30 – an astonishing figure for the length of river. Essentially the District Salmon Board now plays a comparatively passive role, and the club is the main active force. In effect it runs the river: it is entirely responsible for the hatchery and stocking; and it carries out extensive pool and habitat improvements, as well as bank repairs. All of this is done at its own expense, with almost all the labour provided by volunteers.

Although fish stocks are reasonably healthy, the system is not without its problems. Discharges from sand and gravel quarries in the upper reaches have caused significant siltation, which is potentially damaging to redds; one offending company was fined in 2003. There is also a continuing landslip of sand at Aberarder (to stabilize this would be prohibitively expensive). And the fish pass at Loch Duntelchaig (controlled by Scottish Water) is understood to be inoperative, denying fish access. On the positive side, all remaining weirs have either been removed or become derelict, and poaching, which was a great cause for concern, is markedly reduced. The impassable falls on the tributary at Cawdor (which had originally been raised to facilitate the intake to the distillery) were opened up in 2002/2003 and the club has begun stocking the considerable nursery areas above.

The Nairn offers some of the best river sea-trout fishing in Scotland. In recent years fish have averaged close to 3 lb, with specimens in the 5 lb to 6 lb class not uncommon; the record in the last two decades stands at 8 lb 9 oz. Some outstanding baskets have been achieved. The tidal pools, particularly Factor's and the Jubilee, are especially productive.

The main runs of grilse and summer salmon are from mid-June, water levels permitting (there is a local joke that the runs begin at 10.20 a.m. on June 11!). Historically there has always been a fair spring run. The record salmon was an early springer: in February 1949 Alex MacKay caught a fish of 28 lb in the Gauge pool of the Cawdor estate water – he had to break the ice to land it. Then in February 1951 Duncan Ross took a springer of 27 lb from the Howford Bridge pool. Evidence that heavier fish do occasionally exist was provided in February 1939, when David MacKay caught and released a kelt of 33 lb at Whinnyknowe; when fresh-run it is likely to have weighed over 40 lb.

Appearances can of course be deceptive. One day in April 1947 Alex MacKay hooked a salmon at 2.45 p.m. on a 7 lb line. If he had had a gaff he could have landed it in the first minute, but thereafter the fish seemed to be impossible to subdue. During the afternoon he received a procession of visitors, one of whom bet him half a crown that it was foul-hooked. Eventually, at 10.40 p.m., he landed a fresh-run springer of 15 lb, hooked in the scissors. The fish had remained 'lively' for eight hours.

NESS

To anyone attempting to categorize Scottish salmon rivers, the Ness system stands alone. Indeed so many of the accepted norms relating to salmon runs and salmon angling simply do not apply to the Ness. By Highland standards this is a large system, draining some 700 square miles, but what makes it so very different from any other system in Scotland is Loch Ness.

This vast and deep loch has a surface area of 22 square miles and holds three times the volume of water contained in Loch Lomond, its nearest Scottish rival. It is almost an inland sea, and it is perhaps no coincidence that seals are resident almost all year round. Its influence dominates the River Ness as well as the tributaries. The loch acts as a filter, and consequently a dirty spate on the River Ness is unknown. The loch never freezes, and this factor keeps its outlet to the inner Moray Firth comparatively warm (4°F above the rivers flowing into the loch), even in the hardest of winters. And it is the influence of Loch Ness that dictates that the spring runs and fishing are centred on the upper tributaries, which are up to forty miles from the sea.

The Ness is one of those systems where salmon run every month of the year. The numbers of winter fish are now, of course, much reduced. In years past, though, there was no such shortage, and in a bygone era, before it was appreciated that spawning fish should not be disturbed, the season *opened* on 14 November, and there were always fresh-run salmon available for St Andrew's Day at the end of the month. By the mid-nineteenth century the opening date was 11 February, then early in the next century it moved to 2 February and subsequently to 15 January.

The system's winter springers are destined for the upper tributaries. Grimble referred to the lower River Garry (between Loch Garry and Loch Oich) as 'perhaps the best early spring fishing in Scotland'. The quality of the fish, averaging in the high teens of pounds, was legendary, and perhaps only challenged by those of the Tay. But, in contrast to the Tay, the Garry, with its headwaters just east of Knoydart on the west coast, is very much a Highland river, wild yet intimate, and perfect fly water; indeed even by the late nineteenth century it was designated as fly-only. Tenancies were jealously guarded. In 1884 two rods took 420 salmon in the 11 weeks to the end of April, an average of 19 springers per rod per week.

Between 1895 and 1914 the Duke of Portland was the tenant for the spring. In his first season the river was iced over until 4 March, but in the subsequent five weeks to 13 April he and another rod had 146 fish, averaging over 17 lb. However during two springs in the late 1890s very few fish reached the Garry. The Caledonian Canal, built by Telford, had been completed in 1822, and this incorporated a substantial weir (which remains to this day) at the head of the River Ness at Dochfour. In low water large numbers of spring fish congregated below the obstacle, and this location soon became established as a lucrative netting station. In the late 1890s this net had two highly successful seasons, including one 'phenomenal' catch on opening day, which was widely reported. The latter event prompted the Duke of Portland to act to protect his own fishings; he leased the net and mothballed it.

There were other netting locations on the River Ness including the Lower Laggan Pool (980 salmon in 1876), Ness Castle, Friar's Shott (2,946 salmon in 1873), the Cherry Shot and the Longman's Grave. It is worth noting that the export of salmon had long been a lucrative trade for Inverness; according to Colonel Thornton's *Sporting Tour ...* (1804) Ness salmon were 'esteemed of more exquisite flavour than any other'. However from the early nineteenth century the extent of fresh-water netting was a simmering source of friction. The Ness Angling Club's minutes from September 1830 referred to 'the complete failure of the fishing in the last season', and accordingly they were applying to the proprietors for a return of half the rent. The following year they complained that the 'pools are constantly netted'. The spring fish were also netted in Loch Dochfour, between the river and Loch Ness, and in the late nineteenth century a catch of 150 salmon per week in February was not unusual. Netting on the Ness was greatly curtailed from 1904, following the establishment of the Loch Ness Angling Improvement Association, which leased several of the stations and left them dormant. It also negotiated an almost complete cessation of netting in Loch Ness. A system of licensing and regulating boats for angling on the loch was introduced, and soon, according to Calderwood, the average annual rod catch for this fishery amounted to some 500 salmon.

The significant reduction in netting, of course, had a marked impact on the numbers reaching the upper tributaries. This is reflected in the Duke of Portland's records for the Garry in the early 1900s. He readily acknowledged that his better catches were directly related to the removal of nets at the mouth of the River Ness, and particularly to the end of netting at Dochfour below the weir. Red-letter days for his two Garry rods were frequent, including 12 March 1905 (9 fish for 177 lb), 19 March 1906 (12 fish for 192 lb), 20 March 1906 (11 fish averaging 21 lb each) and 17 March 1911 (11 fish averaging over 20 lb). In February 1905 a salmon of 40 lb was taken in Loch Oich.

Between 1905 and 1914 the Duke recorded another two portmanteau fish of over 40 lb, one of them a cock springer of 44 lb to his own rod from Loch Oich, which he (writing in 1933) believed 'to be the largest ever killed in either Loch Oich or the Garry'. Jock Scott (*Fine and Far Off*, 1952) contradicted this, referring to the great Alexander Grant (see below) landing a 55-lb salmon in the Garry. In the early 1950s Richard Waddington was broken by a very large fish in the Little Crooked Pool of the Garry. A few minutes later in the pool below he hooked a strikingly similar fish, and when he eventually landed the 39-lb salmon, he discovered that it was indeed carrying two of his distinctive flies.

Historically the Garry's spring season was largely over by May, when fish dispersed upstream over the Falls. The lower Garry remained an excellent spring fishery up till the early 1950s, averaging some 400 fish a year. The development of the Ness tributaries for electricity generation had first been proposed in 1938; many of the system's proprietors opposed it, spending considerable sums lobbying the authorities, but to no avail. Finally, in the mid-1950s, the whole regime of the River Garry was transformed by the construction of dams at Loch Quoich and Loch Garry, with only the latter incorporating a fish pass – this scheme signalled the demise of one of the truly great spring fisheries. The Hydro Board was (and indeed remains) responsible for a raft of measures to mitigate its effect on salmon populations, including the construction of a massive hatchery at Invergarry, but in the end nothing could really compensate for the loss of natural spawning. Between 1965 and 1979 an average of only 304 fish went through the Borland fish lift in the Loch Garry dam.

Soon after the hatchery was built a cock fish estimated at 52 lb was amongst

The Invermoriston Falls on the River Moriston. The half-mile stretch below is now by far the most productive spring beat of the whole system

the broodstock used, but now salmon of over 30 lb are unheard of. The Hydro scheme feeds the water from Loch Garry by tunnel to the turbines at Invergarry, bypassing most of the classic pools of the river above. The Estuary Pool, where fish congregate, is now the most productive. In recent years the lower Garry has been lightly fished and averages less than 100 fish a year.

The River Oich, which runs between Loch Oich and Loch Ness, is also traditionally a spring river and was thought to depend, as Calderwood put it, on catching Garry fish in the 'bye-going'. This is not entirely accurate, as its six-mile length includes some first-rate spawning and nursery areas, and there are some very attractive stretches, but, since the introduction of the Garry Hydro scheme, the Oich is largely dependent on the release of water to fish well.

The other important spring tributary is the Moriston. The Invermoriston Falls, half a mile up from the estuary in Loch Ness, was impassable to salmon, and fish were regularly netted from the pool below. In 1880 an elaborate fish ladder was built on the left side of the Falls. Whilst some salmon did indeed take advantage, it was not, according to Calderwood, an 'unqualified success', and in 1902 another ladder with a more gradual gradient was constructed on the right bank, which, after some teething problems, afforded easy access to twenty-five miles of virgin

Landing a May springer in the Burnmouth Pool at Dochfour at the
head of the River Ness

The Pot at Ness Castle

river, and a whole new spawning area was opened up. This upper section was however never really exploited as a fishery.

The Moriston was also harnessed for hydro-electric power in the 1950s, and as a result much of this spawning capacity has been lost – the upper dams have no fish passes. The lowest beat, below the Falls, is still (generating levels permitting) a good spring fishery; salmon are held back in the beat until May and the start of summer compensation flows, which allow them to move upstream. This stretch can produce up to 20 fish a week in the early part of the season. In the 1970s and 1980s Moriston springers averaged close to 18 lb, and the river yielded springers of 30 lb virtually every season; one day in February 1971 salmon of 31 lb and 29 lb were landed by Graham MacKenzie (who has the distinction of having caught three salmon over 30 lb from the Ness system) and John Cathcart respectively. Since the 1990s a smaller class of springer has predominated. As recently as the 1980s fish would build up in very large numbers in the spring in the loch by the mouth of the Moriston, and this location became highly favoured by loch anglers.

On Loch Ness the spring fishing tended to be concentrated in the Fort Augustus, Invermoriston and Foyers areas, whilst the summer and autumn fish were more dispersed. Sport with grilse could be fast and furious; in the 1970s and 1980s seven to ten grilse per boat per day was achievable, with the runs lasting

Spring on the Ness-side Beat

weeks. On occasion this is still possible, but nowadays trolling a bait or lure for hours does not have the same appeal as in past decades. It is also true, though, that fish are not staying in the loch as long, and fewer anglers have the necessary knowledge of the lies or the appropriate tactics; one notable exception is Ala MacGruer, who still uses his own special sprat formula and who prefers to row with a following wind (as opposed to using the outboard). Trolling on the loch (dead slow in spring and much faster in summer) requires considerable skill – the angle of a sprat determines depth, and to be effective a Toby must have 'flutter'.

On the River Ness netting operations recommenced on the lower river after World War I on the insistence of the municipal authorities. They continued until 1927, when the Ness De-netting Scheme' was launched. For the sum of between £900 and £1,000 per annum the nets in the river and the estuary (as far out as Fort George) were kept off for two decades. The Moray Firth Salmon Fishing Company paid two-thirds of the cost, with proprietors responsible for the balance (Dochfour Estate contributed the lion's share – £200 per annum – of the latter). Whilst there is no doubt fish stocks increased as a result of the scheme, the arrangement ceased in the late 1940s, as the major players resented bearing such a high proportion of the cost. Nets operated within the river, notably at the Still and Friar's Shott, through the 1950s before being phased out.

Although the early spring fish tend to go straight through the short River

Ness, historically, when the runs were more numerous, both Dochfour and the Town Water (the lower river) beats were able to intercept enough to be viable rod fisheries in the early months. All six miles of the River Ness really become productive from mid-summer onwards. The Ness's great advantage is that it is never too low, even in a prolonged drought, and all beats can score heavily any time from July through to the close on 15 October. Many of the summer and autumn fish show no inclination to migrate up into the loch above, as they spawn in the river itself; it has no adjacent tributaries or even burns of any consequence.

In 1909 the beats consisted of Dochfour, Ness Castle, Ness Side, Holm, The Four Cobles, Bught and the Town Water. Dochfour has belonged to the Baillie/Burton family since time immemorial. Between 1872 and 1877, part of the era of the most intensive netting activity, rod catches at Dochfour averaged 144 per annum, one-third of which were taken in the spring (these figures I have gleaned from the records of John MacDonald, gillie at the time). Catch records from Dochfour Estate for the late 1920s and 1930s (during the time of the 'De-netting Scheme') confirm a healthy spring fishery. William McLellan's party ('two rods at least') were the long-standing tenants for January to June. Their best year was 1927, with 101 springers in this period, averaging 16 lb. Generally they caught between 50 and 80; one spring the average weight of the catch of 58 fish was almost 18 lb.

At this time Dochfour was essentially unfished in July and August; sport resumed in September with the 'autumn fishing'. The lower 700 yards of the Dochfour water (Laggan) was sold to Willie Armstrong in 1978. He retained it until 1989, selling to Prime Salmon Fishings Ltd. They timeshared the beat successfully, creating the Laggan Fishings Club. Since 1992 a syndicate has rented the rest of the Dochfour water.

The next beat downstream, Ness Castle, was owned by Simon Fraser and descendants from 1801. In the second half of the nineteenth century it was probably the most productive angling beat on the Ness, averaging some 200 per annum in the 1870s, for instance. In 1885 tenant Mr Denison caught 120 salmon on the Ness (the same year he took 180 from the Tweed); he had an epic struggle, related in the 'Fur, Feather and Fin Series', hooking a massive salmon at 6 p.m., finally losing it at 4 a.m. the next morning. The proprietors of Ness Castle in the twentieth century included the Hone family, the Wetherspoon family and the Commercial Union. In 1975 the latter sold to Geoffrey Myers, who passed it to Mr and Mrs Turley in 2002.

Below Ness Castle is Ness Side, owned by the Godman family for several generations from the 1880s. In 1975 Major Godman sold Ness Side (into which the short Holm beat had been incorporated) to Hamish Campbell, who retained it until 1998, selling to the Cardrona Charitable Trust. Ness Side's records are virtually complete back to 1888. As with the other middle beats, there used to be almost no fishing before July. On the evidence of the figures, the beat was fished consistently between 1888 and 1900, averaging 108 per annum. The average annual catches from 1901 to 1925 (56) and from 1926 to 1950 (30) indicate that fishing effort was light in the first half of the twentieth century, though a different attitude prevailed in the second half, with the beat averaging 155 per season between 1951 and 1973, increasing to 172 between 1976 and 1993. Between 1888 and 1977 Ness Side anglers recorded 17 salmon over 30 lb; this included a remarkable first-ever salmon of 34 lb for F. Knowles on 13 October 1952. Since 1977 the beat's heaviest salmon has been 26 lb.

The Four Cobles and Bught beats have now been absorbed into the Town Water, a three-mile stretch (partly tidal) upstream from the mouth. This is fished by Inverness Angling Club. Under a charter of 1591 the Town of Inverness was 'vested with the whole of the salmon fishings between the Stone of Clachnahagaig and the sea'. There is a long tradition of public angling on the Ness: in the nineteenth century this consisted of one dedicated public stretch and free access to a much longer section 'every ninth day'. The club's most productive period was in the 1980s, when the average annual rod catch was 385.

In its heyday in the latter half of the twentieth century, the River Ness as a whole yielded some 1,200 salmon/grilse a year. The five-year average catch (1999 to 2003) now stands at just under 750. The three leading beats are Dochfour with 37% of the total, Ness Side with 21% and Ness Castle with 20%.

The Ness is by Scottish standards a large river, and a long line is imperative to cover the water effectively. The casting prowess on display is legendary. The river's most accomplished angler was Alexander Grant, the 'wizard of the Ness', who used a spliced greenheart Vibration rod. In a demonstration with an 18-ft rod on the Thames in the early 1890s he cast 56 yards, *without* shooting any line. Then in 1895, in a competition on the Ness, he cast an astonishing 65 yards with a 21-ft rod, again *without* shooting any line. Grant was a highly practical angler, using his ability to achieve distance to devastating effect, and he frequently caught fish with casts of 40 to 50 yards.

BEAULY

For some six hundred years most of the Beauly system remained under single ownership. The Lovats, chiefs of the Clan Fraser, presided over vast tracts of territory. Their holdings were nearly lost forever following Culloden in 1746, after the then Lord Lovat declared for the doomed Jacobite side at the eleventh hour.

In the aftermath he died, gallantly, on the scaffold in London in his eightieth year; the estates were forfeited, but were returned to his son in 1774.

Of the rivers north of the Great Glen, only the Conon has a greater catchment than the Beauly, which drains 270 square miles. Its uppermost headwaters lie within some of the North Highlands' most awe-inspiring deer forests including Glenaffric and Glencannich. What Calderwood termed the 'mountain valley' sections of the system flow through dramatic high glens overlooked by towering peaks up to 3,700 ft high. The Affric and the Cannich tributaries, both with almost 20-mile parallel courses including major lochs, combine to form the Glass; after seven miles the latter is then supplemented from the west by the Farrar, which itself has run a similarly spectacular course of some 25 miles.

From the junction of the Glass and the Farrar, the river is known as the Beauly – although, confusingly, it still flows through Strathglass. The Beauly itself, ten miles in length, soon enters what was, and to some extent still is, an awesome gorge, before descending through comparatively open country to its estuary at the head of the inner Moray Firth. Incidentally, many eras ago, the whole of the Glass and the upper section of the Beauly are thought, according to geological survey, to have been a 13-mile-long loch, which was finally drained by the erosion of conglomerate rocks at Eilean Aigas in the gorge. According to Calderwood, 'before this erosion took place, it is likely there was a waterfall such as is nowhere now to be seen in Scotland'.

The Beauly has always been immensely productive. Richard Franck, writing in 1658, referred to it as being 'replenished with salmon, whose numbers are numberless'; he spoke of the netsmen often taking 500 in one sweep. Between 1827 and 1832 an average of 9,831 salmon and grilse per year were taken from the lower river and estuary, rising to 11,374 over the next six years. These numbers could not be sustained, given the growing pressure on stocks from bag netting, and by 1856–1862 the average annual take had slumped to 4,243. The statutory extension of the estuary for the Beauly (and indeed the Ness) to include the whole of the inner Moray Firth under the 1865 Byelaw signalled the end of the fixed-engine nets within this area. (The Byelaws of 1864 and 1865 were enactments of the Salmon Fisheries Scotland Act 1862 and they defined the extent of river estuaries across the country; within estuaries fixed-engine nets – the legal term of bag-nets and stake-nets – were not permitted.)

In the meantime the Beauly's reputation for angling was being made. In 1854 Lord Lovat landed 128 fish in eight days in late June and early July. In 1859 Colonel Duff took 108 fish in the first week of July. Then in 1864 Lord Lovat caught 146 salmon/grilse in the five days from 27 June (an astonishing average of 29 per day); Francis Francis referred to this episode as 'perhaps the most extraordinary sport ever had in Great Britain'.

The Silver Pool on the Home Beat of the lower river in July (prime grilse time)

In the latter part of the nineteenth century the netting effort was curtailed, as the Lovats strove to strike more of a balance between angling and the nets; in addition, the periods, during which the in-river cruive-boxes were employed, were greatly reduced. The Lovats were far-sighted and conscientious in their management of the river: for instance, buying up and mothballing an estuary netting station in the early twentieth century, opening a hatchery (discontinued before World War I) and conducting a determined campaign against predators. Another hatchery with smolt-rearing ponds was established in the 1940s (a significant part of the diet provided was hard-boiled eggs!).

In 1920 the Lovats – together with other river and estuary netting proprietors, including Sir John Stirling on the Conon and the Sellar family at Findhorn Bay – were instrumental in the formation of the Moray Firth Salmon Fishery Co, which for many decades gave the partners considerable control over the numbers of salmon legally netted within the Firth. The company bought up many of the area's netting stations before exercising the rights itself, taking into account stock levels. The Atlantic Salmon Conservation Trust acquired all the company's netting rights (excluding those in the Cromarty Firth) in 1987 and closed down these stations, whose ten-year average take (up to 1986) had been 3,536 salmon and 8,023 grilse destined for a number of Moray Firth rivers. Incidentally, netting within the Beauly itself, over two miles above the tidal limit at the cruives (the largest structure of its kind in Scotland), had continued until 1985 – latterly just twice a week during the grilse runs. Between the wars the then Lord Lovat (the 17th Baron) often participated in the netting below the cruives, and in the early 1930s the Prince of Wales (later Edward VIII) visited Beaufort Castle (the Lovat family seat) and watched the lord hauling the nets in midstream in his kilt; he is said to have found the whole experience 'rather barbaric'.

Historically most of the angling was always concentrated in the lower river downstream of Kilmorack. There was a tremendous build-up of fish below the (now submerged) Upper Kilmorack Falls, also known as the Red Falls, towards the bottom end of the gorge. This landmark falls was a formidable temperature barrier, and when the water warmed up a spate was required to enable salmon to run the fish-ladder. Consequently, throughout the spring and often for considerable lengths of time during the summer, there were great numbers of fish immediately downstream. In the legendary 75-yard-long Mare's Pool (so named because a mare once fell into the pool from the cliff above, where a regular horse fair was held), accessed by a steep ladder, the fish would be lined up like 'bunches of bananas', as long-time Lovat Estates' factor Giles Foster recalls. This deep, dark and narrow pool was the best on the river, sometimes accounting for thirty per cent of the catch between the falls and the mouth. On one pre-war occasion William John Matheson was sent down to the Mare's Pool in early summer to

Beauly Angling Club water below Lovat Bridge

30

obtain fish for the castle, and in one brief session he landed 21. (He was the second generation of Mathesons to work on the river; the third and fourth generations are still very much an integral part of the set-up.)

There were two other significant angling pools in the gorge, the Falls and the Mill; most of the rest of this section was virtually inaccessible. The lower river was by today's standards lightly fished, with efforts focused on the spring (often two-thirds of the annual catch was obtained by the end of May). The spring fishing was indeed excellent, with some 70 in February, and 200 in both March and April entirely possible. The river was often left alone during the summer months, before the rods reappeared in September. It was not unusual for only one rod to fish each of the three beats – two rods per beat was the maximum. It could be a big river, particularly in the early months, and an 18-ft rod used to be recommended; Giles Foster favoured a massive 22-ft cane rod to put out a very long line on the pools behind the castle. As the twentieth century progressed, so Lovat Estate's control over the system was gradually diluted. In 1922 they sold Struy Estate, with the lower Glass and the lower Farrar. The process continued with the tributaries, culminating with the disposal in 1990 (when salmon angling values were at a peak) of most the Beauly itself – the jewel in the crown – to Landmatch, which subsequently became the River Beauly Fishings Co. The latter have successfully syndicated both the lower river (above the Lovat Bridge) and upper river. Lovat Estates leases the tidal section of the river (below Lovat Bridge) to the Beauly Angling Club.

The more momentous impact on the system, however, has been its comprehensive harnessing for hydro-electric generation. The Affric/Cannich area was developed first (in the 1950s), with water diverted by tunnel from the dammed Loch Mullardoch on the Cannich across to Loch Beinn a Mheadhoin (also dammed) on the Affric, and thence by tunnel again downstream to Fasnakyle power station; neither dam incorporates a fish pass, as both are upstream of impassable falls. Next the northern part of the system, the Farrar, and the Beauly itself were exploited. Remote Loch Monar, at the top of the Farrar, was dammed (doubling its length to eight miles) and its waters are taken by tunnel to a power station above Loch Beannacharan. The latter was also dammed to supply the next power station at Culligran. Finally two dams/power stations were built in the gorge section of the Beauly, at Aigas and Kilmorack. All these dams, except Loch Monar, included Borland fish lifts. Compensation flows were agreed for all the rivers.

The regime of the system was obviously altered radically – with both advantages and disadvantages. On the negative side, the renowned Mare's Pool was lost for ever. The spring run is a pale shadow of its former self; the small early springers of February and early March have virtually disappeared, and only a limited number of the late March/April/May springers (typically 11 lb) survive. Some spawning areas have been drowned.

On the positive side, the guaranteed water levels throughout the grilse runs have been an enormous boon to catches on the lower river. Very few days are lost to spates; the lower river now clears within a day – before the dams were built it could take three or four days to settle. The upper Beauly and tributaries have also benefited, not least because the lifts are more reliable than spates; previously, in a dry year fish could be very scarce above the Kilmorack Falls before September.

Severe flooding, to which Strathglass was notoriously prone, became less likely. There was, however, an exception to this in 1966, when a combination of snowmelt and heavy rain built up in the lochs before spilling over the dams with serious consequences. Several bridges were swept away, and boulders were deposited on the main road on the Inverness side of the Lovat Bridge. Willie Matheson (snr) and Donnie Morrison were sitting in one of the houses close to the Priest Pool on the Saturday night in question, enjoying a quiet dram; the carpets seemed to be developing wave motions, which both of them put down to the quality of the whisky, before they realized that the water level was indeed rising fast.

The table below of ten-year averages gives much information on catches on the River Beauly between 1900 and the sale to Landmatch; it can be seen that overall rod catches remained remarkably stable in the post-war years, despite the hydro-electric development. There was, of course, a significant increase in the grilse catch.

	Upper river	Lower river	Total rods	Nets	Total catch
1900–09	*	261	261	1,059	1,320
1910–19	*	338	412	1,252	1,664
1920–29	*	369	388	2,062	2,450
1930–39	43	303	346	3,180	3,526
1940–49	166	318	451	1,730	2,181
1950–59	466	755	1,221	*	*
1960–69	420	696	1,116	*	*
1970–79	353	542	895	1,280	2,175
1980–89	547	509	1,056	*	1,264

* Denotes insufficient data.

Nets were phased out during the 1980s.

Upper river: includes all beats on the Beauly itself above the lower river. Figures are thought to be unreliable before 1946.

Since the syndication of the lower river, fishing effort has increased, and the ten-year average (to 1999) for the three beats downstream of Kilmorack was 856, dropping to 664 for the period 2000 to 2003. Upstream the Aigas and Eskadale beats averaged 96 between 1994 and 2003. Perhaps the best indication of the health of the system is the number of fish counted through Aigas Dam (above the lower river) – below are the annual averages:

	Salmon/grilse
1962–70	7,856
1971–80	6,703
1981–90	6,295
1991–2000	4,878
2001–03	3,472

The Beauly has never been noted as a large-salmon river, although every year a handful or so over 20 lb are landed; fish over 25 lb are very rare indeed. What was perhaps the heaviest fish encountered in recent years never made the bank. In 1986 Mike Smith had an eight-hour battle on a 10-ft trout rod, during which the backing broke twice, but was retrieved and reconnected; the salmon was clearly seen and estimated at 40 lb. The fish was always in control, moving at will between the Minister's and the Island Run; finally the hooks straightened. In 1992 a cock fish of over 30 lb was netted for the hatchery – it would have been considerably heavier when fresh. In 1991 a salmon over four feet long was seen in the Aigas fish-lift.

The tributaries have always been summer/autumn fisheries, with little activity before July. Catches could fluctuate wildly. Many of the upper sections were traditionally viewed as nursery areas, and were hardly fished; until recently the lower sections were generally unlet, and retained for the proprietors' use, with fishing effort determined by conditions. Struy Estate, with until 1967 the lower half-mile of the Glass and the lower six miles of the Farrar, was more consistently fished than most; the records, which go back to 1888, show that 150 was possible in a good year. Struy was split in 1967, with five miles of the Farrar going to Culligran Estate; the latter now has a ten-year average (1994 to 2003) of 55 fish. The Glass, the larger and more productive tributary, now averages in the region of 250 fish per year.

Every effort has been made in the past decade or so to utilize all the available nursery areas within the upper catchment that are inaccessible to adult fish due to impassable falls (such as the Dog Falls on the Affric and the Plodda Falls on the Tomich Burn) and other obstacles. Between 180,000 and 350,000 fry are planted out annually, and at the same time intensive efforts are being made to improve neglected juvenile habitat.

CONON

Lower Strathconon, now an open and serene landscape of rolling farm and parkland, used to have a very different appearance. Before it was drained in the eighteenth and nineteenth centuries, most of this terrain was bleak marsh and bog.

The latter played a critical part in one of the most decisive battles of the clan era. In 1491 the Mackenzie army of some 800 men was heavily outnumbered by over 2,000 MacDonalds at the Battle of the Park (*Blar na Pairc*) near Contin. The Mackenzies, who were on home territory, cunningly lured the MacDonalds into a quagmire; as they wallowed and floundered in the peat, thousands of arrows rained down on them, before the Mackenzie line moved in to finish the slaughter. A few MacDonalds managed to flee towards the River Conon. As the river was in spate, they asked an old woman the location of the ford. Intentionally she misled them, and they attempted to cross at the wrong point; many were drowned, and those who desperately clung to the bank had their hands severed by the sickles of the old lady and her associates. No more than 200 MacDonalds survived to return to the Western Isles, and they never threatened the Mackenzies again.

The Conon system, by far the largest north of the Great Glen, drains 400 square miles of Ross-shire's high mountains and moorland. Lying, broadly speaking, between the Beauly to the south, the Ewe to the west and the Carron to the north, it is fed by a fan-like formation of four main tributaries, each between twenty and thirty miles long; in clock-wise order from the south, these are the Orrin, the Meig, the Bran and the Blackwater. The Conon itself has a course of some twelve miles from the Conon Falls. It is initially Highland in character, before flowing through the rich pastures and arable fields to its mouth at the southern end of the Cromarty Firth by Dingwall.

The Conon was a very important source of wealth for the Mackenzies – an apocryphal story that another strain of Mackenzies (of Conan Estate) lost their netting rights in a gambling episode in the 1700s has no basis in fact. The estuary salmon netting was highly lucrative, and remained so over the centuries. The Cromarty Firth, completely protected from the open sea, is an ideal netting location, and by the nineteenth century there was a profusion of nets up and down the

Gillanders Pool on the Upper Fairburn Beat immediately downstream
of Torr Achilty dam

Firth, supplemented by in-river nets and cruives (fixed salmon traps). Between
1828 and 1837 a long legal battle was waged by Cromartie Estate against the use
of stake nets by two other proprietors with land adjoining the Firth. In 1838 the
court found in favour of the Estate, and the estuary was defined as extending as
far as the mouth of the Firth at the Sutors, inside which the use of fixed-engine
nets was prohibited. This was reconfirmed by the Byelaw of 1865.

By the latter part of the nineteenth century, as salmon angling became more
valuable, the cruives at Brahan on the lower Conon became extremely
contentious. Those fish not trapped in the boxes were netted below, and escapement above was thought to be minimal. In 1890 a consortium of river proprietors,
wishing to maximize escapement, leased the Brahan cruives and net fishing. For
the next few years there was no exploitation at this location, which allowed stocks
the opportunity to recover. However, on the face of it the main beneficiaries were
the net and coble operators in the Firth: the district's netting catch increased
steadily from 8,000 in 1892 to 27,200 in 1895. In the latter year the total for the rods
including the neighbouring Alness amounted to only 800.

Evidently the intensity and productivity of the nets dismayed the river proprietors, and by 1901 the cruives were functioning again. According to Calderwood
(1909), as well as the cruives, '27 shots [i.e. nets] are fished here in three and a

quarter miles of water' and 'it will be readily understood that a very complete control over all ascending fish can be exercised and, except during floods or the weekly close times, fish have a poor chance of reaching the upper waters'. The efficiency of the nets was beginning to have a marked impact on stocks, as in 1907 their catch was reduced to little more than 4,000; this included '150 clean fish at the first sweep' on opening day (11 February).

Within a decade the decline in stocks was 'serious', threatening the viability of rod fishings, and the river proprietors decided to act. Sir John Stirling and Lord Roberts, amongst others, joined forces with the Sellar family (who had the Findhorn Bay nets) and the Lovats on the Beauly to form the Moray Firth Salmon Fishing Company in 1920. They bought up most of the area's coastal nets, including those in the Conon estuary and Firth, so that they could be properly regulated and operated to achieve a balance; once stocks built up after a period of little if any netting effort, the company would reactivate their operations to exploit the better numbers. This was the pattern for four decades or so before it adopted a more business-like approach. As salmon stocks started to dwindle in the 1980s, so once again the company reduced the intensity of its operations; between 1977 and 1986 its annual average catch within the Firth was 502 salmon and 1,478 grilse. Ultimately, the company's rights in the Cromarty Firth were acquired and mothballed by the Atlantic Salmon Conservation Trust in 1991.

In terms of angling, the Conon was historically very much a spring fishery, with fresh fish in the lower reaches from opening day (11 February). (Incidentally there seems to be some confusion as to when and by whose authority the opening moved to 26 January.) The main runs of salmon were in March and April. Before 1939 the lower Brahan beat (above the tidal stretch) would typically catch 150 by the end of March, and 300 by the end of April, while between 1898 and 1900, before the nets were brought under some control, Brahan Castle averaged only 96 up to the end of April. Up until the 1940s Fairburn Estate, with the right bank for some four miles upstream from the mouth of the Orrin, hardly fished after the end of June, and thus in most years no more than three grilse were recorded!

The Blackwater tributary, which joins the left bank of the Conon from the north-west some five miles up from the mouth, was also a superb spring fishery; the short Middle beat (below Rogie Falls) could easily produce 500 fish by the end of June.

The Conon system was first tapped for electricity in the 1920s, when a small power station was built to harness the potential of the Falls of Conon. Then, between 1946 and 1961, the whole of the catchment was exploited in the most ambitious and comprehensive hydro-electric scheme in the north. In three sepa-rate stages – the Fannich Scheme, the Glascarnoch-Luichart-Torr Achilty Scheme, and the Orrin Scheme – the Conon catchment was transformed, with seven main dams, twenty miles of tunnels, fifteen miles of aqueducts and seven power stations. Thereafter the character of the system was fundamentally altered. Both the Conon and the Blackwater used to be wilder and less predictable in the spring. There were major floods in 1892 and 1922. There were also four big damaging floods between 1962 and 1989, after the harnessing of the system but before lessons were learned. In the 1962 flood the Marybank to Moy Bridge road was under 16 ft of water. The main stem of the Conon now carries far more water on an annual basis than previously, as it receives great volumes from outwith its own catchment – from the headwaters of the Carron, the Blackwater and the Orrin. Since 1989 there have been no further floods, as more water is released on a regular basis from Loch Luichart, and consequently there is enough spare capacity to hold back flood waters when required.

As the scheme developed, the Hydro Board bought all the salmon fishing rights (including the valuable Brahan Castle fishings, held for generations by the Seaforth family) with one notable exception: the late Sir John Stirling refused to sell the Fairburn beats, despite the threat of compulsory purchase, as he believed that in due course the fishings would actually improve downstream of the dams.

During the 1950s the Hydro Board put into place an extensive programme of works designed to mitigate for the loss of spawning grounds and natural flows. This 'compensation package' included numerous fish-lifts within dams, a

The Boat Pool of the Lower Fairburn Beat, just below the junction with the Blackwater

The Kettle Pool on the Middle Brahan Beat

large-capacity hatchery and guaranteed compensation flows (the Conon no longer becomes unfishably low in summer). New fish-ladders were installed, most notably at the Conon Falls; prior to this the falls had never been surmountable, although blasting them had been considered on several occasions since the late nineteenth century. With these falls circumvented, salmon for the first time had access to the River Bran (the largest tributary) and a vast area of virgin spawning territory. There were considerable teething problems with the downstream migration of smolts, but these have now been resolved, and the Bran is already making a considerable contribution to the system's smolt-producing capacity.

The Blackwater was also radically affected by the Hydro scheme. Its headwaters were dammed and piped across to the Conon. Most of the spawning burns and habitat were lost, and consequently the two dams were constructed without fish passes. By way of further compensation, a large fish trap was built on the Upper Blackwater. This was designed to capture the entire run of adult salmon returning to the Blackwater, and these fish are indeed trapped each year as broodstock for the hatchery.

Whilst the importance of the Blackwater as a fishery has greatly diminished, it is still a vital nursery area. In fact two-thirds of the River Conon's annual rod catch is now landed below the junction with the Blackwater. It is probably fair to say that the tributaries have borne the brunt of the effects of the Hydro schemes. The Meig, which flows from the west parallel to the Bran and joins the Conon below the falls, and the Orrin are no longer so accessible to adult salmon.

The Orrin, the lowest tributary (two miles up from the mouth), was another excellent spring fishery; by virtue of a separate royal charter to Fairburn Estate, the Falls pool was extensively netted, and in some years it yielded 1,000 salmon, with fish taken as early as opening day. The Orrin was impounded prior to the 1959 season. That year the nets took 87 and the rods three, and the following year they had one and one respectively – the reason for the dramatic decline being the amount of dirt and silt being washed downstream from the works above. The tributary was then restocked, but the outbreak of UDN in 1967 meant that it was the early 1970s before adult numbers recovered, with the nets taking an average of 111 salmon and 239 grilse between 1973 and 1982. Fish began to use the four Borland passes in the dam, but the smolts could not get down; modifications were then carried out, and now some smolts are descending. Netting ceased in 1988, and these days there is hardly a fish in the Orrin before July.

The Conon system's run patterns have changed substantially. The spring runs are a faint shadow of their former selves, but the grilse runs are generally excellent. Whilst the Hydro regime has contributed to the demise of the system's spring run, other factors have also contributed, including UDN and marine mortality. There are indications that numbers of multi-sea-winter salmon are beginning to recover as a result of restocking programmes. Thus the Brahan beats' 2004 spring catch was over 70, compared to an average of 39 for the previous three years.

Salmon in the high teens of pounds used to be caught by rods in good numbers, and fish between 20 lb and 30 lb were landed on a regular basis, with heavier examples not unknown. One spring in the early 1920s the Stirling family's German tutor, a salmon angling novice who had never caught a fish, was struggling to put out a line on the Muirton Falls Pool (now submerged at Torr Achilty dam). Somehow he managed a reasonably long cast, and hooked a fish. Realising that this was the salmon of a lifetime, old Forbes the gillie seized the rod without ceremony, and 45 minutes later a cock springer of 48 lb was on the bank. In the early 1900s a baggot was caught by a rod on the Brahan water, and before it was released it was laid out on the sand, so that its outline could be recorded. From the measurements its weight was later estimated at over 60 lb.

By any standards the magnitude of the current stocking policy is impressive. In the last ten years an average of 2,600,000 ova per annum (an astonishing figure) have been handled by the hatchery. The river board's approach is as follows: 'By distributing the juvenile salmon in large numbers and at an early stage of development over the suitable nursery, they are exposed to natural selection for as long as possible in freshwater. The resulting smolts are of indigenous stock, have lived in the wild for two or three years and are well adapted to the habitat that produced them'. In the last decade close to 100 miles of previously inaccessible juvenile habitat have been brought into use; this includes half a mile of a specially created 'nursery channel' (completed in early 2004), with optimal habitat to support a high density of fish, adjacent to the lower river. Each year over 700 holes are dug by hand in the headwaters to create artificial redds. These continuing efforts have ensured that the Conon system remains a significant fishery, as figures for the average annual rod catch for the main river and the Blackwater confirm:

	Salmon/grilse
1980–84	1,428
1985–89	1,960
1990–94	1,861
1995–99	1,726
2000–03	1,290

It is fair to stress that these numbers could not have been achieved without the immense assistance of Scottish Hydro Electric, which has been freely provided on every level for four decades. The harnessing of the Conon is a *fait accompli*, but that said, the company does everything within its power to promote salmon regeneration. In the 1980s the company sold off its salmon-fishing rights (it was really not set up to be a riparian owner). The prolific Brahan fishings, purchased by Peter Whitfield in 1985, were successfully syndicated and now consistently enjoy over half of the system's rod catch; their annual average (1991–2000) was 986, dropping to 690 for the period 2001 to 2004.

On the netting front the Conon District Salmon Fishery Board spent over £250,000 on buy-outs in the 1980s. All that remain are three bag net operators outside the Firth and five sweep-net operators inside the Firth. Their take is approximately 500 fish a year and they have an incentive to restrict their netting to six weeks from mid-June, as if they do so, the board allows a 90 per cent rebate on their rates.

The Conon is afflicted with a formidable and diverse array of predators. Seals have always been a problem, as Grimble noted; 'their depredations are very serious'. Today the population in the Cromarty Firth is close to 400, a considerable gauntlet for salmon to run, and they make frequent raids into the Conon, as far upstream as Torr Achilty dam, some seven miles inland. In 2001 a 25-lb fish was landed with no less than four large seal bites. And recently a lady angler on the

Green Bank Pool of the Lower Brahan beat had played out a salmon and was bringing it towards the net, when it was seized and removed by a seal.

Considerable populations of pike exist in the lower Conon, with specimens in the 12 lb to 14 lb class frequently encountered. It seems likely that the pike emanated from Loch Luichart, where in the early 1960s the Hydro Board netted a 32-lb specimen. The Bran tributary holds considerable numbers of perch, and mink are steadily establishing themselves, especially on the Blackwater. Perhaps the most unusual alien species discovered to date is a cobra; in 1999 one was found, newly expired, in bushes on Moy Island.

Recently there was an unusual case of attempted unsanctioned human predation. In 2001 a local poacher was apprehended in a wet-suit, carrying a spear gun, by the Russian Pool on the Brahan water. At his subsequent appearance at Dingwall Sheriff Court, he pleaded 'not guilty' and stated that he was 'shooting eels in the burn to feed a sick otter'. The magistrate then asked, against a background of considerable mirth, why a wetsuit was necessary in the burn. The defendant replied that the unfortunate otter was on the other side of the river, and so it was going to be necessary for him to swim across with the eels. Rarely has a court of law collapsed so uncontrollably.

ALNESS

The recent history of the Alness is testimony to one of the most remarkable transformations of a Highland salmon river in modern times. Until just a few decades ago this east-coast spate river was of marginal interest from an angling point of view. In terms of salmon rivers the Cromarty Firth, throughout the nineteenth century and for most of the twentieth, was viewed almost exclusively as the long estuary for the Conon, universally accepted as one the north's great systems. By comparison the Alness, with its mouth halfway down the twenty-mile-long Firth, was barely accorded a mention. This was hardly surprising given the level of rod catches, which a hundred years ago amounted to at most 30 salmon/grilse per annum and up to 150 sea trout. The real value attached to the river was the lucrative netting rights at the mouth – taking both Alness fish and passing Conon fish.

The source of the Alness is in the mountains of Kildermorie Forest in Easter Ross, close to the watershed of the upper Carron. The river, known in this upper section as the Abhainn na Glasa, flows for some ten miles, first through flat, high moorland (excellent spawning territory) and then through a fast, tumbling, boulder-strewn section, to reach Loch Morie. This loch, surrounded by precipitous

The Wire Pool on the Alness AC's Burns Water stretch 400 yards downstream of the
mouth of the Blackwater tributary

hills, is some two miles long and very deep. (Incidentally both Grimble and
Calderwood stated that salmon could not 'reach Loch Morie'. This is clearly erro-
neous, as there is no obstacle of any consequence below the loch.)

From the loch, the Alness (also known as the Averon) runs for another 12
miles – initially at a sedate pace through moorland, and then much more swiftly
through gorges and heavily wooded sections – to its mouth below the town of
Alness. It has one of the steepest descents (over 600 ft) of any river of comparable
length in Scotland, although there is no significant waterfall, and is one of the
most stunningly attractive rivers in the north. Two miles below the loch the river
receives its most important tributary, the Blackwater, which runs down Strath
Rusdale from the north-west.

In the early 1800s Sir Hector Munro (1726–1805), a general who had made a
fortune in the East India Company, put together a major estate in Easter Ross that
in due course became known as Novar; the holdings included most of the Alness.
One section excluded was that attached to Ardross Castle, half-way up the river;
here some importance was attached to angling, as a network of catwalks to facilitate casting was built in the mid-nineteenth century.

The Salmon Fisheries Commission of 1863 concluded that the Alness ('owned
by Munro of Teaninich, Matheson of Ardross and Munro of Novar') was 'very

badly managed', but that it 'might be made a very valuable stream, were it not overlapped by two stake nets'. Management did not improve, and in fact became more difficult, as during the first half of the twentieth century Novar disposed of some of its interests in the river; in essence ownership of the salmon rights became highly fragmented.

Right up until the 1960s very little priority was given to salmon angling. In fact, back then the lease of the shooting rights at Novar included seven single-bank miles of the river at no extra cost (in truth the fishing could hardly be marketed separately, as the annual rod catch of salmon/grilse for the whole river often struggled to reach double figures). Then, some forty years ago the late Arthur Munro-Ferguson, descendant of Sir Hector Munro and laird of Novar, determined to realize the potential of the Alness and turn it into a viable rod fishery. The task was immense, but he had a great affinity with the river and, crucially, a vision of what was possible.

He set to work on a variety of fronts. Wherever possible he extended and rationalized Novar's ownership, so that in due course the estate had some seventy per cent of the river (double bank) between Morie and the sea. He hired a huge bulldozer and excavating machine and created a network of tracks, allowing easy vehicular access to all the estate water – a massive undertaking (hitherto, much of the river had been essentially cut off by dense woodland). The same machine was also employed in the river. Initial advice on pool improvement was obtained from fishery consultant the late Neil Graesser, but the hands-on, day-to-day management of a most ambitious programme involving fifty or so pools and extensive other works was under the control of the then River Superintendent Bill Topham, whose attention to detail proved in the ensuing years to be invaluable.

Boulders were moved, creating long large pools wherever there was a flat section of water; in addition, in the faster sections innumerable small runs and pots were enhanced and developed. The amount of holding water was increased immeasurably, and the fish, which had previously tended to run right through to the loch with hardly a pause, now began to move upstream more slowly. Inevitably some croys have been washed out (particularly in a tremendous flood in 1989) but most are still in place and have blended into the natural surroundings.

A hatchery was built in 1980, and since then between 150,000 and 200,000 fry have been planted out annually in inaccessible areas (it is perhaps worth noting that ova from the Helmsdale were introduced to the system in the 1920s). In 1979 a small dam incorporating a fish pass was constructed at the outlet from Loch Morie; judicious use of the stored water allows a spate to be prolonged by a week or two.

Mr Munro-Ferguson split the Novar water into six rotating beats (emulating to some extent the Helmsdale) and a Home beat, though the last was subsequently

A fine late season day on Beat 3 of the Novar Estate water

scrapped in a further reorganisation. Netting at the mouth finally ceased in 1987, and in 1992 the rights were acquired by the district fishery board. All these factors combined to create a viable rod fishery, and the results have been impressive. In the 1980s the Novar beats averaged close to 250 salmon/grilse per season, though, given that the Alness is a spate river, substantial variations are inevitable; in the wet season of 1985 Novar had some 600 (the total for the whole river was some 750). Since the mid-1990s the average for Novar – to some extent reflecting the global downturn in salmon stocks – has dropped to 150; it is also fair to say that angling pressure is less now than it was in the 1980s.

The Alness's main grilse and summer salmon runs are from mid-June. It is a late river with a genuine back-end run; indeed sea-liced fish were caught in October 2003. There is still a race of heavy, late-running, powerful salmon in the 12 lb to 16 lb class with much bigger fish among them, the majority of which come in during late October and November, after the end of the rod season. They are usually known as greybacks or bluebacks (locals in Alness, who regularly watched them surmounting the sluices at Dalmore, refer to them, for some unknown reason, as 'Norwegians'). There is also the remnant of a spring run, with the odd fish taken in May. There was (and perhaps still is) an earlier run. Certainly, bail-liffs' reports from the early 1900s refer to springers running in April, and it appears that rudimentary attempts to develop the spring runs, presumably for the

Raven's Rock – one of the Alness's best holding pools

benefit of the nets, were made in the 1920s by purchasing limited quantities of ova from the Helmsdale. It is thought that early running fish were adversely affected by the absence over many decades of an effective fish pass at the weir at Dalmore; this weir, half a mile up from the rivermouth, was a temperature barrier, below which springers were highly vulnerable. The situation was rectified twenty years ago with the construction of a new fish pass.

The Alness is very much a 'hunter's river'. The larger pools may be fished conventionally, but much of the water is difficult to read and needs a different approach, for small lies are everywhere – the Alness is one of the great dibbling rivers. The finest exponent of this art was Arthur Chamberlain, who fished the river for forty years, finally hanging up his rod when he was 90. His knowledge of the lies was supreme, and, such was his skill, he had an uncanny ability to take a fish from the river at will. His confidence was such that with many lies, if he could not induce an instant take, he would simply declare that 'he's not there'. Some sections of the Alness can really only be tackled with a dibbled fly. Both methods of dibbling are effective – the dibbled dropper and the dibbled tail fly (the latter is usually a version of a Collie Dog skated between the boulders).

Apart from the Novar water, there is also a thriving club, the Alness Angling Club, with two miles of the lower river (from the Douglas Pool to the sea) as well as a mile below the junction with the Blackwater. Between 2000 and 2002 the club averaged 94 salmon/grilse and 60 sea trout.

CARRON

Whilst there are no less than five River Carrons in Scotland, only one, the Kyle of Sutherland Carron, merits a place amongst serious salmon streams. It was formerly in Ross-shire, but in the interests of 'rationalization' was transferred to Sutherland in 1974.

In the mid-nineteenth century the upper Carron glens suffered a far more traumatic rationalization. In the early 1800s some 400 people lived west of Braelangwell, and in the 1840s and 1850s this area was the scene of some of the last large-scale forced evictions in Scotland. The scale of the human tragedies is evident at Croick Church; here the stained glass windows carry poignant graffiti incised by the inhabitants of Glencalvie, who in June 1845 sought refuge amongst the tombstones. Gruinards was cleared of its population as late as 1854, after a brutal episode known as the 'Massacre of the Rosses'.

The Carron drains some 150 square miles and is the third largest of the Kyle rivers. Its source is only five miles from Loch Broom on the west coast. It then flows 14 miles, past Deanich Lodge (as remote as one can get in these islands), to the Falls at Glencalvie. Upstream of this landmark it absorbs the Alladale River, and downstream it receives the Diebidale River/Water of Glencalvie. A mile below that, its major tributary, the Blackwater, comes in from the west, and the river then descends seven miles through Strathcarron to its mouth in the lower Kyle opposite Bonar Bridge.

Anyone who walks the eight miles between Carron Bridge and the Glencalvie Falls will soon appreciate that salmon angling has a long tradition here. Casting walkways and platforms of late nineteenth-century origin abound, and lengths of iron protruding from sheer rock faces indicate where other wooden structures have long since decayed and been washed away. With the possible exception of the long gorge section of the Findhorn, no other Scottish river has been the subject of so much endeavour to make almost every yard of otherwise inaccessible water coverable by rods. Calderwood referred to 'hundreds of yards of wooden paths' downstream of the 'Amat Falls' (i.e. the Glencalvie Falls).

Falls dominate the Carron system, and they dictate the timing of upstream migration. On the lower river, half a mile above Carron Bridge, the Gledfield Falls (now shared by the Gledfield and Cornhill beats) are a temperature barrier in the early spring, although nowadays less formidable, given the trend to milder

The head of the Long Pool at Amat, consistently the Carron's most prolific beat

winters. On the middle river the Moral Falls (shared by Gruinards and Braelangwell) are a more significant obstacle, which fish do not begin to ascend until the water temperature reaches around 40°F, and so up until mid- to late April spring fishing is concentrated on the beats below. Incidentally Young (1857) stated that the Carron was not an early river, having 'no clean fish earlier than April, and but few even at that time'. However, since then the river developed a consistent reputation for February and even January springers. These winter fish are now scarce, and the main spring runs are from March to May, with, in the last few years, April becoming the most reliable month.

The Glencalvie Falls, some twenty feet high, are in a different league, and only negotiable in certain very-low-water conditions. Whether and how they might be eased has been the source of bitter controversy for very many decades. On the one hand, the beats immediately below the falls, Amat and Glencalvie, benefit from having a captive audience of fish – a horrific poisoning incident in July 1995, which killed 1,150 salmon/grilse in a 200-yard stretch downstream from the falls, gave an indication of the density of fish that can assemble below. On the other hand, the middle and lower beats have long wanted to see the falls modified to allow more fish access to the excellent spawning and nursery grounds in the headwaters above. With this in mind 50 rod-caught springers were uplifted from downstream of the Moral Falls and released at Deanich in both 1999 and 2000.

The Moral Falls, an important temperature barrier to the ascent of salmon in the spring

The falls were not always quite so insurmountable. Ronnie Ross, the current gillie at Braelangwell, recalls that in the 1920s his father was one of a group of men, who, in low water around the end of May each year, would with the use of ropes lower one of the party into the chasm half way up, to clear out rocks and other debris, deposited there over the winter; with greater depth in the chasm, fish had a better chance of making a further leap. Evidently this had some effect, as Alexander McConnochie (1923) wrote that, when he was staying up at Deanich, bags of four to six fish per day were possible in favourable conditions – indeed 40 salmon was the normal annual catch at Deanich in the 1920s. A few decades ago the Falls Pool was netted every May, with springers lifted over the obstacle. There is little doubt that the falls alter from year to year; occasionally reasonable numbers ascend (thus in the late 1960s Jim Pilkington once caught 27 upstream during August and September), but in many years few if any are able to make it.

The Glencalvie Falls remain contentious because the system is not over-endowed with easily accessible spawning water. The gravel in the Diebidale River/Water of Glencalvie is highly unstable. The Blackwater is not as productive as a glance at a map might suggest. First, there is quite a daunting waterfall two miles up, below which large numbers of salmon congregate in the summer in anticipation of the right water conditions. The ripping of fish used to be carried out here on a commercial scale, and the situation became so grave that in 1964 the then proprietor eased the falls. This helped, but they remain a substantial hurdle. Above the falls there are two miles of deep canal-like water – a useful sanctuary but devoid of gravel. Upstream, three miles have spawning possibilities. Then there is a gorge section with several small falls, none of which appear to be particularly serious, but mysteriously fish have never been reported above them in what is called the Glasha Burn, which includes over four miles of seemingly ideal spawning and juvenile territory.

The smolt-producing capacity of the Carron system is also compromised by the fact that adult fish, if they manage to surmount the Glencalvie Falls, are now denied access to the headwaters west of Deanich. Two miles upstream of Deanich is a weir, constructed in the late 1950s, above which a tunnel takes much of the flow through the hill to supplement the Conon hydro-electric system. This weir was designed with no provision for fish to negotiate it. Scottish Hydro Electric is now coming under pressure to incorporate a fish pass and a smolt screen over the entrance to the tunnel, although to date there has been no official representation. These comparatively inexpensive modifications would enable the recolonization of Gleann Beag, an area rich in spawning gravel and, given the altitude (well over 1,000 feet), ideal for the production of late-hatching fry.

On the Carron system generally agreement on any plans of action has long been a problem, on account of the politics and factions that prevail. A hundred-and-fifty years ago, Andrew Young wrote perceptively that the 'one great preventive to the increase of salmon in this river, is its being in the hands of so many proprietors'. Then there were seven. Up until 1961 the predominant owner was Balnagown Estate, which owned the catchment above the Glencalvie Falls as well as some six miles of the left bank upstream of Carron Bridge. These assets formed part of the Balnagown dispersal sale of 1961. The Estate had been convinced that the weir and water abstraction on the upper river would spell the end of the Carron as a significant salmon system, and with this in mind guests at Braelangwell (which the Estate ran as a hotel from 1954, offering access to its left bank fishings) were permitted to spin the water in order to boost catches prior to compensation negotiations with the Hydro Board. Thus, in April and May 1955 guests landed 210 springers. Apart from this brief episode, the Estate's waters were not fished intensively. The main effort was on the upper stretch, from the Frenchman to the Scarp pools, which averaged 131 salmon between 1952 and 1960. From the tail of the Scarp to the Mistress Ross was 'hardly fished' and from there to the Whirl Pool was 'spasmodically fished'.

Miss Edith and Miss Eva Godman bought Balnagown's assets within the Carron catchment in their entirety, and later added Forest Farm and Corriemulzie from the Campbell family and Glencalvie from Tony Hickley to their immense empire. They later gave most of the estates to their relations, but a large section remained in trust for some years. Now, including the lower Blackwater, there are ten proprietors – eight of whom share just eight miles of the river's main stem. Current ownership of the beats in ascending order is as follows: Invercharron (one mile double bank), the Macnamara family; Gledfield (one mile single bank), the Swarovski family; Cornhill (one mile single bank), the Speirs family; Dounie (one-and-a-half miles double bank and half a mile single bank), the Hunter family; Gruinards (four miles single bank), Miss Jean Matterson; Braelangwell (four miles single bank), the Godman family; Amat (two-and-a-half miles double bank and two miles single bank), the Holt family; Glencalvie (one-and-a-half miles single bank), Peter Fowler and Nick Forman-Hardy. Paul Lister owns the upper Carron (Alladale and Deanich Estates). Most of the lower Blackwater is now the property of James Hall.

The section of the Kyle of Sutherland immediately upstream and, particularly, downstream of the mouth of the Carron was for the best part of two centuries one of the most productive netting locations in the north. The mouth of the river was altered and moved 100 yards westwards in the 1840s to facilitate the building of the netsmen's walkway (the original channel is still visible). These nets at Bonar Bridge, because of their location, could take a high proportion of the Carron's summer stock, especially in times of drought. In 1907 eight proprietors and one tenant formed the Kyle of Sutherland Fishing Syndicate, and for the following

A late spring spate on the Moral Pool, shared by Gruinards and Braelangwell

decade (as detailed in the Oykel entry below) it sought to moderate the netting catch. Notably the nets did not function before April, and following the Syndicate's demise this remained the case, with the netting season delayed until 15 April. Balnagown's Bonar nets averaged 3,023 salmon/grilse between 1950 and 1963. The Misses Godman acquired the Bonar station in 1961 and subsequently bought adjacent stations. In a 'good year' these nets, worked by five crews and stretching from about a quarter of a mile above the mouth of the Carron to the lowest station at the Scarp three quarters of a mile below Bonar Bridge, accounted for over 10,000 fish. The Bonar Bridge stations finally ceased operations after the 1997 season.

Apart from the brief lapse referred to above, the main stem of the Carron has long been fly-only. The river has also been in the vanguard of 'catch and release'. This began in the late 1980s when two Braelangwell tenants, Dr Hugh Muir and Ian MacDonald, started to question their actions, killing just a brace or so a week; soon this attitude spread, and now, with published catch limits in place, consistently over 75 per cent of the river's spring catch and over 60 per cent of the annual catch is returned. All the river's gillies are staunch advocates of this form of conservation.

I have already indicated how spring runs have altered, but perhaps the most marked change has been the increase in grilse. Until recently most of the summer

The Little Gorge Pool at Dounie

catch consisted of salmon, and indeed grilse were quite unusual. At Braelangwell grilse amounted to just 9 per cent of the average annual catch of 136 between 1962 and 1970. By 1998–2000, though, this had escalated to 56 per cent of the average annual catch of 164. Spring salmon catches (to the end of May) have declined since the 1960s, and more recently there has also been a fall in the number of summer salmon.

Five-year averages for 1999 to 2003 for six of the beats are as follows: Gledfield (25), Cornhill (44), Dounie (85), Gruinards (111), Braelangwell (127) and Amat (192), and the average for the system as a whole – including Invercharron, Glencalvie, the upper Carron and the Blackwater – is now some 700 per annum. In addition, the Kyle of Sutherland Angling Association, with the tidal fishings near the mouth, averages close to 200, although there is no way of determining what percentage are Carron fish.

The size of salmon on the Carron has never been exceptional. Twenty-pound fish are most unusual, and very occasionally salmon of 30 lb have been landed, but this would appear to be close to the limit. In the 1950s Larry MacDonald caught one of 30 lb in the Raven Pool at Gledfield, and in August 1958 Ronnie Ross took a 'horrible thing' of 31 lb in the Whirl at Gruinards. On the same beat Jean Matterson had a fine 30 lb springer in the Washerwoman in 1992. In August 2000 Andy Griffiths released a 42-inch summer salmon on the Braelangwell side of Moral. In late September 2004 Allan Donaldson released a very heavy cock fish (43 inches long and estimated at 33 lb) in Vernons at Amat.

In September 1991 Dounie gillie Kim Sawyer hooked a very big salmon in heavy water in the Hiding Pool. After one hour, during which the fish never lost the upper hand, it left the pool with a surging downstream run. The only way to follow was to enter the water, and this Kim did – a total and frightening immersion through rapids. At last he gained dry land, minus both waders but clutching the rod; he had lost contact with the fish, but steadily retrieved the backing, until he reached the Big Gorge, some 450 yards below the Hiding Pool. Then there was a tug – unbelievably the fish was still on. Kim edged his way to a ledge opposite the deep water, where the salmon had taken up station, sulking fifteen feet down. Two hours had elapsed, and darkness was drawing in. Kim decided that, make or break, the fish had to be brought to the surface.

By now a young lady, Kim's charge for the week, had climbed down with the landing net, pleading to be allowed to net it. Applying maximum pressure Kim winched what felt like a sack of coal to the surface. Against his better judgement, he finally agreed to his companion's request, despite her inexperience. As the great fish 'with scales the size of thumbnails' passed over the net Kim tried to warn her not to lift it like a pan. *She lifted it like a frying pan.* The salmon teetered momentarily on the rim (the fly caught in the net) before slipping away into the deep. Recriminations were not appropriate: 'Everybody loses fish, miss ... What were we going to do with a great muckle fish that size anyway?' The salmon was estimated at 30 lb.

To some extent sea trout are an unknown quantity on the Carron. As was the case on so many salmon rivers, they were for many years considered to be vermin, and so were not recorded. The other factor is that fishing effort for sea trout varies considerably from season to season. A reasonable estimate for the annual catch would be between 100 and 200; Moral can hold good numbers, but the main holding area is the sluggish stretch of the lower Blackwater between Croick and the bridge by Amat; in fact sea trout traditionally run and spawn in this tributary.

OYKEL

Up until the early twentieth century most maps and gazetteers credited the Oykel with the most extensive catchment north of the Spey. The Cassley and the Shin were viewed as tributaries of the Oykel, the lower reaches of which were accepted as extending almost as far as Bonar Bridge. Modern thinking is that whilst they share a common estuary in the Kyle of Sutherland (tidal to just west of the mouth of the Cassley), the three are entirely separate rivers, each with its own distinct runs of salmon.

The Oykel, which drains 137 square miles, emanates from the south-facing slopes of the Ben More Assynt massif. It has a gentle course of five miles through Benmore Forest, punctuated by two sets of falls, to Loch Ailsh. Then it flows down Strath Oykel for eight miles, absorbing several spawning tributaries, to an impressive gorge section just above Oykel Bridge. At the top of this gorge is the Oykel Falls, a temperature barrier that holds fish back in the spring. Half a mile below the bridge the Oykel's main tributary joins from the south-west; this is the Einig, which in turn has two significant spawning sub-tributaries, the Corriemulzie (which runs off Freevater Forest to the south) and Rappach Water (which rises in Rhidorroch Forest in the far west). The great majority of the system's spring fish run the Einig. Below the junction the Oykel proceeds at a more sedate and majestic pace for six miles to the head of the Kyle by Rosehall.

Like the other great straths of Scotland's far north, the tranquillity of Strathoykel hides a darker side. A mile downstream of Langwell is the battlefield of Tuiteam-Tarbhach, where in around 1400 the McLeods of Lewis clashed with the MacKays of Strathnaver and other Sutherlanders. The islanders were outnumbered, and all the McLeods were killed except for one man who escaped back to Lewis, where he died of his wounds. Tuiteam-Tarbhach translates as field of blood or plentiful slaughter, and it is believed that the cemetery, which is miles from the nearest church, marks the spot. It is perhaps not surprising that, according to McConnochie (1924), the Oykel's 'fords had at one time an evil reputation, not on account of natural dangers, but from the water-spirits that were believed to lie in wait for travellers'. (Incidentally, the traditional way to traverse these fords at times of high water was on stilts.)

Despite the troubled past there has been remarkable continuity of ownership. For over 700 years the whole of the Oykel was part of the vast land-holdings of Balnagown Estate. Following the death of Sir Charles Ross in 1942, his widow concentrated considerable efforts on marketing the sporting side of the estate, but with limited success – the debts were crippling. The situation came to a head in September 1961 with a massive dispersal auction. All lots relating to the Oykel were sold to Miss Edith and Miss Eva Godman. The Lower Oykel Fishings – downstream of the Falls, and including the Einig below its Falls – were then syndicated through the sale of five pro indiviso shares. The intention was that they could not be sub-divided, but this has not been accomplished, because in Scotland a share can be sold to a partnership. In 1987 Pat Colvin (Miss Edith Godman's nephew and inheritor) sold Benmore Estate, including Loch Ailsh, the two miles of river below the loch and the headwaters

The Lower Allt Rugaidh Pool on the Allt Rugaidh Beat of the Upper Oykel

above, to Edmund Vestey. The Colvin family retains ownership of the five miles upstream of the Oykel Falls.

In the early nineteenth century Strathoykel, which until then had supported numerous small communities, was cleared – not so much by the direct use of force, but rather by a combination of 'persuasion', attrition, religious blackmail and economic necessity. By the 1830s salmon angling in the Oykel began to gain some limited status, although on restricted terms. Thus in 1837 and 1838 the rod fishing downstream of the Falls was let to John MacKenzie of Cromarty for £30 per annum, but the Estate retained the rights to all fish caught (apart from fish for the tenant's own use), and no angling was permitted after 26 August.

In this era the Kyle of Sutherland below the mouth of the Oykel was systematically netted. In 1851 Andrew Young of Invershin had ten netting stations in the seven miles between the 'junction of the Oykel and the Cassley' and the junction of the Shin with the Kyle. And commercial exploitation was not restricted to the tidal waters; several nineteenth-century accounts refer to the practice of using long-handled hoop-nets to scoop running fish out of the pots on the Oykel Falls, just above Oykel Bridge. There is another important waterfall a mile up the Einig tributary. Both of these falls are temperature barriers, and spring angling is concentrated in the waters downstream.

June on the Flag Pool below Oykel Bridge

An early cast on the Washerwoman, just upstream of the junction with the Einig

A hundred years ago, perhaps reflecting the intensity of the netting effort, rental income from angling on the Oykel was fairly modest at £300 per annum (this compared to a contemporary annual rental on the Shin of £800). The Oykel below the Falls was then divided into just two beats, with the lower starting at the Long Pool; Grimble suggested that to cover the whole of the latter (which now constitutes almost three beats) required 'nine hours' hard flogging', and in view of the distances he advised having the gillie carry the waders! Rod catch records from this era are extremely scarce, with just the odd reference to the likely sport in a particular month. Thus McConnochie singled out April as the 'best month ... when 50 to 60 to two rods can be depended on'.

In 1907 the Kyle of Sutherland Fishing Syndicate was formed, representing eight proprietors and one tenant in the district. Its objective was to work the nets, but with a view to achieving a greater balance between the nets and the rods. The Syndicate leased most of the Kyle nets for £1,575 per annum; it short-ened the netting season (with no exploitation before 1 April), extended the weekend slap (the period during which netting was prohibited) to 60 hours and closed the netting stations above Bonar Bridge. The last restriction was not sustained after the first season, but at least there was a semblance of control. Between 1907 and 1916 the Syndicate's average take was 1,692 salmon, 2,566

Late evening on the lower Oykel's Washerwoman Pool as a heavy summer spate runs off

grilse and 1,767 sea trout. Perhaps its greatest legacy was the cessation of netting before April.

Between the wars the lower Oykel was by today's standards lightly fished. From 1927 to 1932 the average rod catch for the season was 181, of which 115 were landed before the end of May, and fishing effort before March and after July was virtually non-existent. However the reputation of the lower Oykel as a rod fishery grew steadily, and in the years leading up to the 1961 auction it brought in £12,000 per annum in rents. Between 1951 and 1960 these fishings, divided into six beats, had an annual average catch of 494 salmon and grilse. The average annual figures since syndication are as follows:

	Salmon/grilse
1964–69	714
1970–79	738
1980–89	955
1990–99	838
2000–03	676

From the mid-1970s rod pressure increased from eight to 12 (four rotating beats of three rods each). The nets at Bonar Bridge ceased operations after the 1997 season; by then, rod catches had already started to fall, provoking the removal of the nets. The recent drop in the annual average largely reflects a decline in the spring catch – although there was a marked improvement in 2004, with 190 salmon caught by the end of May, out of a season's total of 821.

Above the Oykel Falls the river is more intimate, and one would be hard pushed, except in one or two pools, to put out a full salmon line. This is essentially a summer fishery, with excellent sport whenever good water levels coincide with the main grilse runs. The five miles upstream from the Falls are now known as the Upper Oykel Fishings, with four rotating beats of three rods each; the five-year average (1999 to 2003) is 165 salmon. In ascending order theses beats are Lubcroy, Camus, and then in more rugged terrain Ault Rugaidh and Salachy. Above the latter is the Assynt Estate water, with a five-year average (to 2003) of 92 salmon. This two-mile stretch between the Allt Eileag burn and Loch Ailsh is split into two beats with two rods on each.

McConnochie asserted erroneously that salmon 'do not ascend' beyond the loch. In fact the Oykel above the loch is easily accessible; falls three miles up are not a significant obstacle, and some spring fish spawn at least another two miles further on. The extent of spawning water is indeed impressive. Apart from the

The Perch Pool of the Einig, the system's main tributary for spring salmon

upper reaches of the main river, the most expansive spawning area is the vast and remote hinterland of the Einig catchment, what Calderwood referred to as 'this lonely hill region where man cannot destroy many fish'. The Einig's two tributaries, the Corriemulzie River (where a fall was eased in the 1960s to make it more readily surmountable) and the Rappach Water, provide at least 20 miles of spawning possibilities.

The Oykel is the only Kyle river which has not been harnessed for commercial hydro-electric purposes; a small domestic hydro scheme above Loch Ailsh was dismantled in 2003. The Oykel is now a Special Area of Conservation for salmon and freshwater pearl mussels under the European Habitats Directive. (Bizarrely, the Dornoch Firth has been given a similar designation for common seals, for which salmon are an important prey species.)

There is also a long history of stocking on the Oykel. The main stem was stocked every year from the early 1900s until 1960, though the nursery burns were essentially ignored before the 1950s. In recent years a Spring Enhancement Scheme has been introduced in an attempt to reverse the decline in early running fish. Rod-caught springers have been held for autumn stripping, with the offspring planted out as fry in appropriate locations in the headwaters. It is fair to say that the results have been inconclusive. There was also a programme of 'large-scale introduction of Norwegian sea-trout fry from adults of 15 lb' in the late 1950s. The 1961 auction brochure referred to first-class sea-trout fishing and gave an average sea-trout catch on the lower river of 484 between 1956 and 1960 (one night in 1960 37 sea-trout were taken in the Junction pool alone). To put this in context, the 2003 catch for the whole of the lower river was just 24.

The Oykel, a fly-only river for over a century, has been at the forefront of catch and release. Since the late 1990s no springers whatsoever have been killed on the Lower Oykel: fish have either been donated to the Spring Enhancement Scheme or tagged and returned. Catch limits apply from 1 June, and the five-year average (1999 to 2003) for the main stem of the river downstream of Loch Ailsh was 888; a release rate of 70 per cent or more is regularly achieved. Conservation is facilitated by the fact that ownership of the Oykel remains comparatively unfragmented.

In contrast to so many of the northern rivers, the Oykel has never been a large-fish system. No 30 lb salmon have been recorded. The heaviest in recent years was a springer of 27 lb, landed in 1999.

CASSLEY

The Cassley, draining some 75 square miles of mountainous terrain (notably the north and east slopes of Ben More Assynt), is by far the smallest of the four Kyle of Sutherland rivers. From Gorm Loch Mor, which is just three miles from saltwater on the west coast at Loch Glencoul, its south-easterly course hardly deviates over the 18 miles to its mouth and junction with the Kyle near Rosehall.

Despite its comparatively small size the Cassley has long enjoyed a high reputation in salmon angling circles. Indeed, it is probable that no other Scottish river of comparable size has been so celebrated in print. From the late nineteenth century the lower Cassley attracted many illustrious guests and tenants, including Augustus Grimble, Viscount Grey of Fallodon, Major R. Chrystal and Alexander McConnochie, all of whom were copious in their praise for what amounts to just over a mile of spring fishing.

The building of Rosehall House by Lord Ashburton in 1822 coincided with the development of the area for sporting use; this vast mansion house (now mothballed) was constructed at great expense with brown stone from Moray, which was shipped up the Kyle of Sutherland and then, via a specially cut canal, to the actual site. For some decades the salmon angling on the Cassley was not held in any great esteem. Andrew Young (1857) was rather dismissive, saying that the river 'never continues long in good angling trim', except in April if there was plenty of melting snow. If there was no snow left in April, 'then the river is not worth stretching a rod on, and the principal fishing is lost'. It is relevant that at this time Young ran, on behalf of the Duke of Sutherland, ten netting stations on the Kyle between the mouth of the Cassley and the mouth of the Shin; not all of them operated simultaneously, but there can be no doubt that they put Cassley stocks under considerable pressure.

In 1898, when Rosehall was bought by William Ewing Gilmour, a great local benefactor who already owned Glenrossal, Glencassley and Duchally (the other left-bank estates on the river) and ran his sporting estates with considerable efficiency, the lower Cassley became a serious fishery. The new proprietor was himself a keen angler and took a close interest in improving the river. The falls, a mile up from the Kyle, were a particularly severe obstacle, and, according to MacFarlane's *Collections* (1726), used to provide rich pickings:

> When the water is low the fish endeavour to leap up, but being wearied with leaping, they ordinarily rest in holes and pitts at each side of the cataract or linn, out of which the fishers take them at pleasure alive with their clipps or large hooks and sometimes with their hands.

The Rossal Pool (Glenrossal Beat), one of the main holding pools of the middle river

According to Grimble 'blasting operations' made the lower river falls 'passable to fish'; actually the falls were simply eased, as Young had previously confirmed that there was sometimes 'a little sport' upstream. Mr Gilmour also leased the fishings on the right bank from Balnagown Estate, so that he was able to offer double bank fishing.

Grimble had cited an 'average yield of both banks' below the falls of 30–35 fish. As fishing effort intensified, so catches improved significantly, and Calderwood (1909), who described the river as the 'best of the Oykel over again on a slightly smaller scale', gave a figure of 90–120, 'but it is by no means steadily fished'. From around 1910 the Cassley was generally let to tenants, rather than enjoyed by guests; at this time the lower river reverted to two separate banks, and catches increased significantly. By now netting pressure was reduced, following the formation in 1907 of the Kyle of Sutherland Fishing Syndicate, which leased the majority of the district's nets and operated them much less intensively (its activities are detailed in the Oykel entry above).

Viscount Grey, who had fished the river from just after the turn of the century, then became a Balnagown tenant, and the revised and enlarged (1930) edition of his classic *Fly Fishing* devotes a chapter to the joys of the lower Cassley. The former Foreign Minister (1905–1916) was unstinting in his praise for the beat, and recalls agonizing over the dilemma of whether affairs of state

The Cemetery Pool (Rosehall Beat)

should take precedence when the river was in perfect trim; he did in fact act responsibly, leaving the water for the London train at 4 p.m. in April 1909 to deal with a crisis in Constantinople, on a day when he and his brother landed 16 springers. Two years later he had 44 in eight days, which then became 55 in ten days – a quality of fishing which has few equals. Grey more than anyone sealed the reputation of the Cassley.

Alexander McConnochie reported that in 1923 two rods had 97 springers in March and April. Then in May three rods caught 120 salmon, and another 72 in June. His comment read: 'surely, a record unsurpassed by any river in Scotland of their size and accessibility!'

After the death of Mr Gilmour, Rosehall was sold in 1926 to the Duke of Westminster, who sought to supplement his summer fishing on the Laxford with some quality spring angling. In the late 1920s the Duke's guest Madame Chanel (of perfume fame), who had never fished before, shared 21 salmon with another rod on a single late spring day. She rewarded the gillie with a gold watch. (Incidentally Rosehall House is perhaps the only mansion in the Highlands with an Edwardian bidet in the ensuite bathroom of the master bedroom; this was installed at Madame Chanel's request.)

Evidently the Duke had not studied the sale particulars; on one occasion he was working his way down a pool, when someone began casting from the

Dibbling the head of the Round Pool (Rosehall Beat)

other side. Turning to his gillie, the Duke reportedly exclaimed: 'Who on earth is that? ... Don't I own that bank?' So perhaps it is not surprising that Rosehall was soon on the market again, and in 1930 it was bought by the Graesser family, who still own it today, with the fishings jointly held with the Creasey family. In 1952 they succeeded in procuring the right bank of the lower river also, and since then it has always been double bank. In the last half of the twentieth century the late Neil Graesser, an expert in all matters relating to salmon, as well as a highly skilled angler, did extensive work creating and reinstating pools.

The Falls in the gorge towards the top of the Rosehall beat are, of course, the key to the productivity of the lower river. More accurately, there is a series of falls, each of which is a temperature barrier to the progress of spring fish. Neil Graesser made a detailed study of this section. Furthest downstream is the Round Pool, and fish will not tackle the turbulent water above it until the water temperature reaches 45°F; Grey referred to this magnificent holding pool as the 'greatest certainty for getting a salmon that I have known on the Cassley or any other river'. Fifty yards upstream fish are checked again, until the temperature reaches 48°F, by the falls surrounding Fir Tree Island (named after a small pine tree, rooted in a crevice of a massive mid-stream boulder, which has survived in this precarious position for some 120 years). Another 50 yards upstream is the main Falls Pool ('a fine, fascinating and beautiful place', as Grey put it), and fish are not thought to migrate beyond this until the water temperature reaches 52°F. Incidentally, this falls was last eased with explosives in the mid-1920s, to remove a particularly awkward overhang.

This graduated series of temperature barriers holds all spring salmon back in the lower river, usually until mid or late April, which is, of course, why it has been such a prolific fishery in the early months. The decline in the numbers of multi-sea-winter fish is reflected in the average annual catch figures for Rosehall (although it is worth noting that 2004 saw a considerable improvement, with a total of 261 salmon and grilse for the season):

	Salmon/grilse
1953–60	389
1961–70	456
1971–80	416
1981–90	307
1991–2000	202
2001–04	185

Whereas in the 1950s and 1960s grilse would represent just 10–20 per cent of the total, this proportion has now risen to some 40 per cent.

The recent marked increase in the grilse runs has been of great benefit to the upper river, which is essentially a summer fishery from July onwards, although a few fish are taken in May and June. In the nineteenth and early twentieth centuries the upper Cassley was hardly fished, and even in the 1930s there was little pressure, with the right bank rarely seeing a rod. In recent years both banks have been fished consistently as far up as the diversion dam (see below); however since 1998 six miles of the left bank have not been let.

Immediately upstream of the Rosehall water on the left bank is Glenrossal with 23 pools, including many low-water pods. The Rossal Pool is an important holding pool, which can often give spectacular catches; the immediate area is rich in spawning gravel, and Calderwood noted that 'as many as 70 pairs of fish have been counted simultaneously making redds in the Rosal ford'. Glenrossal (now owned by the Hasson family) has an average annual catch of some 120 fish. Above it, on the left bank up to the upper Cassley falls, is Glencassley, now untenanted. This section has 34 pools and includes the Long Pool, almost a mile in length; this is another significant holding pool, which can almost be treated as a loch and will fish even in a severe drought (especially in a strong wind). Opposite both Glenrossal and Glencassley on the right bank were the Upper Cassley Fishings; these were sold in 2003 and are now incorporated into Glenrossal and Glencassley.

The upstream limit of the Glencassley beat is the upper Falls, which was blasted over a century ago, and again eased in 1966. It still remains a formidable obstacle, which is surmountable in lowish water. At times the pool below can hold great numbers, but it has always had a reputation as a poor taking spot. Regrettably, over the years some tenants have resorted to unsporting methods, and in order to combat this problem the pool is no longer fished. Between these falls and the diversion dam upstream is the Duchally beat. Angling pressure upstream of Glenrossal is now minimal.

In 1959 the headwaters above Duchally were diverted by a tunnel through the hill to Loch Shin and incorporated into the Shin hydro-electric scheme. A dam was constructed below the tunnel, including a Borland fish pass. Two major burns draining the east side of Ben More Assynt, which joined the river below the dam, were also diverted back upstream to above the dam. The river is now fed by a compensation flow, with additional freshets to supplement spates. The fish pass is understood to be reasonably efficient, at least since it was overhauled in 1995, and as a result the high-altitude spawning areas near

A March springer approaches the net in Neil's Pool at Rosehall

Gorm Loch Mor and north of Ben More Assynt can now be accessed more easily by springers, and it is hoped that this will help restore the numbers of multi-sea-winter fish.

The diversion regime, which harnesses approximately one-third of the catchment area, has however had a marked effect on water levels, and this was not fully appreciated when the scheme was first discussed. The compensation payments did spur some proprietors to improve certain pools, so that they were more fishable in low water, but the duration of spates is much diminished; a five-foot flood used to take four days or so to run off – now it is gone in a matter of hours, to the particular detriment of the upper beats. In 1998 maintenance on the tunnel saw water levels temporarily restored, and for several weeks summer anglers enjoyed the full natural flow again.

With access to the Gorm Lochs to a certain extent curtailed, protection of the system's other spawning areas has assumed a higher profile. Thus when a major scheme was proposed to plant much of the west bank of the Cassley with native woodland, local opposition was intense, and eventually the project was scaled down considerably, with the area adjoining the important Gleann na Muic burn and other spawning tributaries excluded.

Cassley salmon do not, as a rule, run large. A fish in the high teens is unusual, and one of 20 lb or more is very rare; in March 2003 a 20-lb springer was landed in the Round Pool, and this was the heaviest fish from the river for at least ten years. The record salmon, which is unlikely to be surpassed, fell to Neil Graesser in June 1957. He received a phone call from his gillie late one afternoon informing him that the river was in excellent order. Arriving at the right bank of the Round Pool, he found that he had neglected to bring a spool of nylon, and all that was to hand was a rather worn 8-lb cast, which he elected to use rather than waste time returning to the house. Soon afterwards he had a 16-lb salmon on the bank. He then walked down to the Upper Platform, and within a few minutes his small Blue Charm was taken in an 'enormous swirl'. The fish then careered up and down the pool and jumped three times – each leap making the 8-lb breaking strain look more inadequate. It then proceeded to sulk below a protruding rock ledge, where a mere touch of the nylon on the rock would have meant disaster. After almost half an hour of stalemate, things had to be resolved one way or the other. Inch by inch, avoiding the slightest hint of a jerk on the line, the great fish was brought to just below the foam-covered surface, where gillie Willie MacKay gaffed it successfully – there would not have been a second chance. The cock salmon weighed 31 lb.

SHIN

Lairg, gateway village to the north of Sutherland at the southern end of Loch Shin, has been the focal point for several ambitious (sometimes over-ambitious) schemes in the last hundred years or so. In the late nineteenth century the Duke of Sutherland spent the astonishing sum of £100,000 reclaiming 2,000 acres of bog between the loch and the River Tirry. Then in the 1920s and 1930s Sir William Edgar Horne, a most generous benefactor, expended a fortune trying to kick-start agricultural and industrial development in the immediate area. But it is the harnessing of Loch Shin for electricity generation in the 1950s, with a massive dam overlooking Lairg, which has had the most lasting impact on the area, particularly the river below.

Those anglers who can remember pre-Hydro days speak of a very different river – at times a truly awesome sight, as it raged untamed down Achany Glen to the Kyle. Draining some 220 square miles it used to be the largest river in Sutherland, at least in terms of the volume of water that it dispensed. Three main tributaries flow into Loch Shin. The furthest west rises in the high terrain of Reay Forest between the upper catchments of the Laxford and Hope systems. Here various headwaters combine to form the Allt nan Albannach, which flows into Loch Merkland, which itself discharges via the Merkland River and Loch a' Griama into the 16-mile-long Loch Shin. The other two significant tributaries, the Fiag and the Tirry, drain less dramatic landscapes to the north of the loch. From Loch Shin the River Shin drops 270 feet in its short seven-mile course. Most of this descent is in the last mile or so, and it is this tumbling rock-strewn section that really established the Shin's legendary reputation as one of the most challenging of salmon rivers.

Close to the top of this section is the Falls of Shin, or Big Falls – a daunting, 12-foot-high obstacle that fish will not generally ascend before May. Half a mile downstream, the river flows over a ledge of rock known as the Little Falls; this appears to be an inconsequential obstruction, but, as Andrew Young explained in 1857, 'the greater part of the fish never go higher up the river than the Little Fall earlier than April, whatever the size of the river may be'. They were blasted around 1870, but to this day they remain an unexplained deterrent.

Evander MacIver in his *Memoirs* recounts the episode, which led to the Duke of Sutherland acquiring the Shin. In the early nineteenth century, by virtue of a crown charter, Murdo MacKenzie of Ardross owned the salmon fishings in the Shin, as well as the rights in the Kyle of Sutherland, the coast of Ross-shire to Tarbetness and the coast of Sutherland abutting the Dornoch Firth. Proprietors in both counties had 'been in the habit of netting salmon *ex adverso* their estates

The Lady Herbert Pool on the upper Shin

long before Ardross became proprietor, without hindrance'. But the latter believed that the fishing in the Shin was 'much injured' by the course of the river through Sutherland Estate land below the bridge at Inveran, so in 1827 'without any permissions' he employed a 'swarm of labourers to cut a new channel for the Shin to the Kyle'. This was completed before the Duke could take steps to stop him. Legal proceedings followed, during which Ardross agreed to sell the Shin and associated fishings on the condition that the Duke also bought his Ardross Estate for £100,000. The Duke agreed, later disposing of the Ardross Estate to Sir Alexander Matheson in 1845.

Andrew Young, who lived at Invershin and managed the Duke of Sutherland's local netting interests and operations in the middle part of the nineteenth century, leased the river from the Duke, letting it out to four rods. He knew the system intimately. He noted that the water temperature of the Shin in winter was several degrees higher than those of the neighbouring Oykel and Cassley, which are not subject to the moderating effect of a large loch. He reasoned that the warmer water led to the earlier hatching of ova, and thus to more early-running salmon. As any fish biologist will confirm, this was wrong, since springers spawn in the upper tributaries. All the same, Young had, perhaps inadvertently, identified one probable reason why the Shin was then the only Kyle river 'that produces early salmon': the comparatively warmer water temperature, which meant that fish were far more likely to move to a fly or lure. Calderwood cited the lower Shin as 'the best spring fishing in the Kyle district'.

In the 1850s and early 1860s Young leased the rod fishings for the significant sum of £450 per annum (the Duke retained the right to fish two days per month). Aware of the river's increasing profile, the Duke took the rod fishings back in hand in 1865, and the following year he abolished the cruives – although tenants still complained that in low water the nets at the mouth took a heavy toll (for instance, the rods took only 12 salmon between 12 February and 26 March 1866). At this time detailed plans for a fish ladder at the Falls were drawn up. They included a channel just above the casting point at the tail of the pool and steps cut into the rock on the west side of the obstacle. Frank Buckland, Inspector of Salmon Fisheries, suggested modifications, notably a dam at the outlet to the Falls Pool, thus raising the level. However in 1870 Archibald Young, Commissioner of Salmon Fisheries, cautioned against the opening up of the Falls because of the 'limited spawning above' and because such action would 'depress the value of the fishings below'.

The nets at the mouth of the river at Invershin were never especially prolific: for example, between 1873 and 1881 they averaged 303 salmon and 626 grilse. However, these were fish (the salmon were almost entirely springers) that had managed to run the gauntlet of nets in the bottleneck at Bonar Bridge and, as noted above, in low water they were unable to gain access to the Shin itself and so were highly vulnerable. By the latter part of the nineteenth century angling interests were in the ascendancy. After the end of George Young's lease in 1888 the Duke closed down the nets at Invershin and increased the angling rents, despite a rod catch of just 72 salmon and 25 grilse the previous season. In 1889 the February and March rod catches were double those of the previous season, but then an extended drought set in, and the gauge at Inveran registered below zero from 15 May to 22 August; inevitably the river was unfishable, and the tenants saw no benefit. The total rod catch for 1889 amounted to only 72 salmon and three grilse. However, from the 1891 season there was a considerable improvement, and by the latter part of the decade angling rents realized £800 per annum, more than double contemporary rents on the Oykel.

The rod-catch figures below are gleaned from the Inveran Hotel, Sutherland Estate and Skibo Estate game books. They relate to the whole river up to 1919, and thereafter to the lower river. It is worth noting that Calderwood quoted figures from the Report of Commissioners on Salmon Fisheries (1902) for the years 1873 to 1899, which, where they overlap, are slightly higher; I can only assume that they included fish caught on the upper tributaries and by the Lairg Estate tenant, who had exclusive rights to the upper Shin for two days a week.

	Salmon	Grilse	Total
1883–90	138	42	180
1891–1900	165	79	244
1901–10	158	65	223
1911–20			290
1921–30			336
1931–40			222
1941–49			232

It is plain that anglers were not drawn to the Shin for numbers but for the superb quality and weight of the fish. The chance to do battle with such powerful springers in a fast yet intimate river, where the odds (particularly in the gorge section) were clearly stacked against the angler, was the attraction that created the Shin's reputation. In 1890 a salmon of 43 lb was taken, and between 1921 and 1949 no less than 27 fish over 30 lb were caught on the lower river, averaging some 34 lb – the heaviest, at 40 lb, was landed by 'T.R.' in Smiths on 8 April 1930. Salmon of 20–30 lb were commonplace; for instance in April 1921 the river produced 16 in this class, and the following March another 15 were caught. In April 1944 the catch of 70 averaged 17 lb. Typically, each season the average weight of salmon (excluding grilse) was close to 14 lb.

Tales of epic battles, both successful and unsuccessful, with very large salmon abound. On 13 April 1949 a spring tenant from Inveran Hotel hooked a massive salmon at 8.30 p.m. in the Garden Pool; at 9.45 p.m. the line was cut and tied to a tree. The next day the line was reconnected and the fish played for a further hour before the line eventually broke. (Incidentally, the Inveran Hotel, the haunt of Shin anglers for almost a century, was destroyed by fire in June 1949.) Also in the late 1940s, the teenage Neil Graesser was playing a heavy fish in the Black Stone on a March afternoon. In due course the springer began to sulk, and no amount of pressure would move it. The gillie, Tommy, then tried a trick his father had taught him: he looped a length of heavy-duty rolling tobacco around the line, and slid it down to the fish. Almost instantaneously it erupted, and soon afterwards a salmon of just below 30 lb was on the bank. In the 1970s Lord Balfour (with gillie 'George') hooked a very large fish in Thompson's Pool. When eventually they saw it, 'they decided that it was so big that they would never land it', so the line was cut.

Weights on the upper river, where many of the pools are more open (thus favouring the angler more than the fish), were also impressive. The Lairg Estate gamebook (for the upper river) for 1921, which was by no means an exceptional year, details 77 salmon with an astonishing average weight of 16 lb 2 oz; June and July produced fish of 21 lb, 26 lb, and two of 31 lb. Over the next three decades there were fair numbers of salmon of over 30 lb, and the 40 lb barrier was breached. Before the war a fish of over 40 lb was hooked in the Grudie Burn Pool and finally landed a mile downstream in the Beech Pool; a rudimentary image of the fish, carved into the trunk of a beech tree at the spot, is still visible, although distended with time. Then in the late 1950s Sir Nigel Davidson caught a July salmon of some 44 lb in the Wall Pool, reputed to be the biggest on fly.

In 1898 the Duke of Sutherland sold some two-thirds of the river, from Gruid's Mill to the Kyle, to the great philanthropist Andrew Carnegie, who added it to his extensive portfolio of properties centred on Skibo Castle (he was generous enough not to displace the existing tenants). Carnegie, a keen angler, had a path made down half a mile of tortuous, steep terrain from his lodge at Aultnagar, under the road and railway, to a point above the Angus Pool. There a hut was built from which he could look up to the Falls. Carnegie also developed the path, much of it cut into the rockface, along the lower river.

For years the focus of Shin tenants' anger had been directed at the devastating efficiency of the Bonar Bridge nets, and in 1907 eight of the principal Kyle river proprietors formed the Kyle of Sutherland Fishing Syndicate. They leased local

The Culag Pool, with the Falls Pool behind, on the lower river

netting rights, most notably those at Bonar Bridge, and operated them in a much less intensive fashion (full details of their activities and legacy are given in the Oykel entry). In 1908 plans were drawn up to dam Loch Shin in order to hold reserves of water (90 days' supply) for summer angling, but they were never acted upon.

In 1919 Sir William Edgar Horne bought the upper Shin from the Duke, and he proved to be another benevolent proprietor. In due course his daughter Miss Phyllis Horne inherited Lairg Estate, and after World War II she was often seen driving up and down the river in Göring's armour-plated Rolls-Royce. When in 1955 the Hydro Board unveiled its plans to dam Loch Shin, Miss Horne decided not to sell her section of the river to the Authority; in contrast, Andrew Carnegie's descendant Mrs Carnegie-Miller elected to sell the lower river to the Hydro. In due course Miss Horne agreed a compensation package, which doubled her fishings on the Shin by giving her from the Mill Stream down to the Grief, some half a mile above the Falls; she had, however, lost the pools in the upper gorge below the Loch, which were submerged in Little Loch Shin, as well as fishings on the River Tirry, which could provide excellent sport with sea-liced fish from late May onwards. In the 1960s she sold the estate and fishings to the Bibby family, who resold in 1971 to the Greenwood family, the current owners.

In 1969 Sir John Egerton acquired the remaining lower river from the Hydro Board (once they had increased catches again to a reasonable level in the post-dam era), after responding to an advertisement and only seeing it at minimum flow. In 1974 he sold a half-share to the Douglas-Miller family, followed by the other half in 2000.

There is no escaping the fact that the hydro-electric scheme radically altered the system. Completion of the dam in 1959 raised the level of the loch by 30 ft, and the diversion dam downstream flooded half a mile of the upper river. Both dams included fish passes, but now very few salmon reach Loch Shin. A tunnel was built from the diversion dam (picking up the flow from the previously important Grudie Burn tributary) to Inveran Power Station by the mouth of the river. The Shin became subject to compensation flow, with additional freshets throughout the season. It is no longer subject to the full-blown spates that used to flood all the meadows by Lairg and turn the lower gorge into a solid mass of water. (In high water the path along the lower Shin would often be submerged, and what are now known as 'poachers' paths' were in fact established to allow anglers access and a means of escape at such times.) On the positive side, being 'washed off', which used to be a regular occurrence, is now almost unheard-of, and the Shin remains fishable all summer, even in the severest drought. Before the war much of the lower Shin, which is now heavily wooded, was open country – at Skibo Castle there is a fine painting of the view up to the Falls and beyond, which confirms this. In the 1950s the sheep were removed, allowing the scrub to develop unchecked.

Given that the upper tributaries have become effectively inaccessible to spawning fish, and almost all natural spawning is in the main river below the diversion dam, each year some 350–400 salmon are netted and held for autumn stripping, resulting in 600,000 eggs; unfed fry are planted out in the Merkland, Fiag and Tirry tributaries, and artificial redds have been created high up the Crask Burn at the top of the Tirry. However, when descending smolts reach Loch Shin, the new regime since the dam has, in all probability, compromised survival. When the loch was shallower with more flow, the outlet was easily discernible. Now with much greater depth, the smolts are liable to spend a considerable time trying to locate the exit – all the while being vulnerable to the loch's extensive population of predatory ferox trout. Below the loch the upper reaches of the Grudie Burn are also planted out with fry, with descending smolts caught in a trap before being released into the main river itself.

Since the regime was altered, catches on the lower Shin held up well, with some decline recently, as indicated by the annual averages below:

	Salmon/grilse
1971–80	369
1981–90	328
1991–2000	322
2001–03	208

However, totals for the spring to the end of May have been less encouraging, with average annual catch figures of 74, 36 and 40 for the three decades since 1970. With the flare-up of UDN at the start of the 1980s, early-running fish declined and have never recovered. The remaining spring run has become ever more concentrated into May, and sadly there are no longer the great number of 'thumpers' that were there up to the 1950s and 1960s, when anything under 12 lb was almost an irrelevance.

The upper Shin, less dramatic in character (with less hazardous pools) but just as attractive a stretch of water, of course has a shorter season. Before the Hydro scheme, it used to fish well in May, but now, with the river fed with cold water from the foot of the dam rather than the surface of the loch, fish are slower to surmount the Falls. However these are highly productive beats from June to September, and in recent years the average annual catch has been enviably consistent:

	Salmon/grilse
1975–80	301
1981–90	294
1991–2000	275
2001–03	248

The average weekly catch for eight rods is close to 15 fish.

Whilst the character of the Shin has changed radically, its tenants are as loyal as they were a century or so ago. Some of today's tenants have been on the river since the 1950s or earlier. One such was George Raikes, who, on his last visit to the upper river in August 2000, landed three fish, shortly before his death aged 93. The Buxton family's tenancy on the lower river dates back to 1892.

The Shin has been blessed with some very accomplished gillies. Perhaps the best known in recent years was Hughie Mackintosh, who began work on the lower river towards the end of the Hydro Board's tenure. Hughie was a 'quiet, wise and wonderful wee man', a first-rate gillie and expert angler. He also had his jocular side, apparent at the time when three members of the same angling family managed to fall into the Hardings Pool almost simultaneously, after one of them had hooked a fish; Hughie rescued the rod and remained dry! He retired in 1983 aged 79, although he still gillied on request until his late eighties, retaining his uncanny ability to hop from rock to rock.

Hughie Mackintosh perfected a technique, which has been highly successful on the lower Shin's gorge pools, as well as the faster streams of the upper river. With a short line, a square cast is made, followed by a quick mend; then the rod point is brought back, behind the angler's shoulder and down, causing the fly (or flies if a dropper is used) to start to work immediately. Often the line is not in the water, and the fly (or flies) is given no time to sink. Using this method Dr Victor Bruce, who has fished the Shin since the early 1950s, has on several occasions hooked two fish at once (only once did he manage to land both). In the 1970s and 1980s Dr Bruce also had success on the upper river with a form of dry-fly fishing, using a Red-faced Sassenach (like a muddler) fished on 6-lb nylon.

Given the fast and rocky nature of the pools in the gorge section, there are particular hazards when a fish elects to leave a pool. Hughie Mackintosh's advice was that, if a fish was going upstream, 'keep with it', whilst if it was going downstream, 'no worries' (because the fish was bound to remain attached).

EVELIX

Rising east of the lower Shin, the Evelix drains a narrow strip of land to the north of the Kyle of Sutherland and the Dornoch Firth. The headwaters pass through two small lochs (Laro and an Lagain), following which the river tumbles down through rough moorland and then flows in meandering fashion through farmland to Loch Evelix and thence to the firth three miles inland from Dornoch.

During most of Sutherland Estates' ownership in the nineteenth century some six miles of the Evelix was included with the lets of the Dornoch Shootings. In 1896 the steel magnate and philanthropist Andrew Carnegie rented Skibo Estate and much of the river. Two years later he purchased the estate and began an awe-inspiring programme of works to create the most opulent property in the north. In 1901 Loch Evelix was greatly expanded by damming the exit, and a fish ladder was built to ease access into the system from the firth.

Before the dam was built there was considerable concern that it would contravene salmon fisheries legislation. The Duke of Sutherland, who still owned much of the river, finally agreed that the project could proceed, but only on the basis that it was entirely at Carnegie's risk; Carnegie thanked the Duke and stressed that his intention was to improve the Evelix fishings. Over the ensuing decades angling pressure was usually intermittent, with fishing on the loch just an occasional diversion; in any event Skibo had far more reliable water on the Shin.

Skibo remained in the ownership of the Carnegie family until 1982, when Derek Holt acquired 7,000 acres and Loch Evelix. He sold to the Miners' Pension Fund in 1990, which in turn divested the estate to Peter de Savary in 1992; the latter created the Carnegie Club, which now owns the loch. The first three-quarters of a mile above the loch is currently the property of Anthony Fraser, the next two miles belong to Donald Munro, and upstream most of the river is still held by Andrew Carnegie's descendants Margaret Thompson and William Thompson.

Netting rights (a sweep net) at Newton Point and within the almost enclosed bay south of Skibo Castle (employing a look-out at the entrance) were exercised infrequently between the wars. In the 1980s on at least one occasion several hundred fish were netted at the mouth in low water. There can be little doubt that stocks could not sustain such levels of exploitation for long.

Aside from Loch Evelix the system has been largely untouched. Loch an Lagain was dammed around 1920 to allow for the possibility of artificial supplements to the water level, but the structure was washed away.

There has never been a spring run; the main influx is from July, with angling concentrated between then and September. Inevitably, in low water fish do not ascend above Loch Evelix, where, traditionally, access has been limited to three boats. Andrew Carnegie's son-in-law Roswell Miller, a deputy sheriff in the US, used to cover it from a canoe. An expert shot he regularly overcame the difficulty of landing a salmon in such an unstable craft by dispatching hooked fish with a single shot from his Colt 45. Rod catches for the system as a whole used to average in the order of 100 salmon/grilse per annum. However, recently they have declined, with no more than 50 expected in a good season – i.e. one with plentiful water.

FLEET

With its limited catchment sandwiched between those of two illustrious neighbours, the Shin and the Brora, the Fleet was never going to have a high profile in the Sutherland Estate portfolio of rivers. Calderwood never afforded it a mention. In fact in the early part of the nineteenth century the focus of attention in terms of the river was on land reclamation and making the lower section navigable.

The Fleet drains some 70 square miles, most of it moorland, with none over 1,000 ft. The system has no fresh-water loch of any consequence, and the main stem of the river runs a south-easterly course of 12 miles to its estuary in tidal Loch Fleet.

In 1815 and 1816 the estuary was radically altered. A massive causeway of earth and stone, with a bridge at the northern end, bisected Loch Fleet. Designed and built by Thomas Telford, the Mound extended for 1,029 yards and cost £9,600. The Duke of Sutherland agreed to contribute £1,600 of this, as the causeway allowed the reclamation of valuable land to the north-west (sea-shells are still found in farmland over three miles upstream of the Mound). Above the bridge an ingenious system of sluices was installed, allowing migratory fish access only at times of high water. Soon after this major undertaking the Fleet was dredged and straightened to make it navigable for small boats (carrying coal in particular) for four miles above the Mound. Only in the last few decades has the channel become unusable because of silting.

One other notable piece of engineering enterprise during the nineteenth century was an extraordinary salmon ladder built in 1864 by Mr Bateson, an inventor, on the River Carnaig (or Torboll), the Fleet's major tributary, which joins from the west a mile upstream of the Mound. Still in remarkably good order, this circumvents a 60-ft falls and is thought to be the first-ever fish pass on such a scale: it is 400 yards long (average width 10 ft), and salmon ascend the steepest part by a series of 23 pools. The pass opened up access to eight miles of the Carnaig above, including Loch Buidhe, as well as the Tollaidh tributary.

Before 1893 there were just three rods on the Fleet – the shooting tenants of Cambusmore, Morvich and Rovie. During this period these were some of the best shooting estates in the north, so Sutherland Estate's interest in the rod angling was minimal, and there was little incentive to improve the fishings – in fact the income from the angling rental in the mid-1870s was just £15 per annum. In 1877 the netting season was actually extended (a rare occurrence) by statutory instrument – previously the nets were off after 27 August, but the end of the season was deferred to 9 September. Netting was concentrated at Little Ferry, the mouth of Loch Fleet. By the 1890s, though, the angling tenants were beginning to flex their muscles. In 1893 the Cambusmore tenant, Henry Graham, complained to the estate factor about the activities of the estate's netting tenant, citing the 'incessant operations' and arguing that the 'netting in that narrow channel is perfectly ruinous'. This area could hold significant numbers (legend has it that at high tide one night in the 1930s a boat from Embo slipped into the loch and took 294 salmon in one sweep). Regular netting gradually reduced during the twentieth century and finally petered out in the early 1980s.

The 'narrow channel' in Loch Fleet has long had a special place in angling folklore. Andrew Young referred to it as the 'only spot in the kingdom' where 'salmon take the fly very well in the saltwater' at certain states of the tide; Grimble agreed that it was unique in this respect. In recent years other such places have been discovered, but clearly Loch Fleet was the first.

Inevitably angling catches on this small spate river have varied dramatically. For instance, in 1911 the recorded total was just 39. The following year a remarkable 448 salmon and grilse were landed – more than on the Brora. In the 1960s a 'good' (i.e. wet) year was likely to produce between 200 and 300 to rods; now this has fallen to perhaps 60. The decline is due to a variety of factors. There are now more seals in Loch Fleet than ever before, discreet control is near impossible, and in low water the fish are extremely vulnerable. The otter population, too, is thriving. In many sections pools have filled in, and bank maintenance is generally poor. The increasing fragmentation of ownership since the early twentieth-century break-up of Sutherland Estate has probably exacerbated matters; six estates now have rights on the system – Cambusmore, Rovie, Morvich, Pittentrail, Tressady and Kinnauld. In the last two decades clearly the Fleet would have benefited from a concerted management plan to counteract marine mortality.

Rogart Angling Club leases various sections, amounting to some three miles in total, and it has paid for some stocking with fry. Much of the remedial work on the river is now carried out by the club, in conjunction with Morvich Estate, including bank clearance and the opening up of particular pools.

There is hardly a spring run of salmon in the Fleet, probably reflecting the lack of high-altitude spawning tributaries. The earliest recorded fish in modern times was taken at the start of May in the late 1960s. The main run – of grilse and the odd salmon in the teens of pounds – is from early July, and there are indications that fish are arriving later (the legal angling season extends to the end of October). The record salmon is 34 lb (caught by Neil Sutherland in the Wash Pool in the late 1960s). There is a spring run as well as a late run, of sea trout.

Although not the most fashionable of rivers, the Fleet has certainly had its devotees. Lord Balfour of Inchrye (then owner of Tressady) was fulsome in his praise for what he called 'that silly little river' in his 1978 volume *Folk, Fish and Fun*: 'I have been lucky enough to have fished fine beats on rivers like the Spey, Dee and Tweed, yet on the all too rare times when the Fleet is in order, I would choose it before the great ones.'

BRORA

Flanked by tributaries of the Shin, Naver and Helmsdale, the upper reaches of the Brora system penetrate deep into Ben Armine Forest in a fan-like formation, draining the southern slopes of central Sutherland's highest terrain. Furthest west is the Brora itself, rising north of Lairg; emasculated by man's diversion of the headwaters in the late 1950s, it is a rather thin stream above its junction with the dominant tributary, the Blackwater. It is in fact the latter that drains the majority of the 160-square-mile catchment, and it and its own tributary the Skinsdale are the main spawning areas for the system. From its junction with the Blackwater, the Brora flows two-and-a-half miles to Loch Brora; this section, together with the half-mile of the Blackwater below Balnacoil Falls, is known as the 'Upper River'. The waterfall is an effective temperature barrier until the water reaches 48°F; consequently spring fish stack up below it particularly in the legendary Pheadair Pool. Unusually, the system's main loch, Loch Brora, is in the middle of the system and fish can safely fall back to it from the river above in times of low flow. The loch is over three miles long and split into three sections by two sets of narrows; it discharges into the Lower River, which has a course of four miles to the sea.

Writing in 1638 Franck noted that the loch was 'very full of salmon', which were exported to 'France and other parts annually' to the value of '£300 sterling a year'. In the early nineteenth century the Brora, fished by both cruive and net, was one of the three rivers (the others were the Naver and the Helmsdale) that produced the bulk of Sutherland Estates' revenue from salmon; in 1812 the Sutherland family had established complete control over the Brora system with the purchase of Gordonbush Estate, including the Upper River, from John Gordon.

Between 1807 and 1817 the boiling house at Helmsdale received on average 1,652 salmon and 2,181 grilse from the Brora fishings annually.

By the middle of the nineteenth century angling on the river was coming to the fore, producing an annual rent between 1853 and 1888 of £150. The estuary nets, which only fished from 1 May, appear to have been less intensive in their operations in the latter part of the century, averaging 937 salmon and 1,073 grilse annually between 1864 and 1900. The nets in Loch Brora (at the Carrol narrows), which fished from 11 February to 1 May, averaged 363 salmon annually during the same period. The Brora clearly benefited from the 1899 buy-out, led by the Helmsdale tenants, of the remaining part of Colin Sellar's lease of the coastal netting rights. This signalled the end of fixed-engine nets on the east coast of Sutherland north of the mouth of the Fleet; there had been stake nets operating by Golspie since 1815.

The Brora's reputation as one the north's best spring angling rivers was soon established. In 1899 Grimble eulogized: 'I know of no stream that is more certain to give good sport in February and March.' He referred to the two rods on the Lower River on occasion landing up to 400 fish between the (then) opening day of 11 February and the end of April; the average rod catch between 1898 and 1920 was 344. To put this in context, one should note that generally no more than three rods fished, little attention was paid to salmon fishing after the spring run and also the system above Loch Brora was largely ignored, with the exception of the

Midsummer at the Falls on the Blackwater, an important temperature barrier pool in the spring

The Blackwater's Stream Pool, downstream from the Falls

half mile of the Blackwater below the Falls. The shooting tenants of Gordonbush and Balnacoil had a rod each, and the Scibercross tenant had a partial rod. During this era the Duke of Sutherland reserved the right of fishing one rod anywhere on the system with one day's notice (the Brora is only four miles from Dunrobin Castle, the family seat). By 1900 angling rents totalled £373 per annum.

Perhaps the most celebrated Brora angler of the late nineteenth and early twentieth centuries was Charles Akroyd, originator of the Akroyd fly. A man of very great wealth with his own luxury yacht, he could afford to fish anywhere. He was introduced to the Brora whilst fishing the Helmsdale. Thereafter it was his favourite river – so much so that he came to live in Brora, building what is now the Royal Marine Hotel.

In terms of pool improvements, little work was done to the river during the nineteenth century. Early in the twentieth century the Haig-Thomas family, tenants of Balnacoil until soon after World War I, carried out some works on the Lower River. Walter and Jessie Tyser's purchase from Sutherland Estates of the north bank of both the Lower and the Upper River in 1921 heralded a period of great change that in due course fundamentally altered the balance of exploitation on the system (it is noteworthy that the spring netting that year in Loch Brora was highly productive with 1,056 salmon taken). Mrs Jessie Tyser – an extraordinarily dedicated angler, who landed some 8,000 salmon to her own rod over half a century – brought to the Brora a wealth of knowledge gained in Ireland and southern Scotland, and she appreciated just how to turn the Upper River into a first-class fishery. This was impossible without the ownership of both banks, and so in 1923 she managed to persuade Sutherland Estates to sell the south bank as well.

A major programme of work then began, which transformed the two miles of river from just below the junction with the Blackwater to the dead water above the loch. Mrs Tyser directed operations on a daily basis, confining the river to a proper channel (previously its path had shifted regularly) and creating new pools and holding water. By 1925/6, when the improvements started to bed in, the top river (hitherto largely seen as a diversion for youngsters whilst the adults were on the hill) began to produce more fish than the lower; it soon became and indeed remains one of the most prolific stretches of salmon fishing in the north.

Fishing effort upstream of Balnacoil Falls has always been limited by the remoteness of the terrain. Much of the Blackwater and all of the important Skinsdale tributary is not fished at all; this vast hinterland of wilderness, with close to 40 miles of spawning and nursery water, is by and large a sanctuary. There is very little conifer forestry, and what there is has been planted at least 30 metres back from watercourses. Fish can navigate almost as high as 1,500 ft, where low-water temperatures persist and delay hatching – a prerequisite for promoting offspring that will develop into spring stock.

There is an extraordinary loch, Gorm Loch Mor (at almost 1,000 ft), which is accessible from the Skinsdale. Salmon can reach here via a spillway over a natural pavement ledge in high water, and they may sit here, unmolested all summer, before dropping back downstream to spawn. The loch is like something out of a Tolkien movie – dramatically windswept, very deep, virtually a cubic triangle, and bordered to the west by an almost sheer 800-ft cliff.

Sadly, the upper Brora, above the junction with the Blackwater, is no longer a significant spawning area. In the late 1950s the Hydro Board negotiated the right to divert much of the flow from the headwaters across to the Shin system via a dam and tunnel at Dalnessie. Now the river below (often known as the Rogart Brora) is a pale shadow of its former self, and only a localized thunderstorm can produce a flood. Consequently salmon are very scarce, particularly above Dalreavock. The system's heavier sea trout (fish of 4 lb or 5 lb were quite common) tended to spawn above the dam and, since they have been denied access, their numbers have dwindled. Inevitably this has had a detrimental effect on Loch Brora as a sea-trout fishery.

The Brora has a long history of hatcheries. The first, at Carrol, was built in 1878 (bizarrely in the 1880s it was handling eggs from as far away as the Rhine) and by 1900 was supplying fry to many of the Sutherland Estate rivers, including some on the west coast. A major new hatchery was constructed at Gordonbush in the early 1920s. It was dormant for many years after World War II but was reactivated in the mid-1980s and is now operated on a fairly small scale, producing some 70,000 fry annually, which are mainly planted out in the Skinsdale.

There was a commercial eel fishery in the lower loch until the 1970s. And the Carrol Rock, a towering structure that overlooks the middle section, is a traditional nesting site for ravens. The demise of the ravens at the Tower of London would, it is said, have serious consequences for the monarchy, and when it was deemed necessary to restock the Tower in the 1960s, ravens from Carrol Rock were chosen.

Netting at the mouth of the Brora finally ceased in 1979, considerably earlier than on almost any other significant northern system: for many years efforts had not been consistent – in the main, the nets concentrated on the grilse runs, when low water prevented access to the river (a sentry on a watchtower was often employed to warn of fish approaching from the sea). Rod pressure increased in the mid-1970s, when the number of rods on the Lower River was doubled from four to eight. Since then, catches of salmon/grilse on the Brora have been extraordinarily consistent, and, in contrast to so many rivers, grilse have not become predominant. Below are the average annual rod catches for the system as a whole:

A good drift on Loch Brora close to the mouth of the Upper River

	Salmon/grilse
1981–90	753
1991–2000	745
2001–03	731

The spring catch to the end of May now averages between 200 and 250. The figures are testimony to consistent and sympathetic management for decades, facilitated by the fact that ownership has not become significantly fragmented. For seventy years from 1922 there were essentially only two proprietors, Sutherland Estates and the Tyser family. This was diluted to three in 1992, when Lord Cadogan purchased the North Bank of the Lower River.

Special mention should be made of the Upper River – the three miles downstream from Balnacoil Falls. Below the road bridge the Brora itself meanders sedately between exquisitely formed pools created from virtually nothing by a thoughtful angler for like-minded souls. The exception is the dead water above the loch, which will fish as long as there is a good wind. Upstream of the road bridge the Blackwater is, by contrast, entirely natural: the dramatic Falls Pool leads into a short series of fast-flowing pots and pools before opening out into the 200-yard-

The Ford Pool on the Lower River in May

long Pheadair Pool. The last, a magnificent holding pool, can be phenomenally productive in the spring. There can be no doubt that over the last fifty years or so the Upper River has proved to be the best spring salmon fishery *anywhere*. In the 1970s and 1980s it regularly yielded over 300, sometimes over 400, salmon to just four rods, with the great majority in the 13 weeks between March and May. In 1977 the spring catch was 419, including 197 in April. Two years later the total for the spring was 448, including 252 in April.

The following anecdote illustrates the Upper River's amazing reliability in the spring. One morning in March 1984 the tenants for the week, who were by the Pheadair Pool, complained vehemently to the gillie that there were 'no fish'; he explained that in the cold water they were unlikely to show. Minutes later he met the proprietor, the late Richard Tyser, on the bridge and relayed the comments of the tenants. Saying nothing, Tyser jumped into the Land Rover and roared off. Ten minutes later he was back with a rod and parked the vehicle on the opposite bank to the tenants, placing a straw bass on the bonnet. Taking the rod, he walked deliberately to a particular spot by the river and then took fifteen paces upstream. He cast three times, with the fly hitting the water like a bullet – he was an immensely strong as well as a knowledgeable man. With the third cast a fish was on, and within seconds the springer was on the bank and dispatched. He held it up to the opposite bank before placing it in the bass. He then marched back to his previous stance and began casting again. After ten casts another springer was hooked and dealt with in similar fashion. Holding it aloft, Tyser shouted across the river: 'Don't you ever say that there's no bloody fish in my river!' He then added the fish to the bass, slung it into the back of the Land Rover, and departed. While the second fish was being brought to the bank, there was a sound like a rifle shot from the other bank. One of the tenants had taken his brand new rod and broken it over his knee in frustration; he then stormed back to the lodge, where he ordered an immediate taxi for the airport.

Over the years some quite exceptional fish have been encountered on the Brora; the river has the remnants of a race of very large salmon (just possibly of Rhine origin), unmatched anywhere north of the Great Glen. Their numbers are limited, but they certainly occur on an occasional basis. In the late 1940s a salmon, taken illegally in the river mouth, was sold to a local butcher who had just installed a new fridge that was six foot square externally. The salmon just fitted in on the diagonal, and is understood to have weighed 65 lb.

The landing on rod and line of a salmon of over 50 lb or so presents particular problems in a river like the Brora – not least because the restricted nature of the pools is a major handicap in terms of tiring such a fish. Anglers are either broken or the hooks tear free. There have been many tantalizingly close encounters. Over a two-day midsummer period in the 1970s a leviathan, 'the size of a pig', was seen

February on the Bengie Pool with snow on the far hills

by many and hooked and lost by two fishers on the Lower River. Then, in early December the same year, a keeper came upon a disintegrating skeleton by the Blackwater. The jawbone was sent south for analysis and the report came back estimating the original weight of the fish as at least 65 lb. In April 1973 a very heavy springer was lost in the Bush Pool on the Upper River, and two months later Richard Tyser found the remains of a huge fish (which had succumbed to UDN) by the same pool – what was left weighed 38 lb. In the winter of 1998 he discovered a complete fish skeleton by the Balnacoil beat that was 49 inches long.

The most recent encounter with a salmon of massive proportions was in October 2001 (three weeks earlier a 38 lb salmon had been caught). Captain Ritson and gillie Donald MacKay, both highly experienced, played a great salmon for over an hour in the Well Pool. Eventually it moved downstream, and they were broken in the New Pool. The following February a huge decomposing female kelt was found half a mile below. It was 54 in. long, the same length as Miss Ballantyne's record, and its girth was at least 30 in. (the Tay fish had a girth of 28.5 in.); its weight prior to spawning was estimated at between 65 lb and 70 lb.

Some portmanteau fish have not evaded capture. In the 1920s Charles Akroyd had one of over 40 lb, and on 25 September 1929 'M. L.' landed a 43 lb salmon (a 'very black hen', 47 in. long with a girth of 25 in.) in the Bengie Pool. In the early 1950s Jock Wilson was fishing the Bengie in September low water with a 9-ft rod and 8-lb cast. He moved a fish seven times, before hooking it. Jock could exercise no control at all, but he noticed that the salmon kept taking the same circular route. After an hour Jock waded out and managed to gaff the fish with a small trout gaff as it swam past. The gaff handle then broke off, and what now appeared to be a submarine complete with periscope continued to circle the pool. At last the pressure began to have some minimal effect, and the fish's regular path came closer to the bank. Once again Jock stepped into the river, and as it swam within reach, he flung the rod onto the bank and in the same movement he got both hands under the fish and heaved it out of the water. He then fell upon it and subdued it whilst he located a suitable priest. The clean cock salmon weighed exactly 40 lb. Most remarkably it was hooked in the shoulder, although the nylon passed through the gills (clearly the fly had initially been swallowed, before being passed out of the gills). The story has an ignominious postscript: at the smoke-house the fish fell off the hooks and was burnt to cinders.

HELMSDALE

There can be few significant salmon rivers that have actually undergone a complete name change in the last 200 years. In the early 1800s the River Donan, also called the Ullie, flowed through the Strath of Kildonan. It was not until the second half of the nineteenth century that the 'River Helmsdale' was preferred, and essentially this progression reflected the realities of the area's recent history. The village of Helmsdale, at the mouth of the river, was developed as a 'planned town' from 1814 and largely populated by those cleared from the Strath of Kildonan who had not opted for emigration. Before that it had been little more than a hamlet, with the remains of a notorious castle where in 1587 Isobel Sinclair's plot to instal her son as the Earl of Sutherland was dashed; the poison with which she killed her guests the current Earl and his Countess was mistakenly taken by her own son rather than her third intended victim, the son and heir of the Earl and Countess.

As the status of Helmsdale grew, so the river became renamed accordingly. Today perhaps the most poignant reminder of the location of the earlier centres of population is the isolated and tiny Kildonan Parish Kirk, half way up the strath and close to the river, which was built in 1786, abandoned after 1813, briefly re-occupied by gold miners in the 1869 Kildonan Goldrush, and restored around 1900 (a replica exists in Nova Scotia, built by descendants of some of those evicted from the area). The Pulpit Pool on Beat 4 Below is so-called, because on occasion the minister stood here to preach to his congregation gathered on the opposite side of the river.

The Helmsdale has the second-largest catchment of all the systems north of the Kyle of Sutherland. The headwaters drain into a vast complex of lochs, including Rimsdale, nan Clar and Badanloch. Below Badanloch is Loch Achnamoine, which is the uppermost beat on the river. Two miles downstream the Helmsdale's major tributary, the Bannock Burn, joins from the north, carrying the water from Loch an Ruathair amongst other lochs. The river then flows south-east for twenty miles to the sea at Helmsdale. During this course the only tributaries of any angling consequence to join it are the Abhainn na Frithe (known as the Free) and the lower part of the Craggie Burn.

Historically, the mouth of the Helmsdale, and indeed the river itself, was always an important netting station. Statements of account for 1732 and 1733 between London merchant William Garden and the Earl of Sutherland confirm annual shipments south of, respectively, 30 barrels and 25 barrels of salmon (each containing 35 to 40 fish) – and, of course, the Estate may have supplied other merchants as well. By early in the nineteenth century the volume of trade was substantial; the records of fish processed by Mr Calder, operator of the salmon boiling house in the village, show that between 1807 and 1817 he handled on average 2,475 salmon and 3,485 grilse annually from the Helmsdale. The best year for salmon was 1807 with 4,767, and the best year for grilse was 1816 with 8,252. The Helmsdale nets generally fished from February (catching 100 to 200 springers); March could produce up to 300, and April up to 500.

The Garden Stream on Beat 2 Above

Dibbling Parapets 1 Pool on 2 Above

The status of angling in the river was first formalized in 1849 when the Sutherland Estate agreed to let the river above Helmsdale Bridge to the five shooting tenants from the 1850 season for a rental of £250 per annum, divided between them. The nets then became restricted to fishing below the bridge. In 1881 the angling tenants (by now six in total) agreed a set of arrangements and rules for the river, which were subsequently approved by the Duke. Over the next three decades these rules evolved steadily; the Duke took a keen interest and held regular meetings with the tenants. Many of these rules are still in place, including the ingenious rotational system, which originally applied only until the end of July. The river was divided into 12 beats, six upper and six lower, with each lodge having two beats a day – one downstream of Kildonan Bridge (the point that separates the upper and lower beats) and one upstream. The rotation works down the river, so that for instance the estate, that has Beat 6 Above and Beat 6 Below on one day, will the following day fish the two beats immediately downstream, Beat 5 Above and Beat 5 Below. Each estate now has two rods and a total of up to four miles of water a day. In early spring, generally up until late April, angling is restricted to the lower beats, as the Kildonan Falls form a temperature barrier to upstream migration.

Returning to the development of the Helmsdale for angling, the tenants were responsible at the turn of the twentieth century for two landmark achievements.

And what is remarkable is precisely that the instigators were tenants, albeit tenants with a fair degree of security (it is worth noting that there were very few changes to the tenants of the six estates between 1850 and 1919). Their first achievement was to gain absolute control of the netting interests. In 1896 Sutherland Estates had granted a 15-year lease of the local coastal netting rights to Colin Sellar. He then operated 28 bag nets between Navidale to the north and Little Ferry (the mouth of the Fleet) to the south, declaring an average of 6,092 salmon/grilse per annum between 1896 and 1899. In the latter year the bag nets took 8,658, whilst the rods managed just 307; in the same year the Duke's own sweep-net in the river mouth took only 342, compared to an annual average of 2,557 between 1864 and 1896.

The tenants, led by the Duke of Portland, determined to curtail what was clearly damaging their interests. They had bought off the nearest stations at Navidale and Portgower in 1898 and in late 1899 reached an agreement with Sellar to buy out the remaining period of his lease for £5,300; the tenants' share of this was £4,416, with the Duke of Sutherland paying the balance – he now appreciated that Sellar's nets were a serious threat to the health of his own fisheries. Sellar had driven a hard bargain (his annual rent was only £350) but the deal did confirm, according to his receipt, 'the entire withdrawal of bag and stake nets from the east coast of Sutherland'.

At the same time, from the 1900 season the tenants committed to a ten-year lease (subsequently renewed) of the Duke's river-mouth nets for a rent of £450 per annum. The tenants did certainly exercise these netting rights on a limited basis between 1906 and 1910 (Calderwood was apparently unaware of this), and they also netted Loch Achnamoine in May, June and July of 1917 and 1918 (taking almost 300 fish each year), with the proceeds divided between the Red Cross and one of the ambulance services operating in France during World War I.

The other major achievement, and another example of the vision of the tenants, was their execution, despite opposition from several authorities on fisheries, of a plan to impound the bulk of the system's headwaters behind dams, in order to have reserves of water available to keep the river in good angling trim during dry weather. In 1901 a dam was installed at a cost of £230 at the outlet from Badanloch, raising the level of the loch by six feet; a further £293 was paid out in 1905 to heighten and strengthen the dam. In addition Loch an Ruathair at the head of the Bannock Burn was dammed. Both dams incorporated sluices and fish-passes. Initially Loch an Ruathair was used to supplement spring flows, whilst Badanloch was saved until the summer. Although the spring fishing clearly benefited, the real boon was to the summer fishing (previously hopeless except in times of spate), which, the Borrobol tenant Frank Sykes observed, 'has wonderfully improved'; Borrobol's summer

Playing a heavy April springer downstream of the Falls on Beat 6 Below

average in the six years after the opening of the dam was 89, more than triple the average for the previous six years.

The above alterations to the exploitation of stocks and to flow levels are inevitably reflected in the average annual rod catches:

	Salmon
1882–85	721
1886–90	748
1891–95	1,202
1896–1900	760
1901–05	950
1906–10	1,245
1911–15	1,639
1916–20	1,731

The Helmsdale is by no means a big river, and its prime claim to fame was as an 'early river'. Grimble paid it the following accolade:

A bitter January morning at the Tail of the Bay on Beat 3 Below

One of the best, if not *the* very best, of the early angling rivers, so much so that in the beginning of the 19th century it is recorded that on the day before Christmas Day 60 clean salmon were taken from the Manse Pool at one haul of the net.

Analysis of the monthly figures for the period 1912–17 shows that of the average annual total of 1,618 caught by the rods, 895 (or 55 per cent) were taken by the end of May; the full breakdown consists of 7 in January, 53 in February, 250 in March, 240 in April, 345 in May, 200 in June, 231 in July, 163 in August and 128 in September.

Whilst the Helmsdale was a spring fishery *par excellence*, and indeed the nineteenth-century tenants hardly ventured near the river after July (Borrobol's 1895 annual total of 249 included 206 taken in the spring), what Calderwood considered the greatest angling performance ever took place on 9 June 1896. Mr T. E. Buckley, using light tackle and without a gillie, was on Beat 5 Above, just below Loch Achnamoine. He had five fish before departing for breakfast. On his return he concentrated on the tail of the Still Water Pool with 'fish rising keenly all the time'. His 12-ft single-handed trout rod broke and he had a nine-mile round trip walk to obtain another – this time a 10-ft trout rod (he passed up the chance to procure a salmon rod, or indeed a gillie). By 7.30 p.m. he had landed 22 (averaging 10 lb), including two at 15 lb, and lost only three. With stronger tackle far less time would have been expended in bringing fish to the gaff. It seems that he stopped fishing because he had beaten the previous record of 21 (mainly grilse).

In 1919 Sutherland Estates sold off five of the lodges and associated land, together with one sixth *pro-indiviso* shares in the fishings, to the existing tenants. The exception was Badanloch, where Sutherland Estates retained the lodge and land until 1949 and the fishings until the 1970s. There has been very little change in ownership to the estates since 1919. The rules for the river, written into the sale agreements, have by and large not been compromised in the interim, and they have indeed served the river well. Remarkably, aside from the opening up of the Town Water (as detailed below), the number of private rods (12) has not altered since the early twentieth century, in sharp contrast to the pattern on most rivers. Similarly, there cannot be many rivers where it has been a strict regulation for over a century that all hen fish caught in September *must* be returned.

The Badanloch dam, which holds sixty days of water at a moderate fishing level, has proved to be a truly invaluable asset, as it keeps the Helmsdale eminently fishable throughout the summer, even when the majority of Highland rivers are down to their bare bones. The original dam was washed away in 1970, and then rebuilt at a cost of £40,000, but the new dam's fish pass was not thought to be entirely satisfactory and was replaced in 1989 at a cost of £21,000. The dam at Loch an Ruathair had become unstable by the late twentieth century and it was dismantled. Once fish reach the seven lochs in the upper catchment, there is virtually no angling pressure on them. The burns feeding these lochs do not originate from any great altitude – there are no high mountains – but what is critical is the size and slowness of water run-off, giving ideal nursery areas and minimal redd wash-out.

After 1919 the proprietors netted the river mouth and occasionally Helmsdale Bay, with efforts concentrated on the summer runs. All netting finally ceased in 1988. Whilst there were two small hatcheries on the river in the late nineteenth century, a more substantial facility was built at Torrish in 1902; adults were held in ponds at Borrobol and Kinbrace. In 1911 860,000 fry were 'turned out'. The Torrish hatchery was mothballed in 1939, and then for several decades the river bought in fry from elsewhere, including fish of Oykel origin. Hatchery operations on the Helmsdale were reopened in the late 1980s, with the focus of attention on planting out in underutilized or inaccessible parts of the catchment.

In 1909 Calderwood praised the river's tenants for realising 'to the full the value of conserving the stock of fish'. In the intervening years this tradition has been maintained, not least by the fact that there has been little increase in angling pressure. It is probably fair to say that no other Scottish river has been so consistently well run for so long. The average annual rod catch figures for the six estates over the last fifty years endorse this.

	Salmon
1953–60	1,568
1961–70	1,631
1971–80	1,973
1981–90	1,837
1991–2000	1,772
2001–04	1,751

But what is masked by recent figures is the decline, as elsewhere, in the numbers of spring fish. In 1961 two estates (i.e. four rods) shared over 300 in May alone. All the same, spring catches in 2004 were encouraging, with over 500 landed on the river by the end of May, which was 174 up on the ten-year average, while the figures for April were the best since 1979. If the spring fishing is no longer as reliable as in the past, today's summer fishing can still be truly spectacular, with the occasional week producing an average of close to 20 fish per rod. The season's total for 2004 of 2,340 was the highest for 12 years.

To any salmon angler the Helmsdale has enormous appeal. Every pool oozes tradition and history, and the great majority of the pools are entirely natural. It is a truly wild place, as anyone who fishes it in the winter months can testify; 'backing up' one of the great spring pools such as Kilphedir or Upper Torrish in a horizontal blizzard is an unforgettable experience. It is also, paradoxically, a very intimate river; in the summer months there is particularly close contact between angler and quarry, as most of the fishing is on short lines with the dibbled dropper the favoured method.

And the river has its share of large salmon, with fish over 20 lb hardly remarkable. On average between 1912 and 1917 there were 16 salmon annually above this weight. The heaviest fish of these years make an impressive array:

1912: 35 lb (to a Badanloch rod in September – the mounted head hangs
 in the lodge) and 36 lb (to Harold McCorquodale in September);
1913: 32 lb (to Harold McCorquodale);
1914: 36 lb (to Frederick Nutting);
1915: 31 lb (to Harold McCorquodale in March);
1916: 32 lb;
1917: 33 lb (to Captain Wild in April).

February on the Salzcraggie Pool at the top of Beat 1 Below

In the 1950s a fish of 45 lb was taken by Dougal MacKay from the Town Water – at this time only sea trout could be killed on this stretch, so its capture is 'off the record'. The heaviest salmon 'on the record' weighed 37 lb and was landed by renowned gillie Johnnie Sutherland (aka Hardy) in the Bend Pool in April 1967. A fish 46 in. long, and estimated at over 35 lb, was returned in September 2001, and a fair number of fish in the 20–25-lb class are still landed each season. Interestingly there is a run of very heavy fish that come in and appear on the redds in November.

Perhaps the greatest Helmsdale angler of the twentieth century, Ina Lady Wigan, came to salmon fishing at the comparatively late age of 43. She started her career on the river in some style, with a salmon of 27 lb from the Salzcraggie Pool in 1934, and in the decades that followed she never bettered it. She acquired the Borrobol fishings in 1947 and thereafter took one of the two rods herself from the last week of April to the end of September until she finally stopped fishing at the age of 89. She usually caught between 200 and 250 fish a year, amassing well over 6,000 before her retirement. She was an incredibly resilient character, always in a hurry and involuntary immersions were not unusual. At the age of 85, when fishing the Falls Pool, she sent her gillie Johnnie Hardy up above to see whether fish were going over. On his return, she was nowhere to be seen. A minute later he found her hanging on to the Dog's Nose rock at the tail of the pool, still clinging to her rod: she had slipped in whilst trying to gain an extra yard.

Whilst the beats accommodate only 12 rods, the sharing of rods (especially in the summer) is commonplace, and in fact some 1,500 anglers now fish the river in the 31-week season. However the Town Water, on the lower river, is entirely accessible. Before 1967 there was local access to the lower river up to the Alan Pool, but all salmon had to be released. Then a club was started, the taking of salmon was permitted, and the beat was more than doubled in size by the inclusion of the long and productive Flat pool, previously part of Beat 1 Below. The club was short-lived (though the stretch is still often referred to as the 'Club Water'), but access for residents and visitors has continued.

BERRIEDALE

The Berriedale is the least typical of all the Caithness rivers. Its catchment of 72 square miles adjoins that of the Helmsdale, and it flows off high hills. From source to sea it is Highland in character, in dramatic contrast to the county's other systems, where long flat meandering sections tend to feature prominently. The Berriedale is some twenty miles long, whilst its major tributary the Langwell, which joins the main stem 500 yards above the mouth, has a length of some ten miles.

The whole of the Berriedale system has been in the single ownership of the Cavendish-Bentinck family (the Dukes of Portland) since 1881, when the sixth Duke incorporated Braemore estate (including the river's upper reaches) into Langwell estate, which the fifth Duke had bought in 1858. The sixth Duke was a redoubtable sportsman, who recorded his memories for posterity in his *Fifty Years and More of Sport in Scotland* (1933). He fished extensively outside the estate, notably on the Inverness-shire Garry, the Tay and the Helmsdale (he bought Suisgill in 1919, mainly to gain access to the latter, selling it on in 1932).

In truth, the Berriedale could not be deemed a reliable angling river – which explains the sixth Duke's tendency to fish elsewhere, although one July in the 1870s he did take 15 salmon/grilse in a day. Without a loch, it is a quintessential spate system that, as Grimble put it, 'requires eight to 12 hours' rain to put these waters into good ply, while a 24 hours' drought brings them nearly as suddenly to a standstill'. Sometime towards the end of the nineteenth century, according to the Duke, there was 'an expensive but useless attempt' to improve the fishing by constructing a complicated arrangement with channel, sluice and fish ladders half a mile up from the sea; apparently the idea was that released water would clear the gravel bar at the mouth, which could completely prevent access to the river in low water.

To run the Berriedale, fish also had to negotiate a gauntlet of nets and (in the mid-nineteenth century) a cruive within the river itself. The coastline immediately adjacent to the mouth was always a highly profitable one for bag nets. Grimble commented that five or six nets were 'unusually close' and the 1884 Fishery Board report refers to between 6,000 and 8,000 salmon/grilse taken in the 'district' – probably including Dunbeath. By the 1960s and 1970s a sweep netting operation had taken over. In 1979 the estate brought the nets back in hand and reintroduced bag nets, which in a good year could still take some 4,000 fish, although fishing never started before 1 July. Commercial netting has now ceased, and in recent years the bay has just been swept occasionally to provide a few for the house.

The Berriedale nets were, of course, a classic interceptory fishery, exploiting salmon as they migrated down the east coast. In the 1980s the Department of Agriculture paid for numbers of fish to be tagged and released, and some were recaptured as far south as the Tweed. The heaviest salmon taken by the nets is mounted in Langwell House: it weighed 62 lb and was caught in June 1894.

Rod catches have remained fairly consistent since the mid-nineteenth century, with the main stem of the Berriedale averaging between 50 and 100 per year. The Langwell could produce up to 50 per annum but historically it has been lightly fished, and the lower section, which runs through a steep gorge, is

Difficult low water conditions on the lower Berriedale

extremely dangerous; the tributary is now entirely private and yields in the order of 20 per year.

The odd Berriedale springer has been landed as early as February, but the main runs, water permitting, are from July. According to Grimble, the heaviest rod-caught salmon was 25 lb. The river is now split into three rotating beats with some 38 pools; one beat is reserved for the Berriedale Angling Club. For the past two decades considerable attention has been paid to habitat improvement, with regeneration aided by a reduction in the deer population from 4,000 to 1,500. Recent juvenile surveys indicate that both the Berriedale and the Langwell are stocked to capacity.

DUNBEATH

For centuries salmon were of great importance to the Caithness village of Dunbeath. There is understood to have been a cruive in the river since Viking times, probably until some time in the nineteenth century, although exactly when this was discontinued is unknown. For most of the past two centuries the focus of attention has been on the sea fishings rather than the river itself. The Dunbeath is a small system with no loch of any size, draining some 23 square miles and flowing 16 miles from source to sea. Given that it is little more than a substantial burn except in times of spate, the river always required consistently careful husbandry to be a useful rod fishery.

Andrew Young described it as 'one of the long-neglected rivers ... whose race of salmon have from time to time been exterminated', and he deplored 'the management of a careless proprietor'. On the whole, the river was of marginal importance to the proprietors, the Sinclairs of Feswick, who owned the estate from the seventeenth century. In 1798 the estate's most valuable asset was the net fishings, producing an annual rent of £115 – double the next highest rent in Dunbeath.

By the late nineteenth century the average rod catch of salmon and grilse was in the order of 50, and for much of the twentieth century similar catches were recorded, with a good year yielding perhaps 100. Fish could be taken on opening day (11 February) with the best chance of a springer from mid-March to mid-April. In the right conditions spring fishing could be highly rewarding, though nowadays numbers of early fish are much reduced. The main grilse runs have always been in July and August.

The Sinclairs finally sold the estate in 1938, since when the river has had a chequered history. Ownership has passed from Captain Currie (1938–50), to an

American, Mr Sinclaire (1950–60), then to Mrs Blythe (1960–77), Mrs Avery (1977–96) and current proprietor Mr Murray Threipland, who hails from Caithness. Captain Currie carried out regular stocking but for much of the second half of the twentieth century the river was left to fend for itself, apart from some ill-conceived use of concrete to 'improve' pools.

Mr Murray Threipland has initiated an ambitious programme to radically improve the river, which had been 'fantastically poached'. In the past the rod fishing had been entirely private, but an angling club of local members was formed in 1997 which fishes all three beats; poaching incidents have reduced dramatically. Commercial netting at the mouth has ended (now just 100 fish are taken each year to help pay for restocking). Since 1998 150,000 fry per annum have been stocked, and it is intended that this will continue until there are enough adult returning fish to give an annual rod catch of over 100. Recent electro-fishing surveys have been particularly encouraging.

The official record for the Dunbeath is a 42-lb salmon taken by Kenny MacDonald, the then head keeper, sometime in the 1920s. Over the decades, though, the poaching fraternity accounted for several fish in the 30-lb class, including one of 36 lb in the Houstry Burn tributary in July 1952. Local folklore suggests that a true leviathan of a salmon of over 60 lb was extracted by illicit means from just upstream of the harbour in the 1920s. This was possibly the inspiration for the 'great fish' episode at the start of Neil Gunn's classic novel *Highland River*, first published in 1937; Gunn was born and bred in Dunbeath, and his central character (at just nine years of age) has an epic battle with a more modest 30-lb salmon in the Well Pool by the old road bridge.

Before its demise the sweep net just outside Dunbeath harbour was devastatingly productive, intercepting passing fish as they moved south to other systems. One single drag in the 1960s captured 800 salmon/grilse, with the whole community helping to bring the net ashore. In July 1984 the crew netted 990 fish in a morning; only an appointment at the Dunbeath Highland Games prevented the day's catch from being rounded up to over 1,000 that afternoon.

WICK

If one draws an imaginary line between Dornoch at the south-east point of Sutherland and Cape Wrath in the far north-west, the triangle of territory to the north includes many of our best known salmon rivers. The four most productive are easily identified: in anti-clockwise order, the Brora, Helmsdale, Thurso and Naver – all illustrious names. However, I would hazard a guess that most salmon

September on the Wash Pool

anglers would be hard pushed to name correctly the river that now ranks number five in this area in terms of rod catches. The answer is the Wick.

This river, with the second-largest catchment in Caithness, has never been fashionable. It was always deemed too flat, although much of the Thurso (which has never had such an image problem) is similar in this respect. Perhaps what has created the Wick's reputation is the almost uniformly flat character of the lower river between Watten and the sea; in this eight-mile stretch, where the majority of fish are caught, the gradient is close to 1 in 800. Further upstream the river's character is progressively less lowland, and at the very top of the catchment (the total length of the system is some 18 miles) Stemster Hill stands at 815 feet. Incidentally, many are under the misapprehension that the main stem of the river emanates from Loch Watten, but the outlet from the loch (which drains a comparatively limited area) is just a small burn that runs for a quarter of a mile before it joins the Wick.

The fact that the river was historically never in vogue has, over time, created the circumstances which culminated in the whole system being controlled and managed by the Wick Angling Association, whose efforts and dedication have created a substantial rod fishery – very much a success story by today's standards.

A century ago the sporting tenants of Hempriggs Estate, the owners of the salmon fishings in the Wick, showed little interest in the river. They would perhaps have a cast if conditions were ideal but, on the whole, the rod fishings were neglected; the estate derived more income from the nets in Wick Bay. Wick Angling Association was founded in 1913, and, like many clubs, its *raison d'être* in the early days was access to trout fishing for its members. Thus it obtained permission from various riparian owners to fish for trout in the Wick. By 1920 it had also gained permission from the owner of Hempriggs for members to fish for salmon on Saturdays during the shooting season. This was the start of a lengthy arrangement between the estate and the club under which the Association 'enjoyed privileges' in the river on an informal basis. Right up to the late 1940s no money was paid, even though access had increased significantly, with members permitted to fish for salmon and sea trout throughout the season except when the estate's sporting tenant was 'in residence' (then fishing was allowed only on Wednesdays and Saturdays). The club generally showed its appreciation of the generosity of the owner, Mrs Duff Dunbar, by sending her an annual gift of a salmon purchased from the nets.

Over the decades the club progressively took on the management of the river, despite the fact that it had no security of tenure. Its activities included stocking the river with fry from 1947 (by definition, a long-term investment), and it paid half the wages for a watcher for the estuary from 1923, and employed a full-time bailiff from 1950. Poaching (illegal netting) in Wick Bay had always been a problem. The

Bilbster Bridge Pool

minutes of the Association's 1946 Annual General Meeting indicate that some of those attending had wartime naval experience: 'Several members suggested that the boats used for poaching in the Bay were well known, and that a depth charge or two might reduce it a little … members then joined in the chorus "Let them sink or let them swim". This idea found little support'!

For decades Wick AA members had been, as a minute from 1924 put it, the 'only persons protecting and improving the fishing on the river'. But at last, in 1964, the club's status was recognized by the granting of a formal lease of the river; the current lease is for 30 years. Over the past four decades the club has carried out a continuous and extensive programme aimed at fulfilling the principal objective in its constitution, 'the improvement and regulation of the fishing on Wick River and its tributaries'. (In this respect it is probably unique in mainland Scotland – but then, I believe no other club has complete control over an entire salmon system.) The Association now works to one-year, five-year and twenty-year plans.

The hatchery is an excellent example of the club's ingenuous use of limited resources. It is located in a small building in Wick and uses the local domestic water supply; filters remove the chlorine, and a chiller is used to prevent the eggs from hatching too early. Between 1971 and 2002 an average of 94,000 eggs were obtained from stripping, and fry are planted out every spring. A study by Colin Carnie in 1999 noted that two peak years for fry production (1985 and 1988) were both followed four years later by peak years for catches. Accordingly, he concluded that there is 'sufficient correlation between fry production and catches to justify continuation of production of fry from the hatchery'.

Working parties are organized on a regular basis, and each year an impressive schedule of works is completed, including the creation of new pools, improvement of existing pools, bank stabilization and the building of bridges. Increasingly, the focus of attention is on the headwaters, so as to improve the spawning areas (in some instances by introducing suitable gravel) and enhance the habitat for juveniles. It is worth noting that the water quality is excellent (a high pH), since much of the catchment runs off old red sandstone (which includes limestone), and there are high numbers of invertebrates and freshwater shrimp. Food availability is good (indeed the fertility is more akin to a lowland river), and most juveniles spend only two years in fresh water before going to sea. In September 2002 two sites on tributaries were electro-fished; at one site parr density was four times that found at the same location in 1995, and at the other site it was double.

In order to maximize the number of adult fish returning to the river, the club has bought the netting rights in the south of Wick Bay and leased the netting rights in the north of Wick Bay, as well as those at Brough seven miles up the coast; none of these rights are exercised.

All these factors have contributed to buoyant salmon/grilse catches over the past two decades, reflected by the annual averages in the table below.

	Feb-May	Whole season
1982–85	10	214
1986–90	11	432
1991–95	15	548
1996–2000	24	333
2001–03	12	354

The best years were 1990 (828), 1993 (993) and 2001 (860). Of the annual catch, 77 per cent is concentrated in July, August and September and fairly evenly split between these months. At times of low flow catches are minimal, and inevitably an extended drought depresses the figures drastically – and a total of just 75 were caught in 2003, a year when nearly 80 per cent club members never wet a line all season, since there was nothing resembling a spate between mid-May and October.

Most of the angling effort is downstream of Watten, and here catches are usually half on the fly and half by other methods, particularly the worm. Whilst the terrain here is flat, there is still plenty of good fly water, notably between the Bilbster area and Watten, where favourite pools include Shepherd's, the Wash, Taroull, Katie Gow's and the Pot. Even the slowest sections can be worked with the fly, and significant numbers of fish are taken by backing-up, especially in a strong upstream wind. There are also some excellent fly pools above Watten – for instance in the Badlipster area – but here high water is a necessity.

Wick grilse tend to be in the 6–7-lb class, whilst salmon average some 12 lb. The heaviest fish in recent years (22 lb) fell to Willie More in 1979, but Jasper McKain (who once took a brace in a day at 20 lb each) holds the all-time record for a rod-caught salmon: a massive cock fish of 30 lb 8 oz landed in the Corner Pool on 28 August 1958. There is no doubt that fish were drawn to Jasper McKain. He was once sitting quietly at the Pot watching the pool, when to his immense surprise a salmon jumped out of the river and into his lap. Not one to look a gift-horse in the mouth, he departed for home a happy man. A fortnight later Jasper was sitting at exactly the same spot when the river-keeper appeared. The conversation soon turned to the bizarre story that was circulating about the suicidal fish. As Jasper was relating the tale, both men were utterly amazed when another salmon gave a repeat performance.

THURSO

It is well-documented that the largest ever haul, anywhere, of salmon/grilse with a single sweep of the net occurred in the Thurso's Cruive Pool (upstream of the town) on 23 July 1743, with an astonishing 2,560 fish accounted for. Caithness's premier river has long been renowned for its capacity to produce prolific numbers of salmon, which is all the more remarkable given its comparatively limited catchment.

Draining 162 square miles, the Thurso is not a large system. The main headwaters flow off the north-east facing slopes of the Knockfin Heights, close to the Sutherland border. Many of the spawning tributaries in this area, including the Glutt Water, are between 500 ft and 1,000 ft, belying Caithness's image as exclusively a low, flat land. The upper reaches combine into the Strathmore Water, which empties into Loch More. From these the Thurso itself takes a meandering course northwards, first through undulating moorland and then farmland, for 24 miles to the town of Thurso and its mouth in Thurso Bay; the principal tributary is the Little River, which joins from the south-east.

The Barony of Thurso, including the river from source to sea, passed in 1718 from the lords of Berrydale to the Sinclair family, who have retained it ever since. Until 1852 salmon netting was the primary activity on the Thurso, with the fishings leased to Messrs Hogarth of Aberdeen, who, according to Grimble, 'netted Loch More and had the river cross-lined by ghillies, they being paid fourpence a pound for clean fish and keeping all kelts for themselves'. In 1846 the nets in the river and around the bay were reported to produce an annual rental of £1,000. Sport angling gained in prominence, at least in the fresh water, when John Dunbar took a long lease in 1852. He marketed the rod fishings, and according to Andrew Young (1857), by paying 'due attention to the protection of the river at all seasons, he has increased the number tenfold since it came into his occupation; for at that time the river was in an ill-used and reduced state'.

Angling on the Thurso became increasingly sought after, as its reputation spread. Andrew Young was unequivocal: 'No river in the north of Scotland will give better sport.' Calderwood (1913) confirmed that 'for very many years the Thurso was regarded as the earliest river in Scotland, as well, perhaps, it may even be said, as the best early river'. Indeed, according to Young, before the introduction by an 'ignorant English Parliament' of the close season, large numbers of fresh-run salmon were caught in December and January. A few of these very early-running fish still survive today.

In the second half of the nineteenth century the Thurso was fished by no more than eight rods (on a similar number of beats), and the river attracted some of the

March on the Weedy Pool (Beat 13), just downstream of Loch More

most illustrious anglers of the time, including Lord Lovat, Sir Francis Sykes, Francis Francis, Frank Enys and G. Ashley Dodd. The spring fishing in this era was truly remarkable, as confirmed by the average catch figures for the early months:

	Spring salmon
1853–60	496
1861–70	723
1871–80	643
1881–90	430
1891–1900	407
1901–04	239

The above averages are for catches to the end of May, except for the period 1891–1900, which includes June. The best individual year (1863) produced 1,510. The river was virtually unfished after May, apart from the 1890s, and all the most numerous individual catches were taken between February and May – for instance in mid-April 1874 Mr F. Hardcastle had 41 in three days on Loch More.

From 1853 to 1904 the overall average annual spring catch to the end of May was 518. This breaks down into 4 for January, 39 for February, 111 for March, 202 for April and 162 for May. What is perhaps most interesting is where the spring fish were caught; between 1878 and 1903, of the average annual catch of 418, just under half (191) were taken on Loch More.

From the figures above, the slump in catches at the turn of the century is starkly apparent. Following the death of John Dunbar in 1888 the river was let to a syndicate of rods, but their average catch soon declined to just 263 for the period 1897–99. Not for the last time the finger of blame was pointed at the nets. By 1900 there was no longer any netting within the river itself, but coastal nets in the 'neighbourhood' had more than doubled to 46. And scant regard was paid to any weekly close time, for, with the great improvement in the means of trans-porting fish to market, the temptation to net round the clock was irresistible, especially when wages were directly related to the number of fish caught. Between 1901 and 1904 the average declared catch for the coastal netting stations leased out by Sir Tollemache Sinclair was 3,394.

All the above numerical information was included in an elaborate brochure produced by the Estate in 1905, which offered to lease out the spring angling and the sea and estuary nets, as well as the Braal and Strathmore residences. There were no takers. Sir Tollemache then proceeded with a programme to close down the local sea nets. By 1908 a net-free coastal area, stretching from nine miles west of the estuary to four miles east, had been established.

In the meantime another important project, designed to extend the angling season well beyond the spring, was in hand. A dam, incorporating a fish pass, at the outlet of Loch More was completed in 1908, raising the level by 12 ft and tripling the size of the loch to 511 acres. This was essentially a small-scale attempt to emulate the storage of water behind the Badanloch dam on the Helmsdale. However Loch More holds just a small fraction of the volume in Badanloch. The original intention was to use the reserves of water in the loch to create brief arti-ficial spates at times of low water, in order to lift fish into the system. In practice, though, they have largely been employed to augment and extend natural spates.

Grimble was vehemently opposed to the dam, believing that it would spell the end of Loch More as a superb salmon loch. To a great extent he has been proved right. In the nineteenth century it was probably the most productive and reliable spring salmon loch in Scotland – so much so that, once anglers were allowed access to the boats from 1 April, they were then reluctant to return to the river below. The consequence of raising the level was that all the traditional spring lies were lost. Nowadays the loch only fishes well when the water level falls back (in times of drought) to pre-dam levels; fish are then taken very close to the bank (wading is discouraged and there are no longer any boats).

On the positive side, damming the loch has considerably benefited the summer and autumn runs, allowing rods a far better chance of sharing in the grilse runs. Since the building of the dam, the system has seen no radical changes, and its management has been fairly consistent, helped by the fact that it has remained under single ownership. The late Lord Thurso developed the current regime of 13 two-rod beats in the 1960s and 1970s by rationalizing various sections of water; one beat is 'the Private', and the others rotate.

One of the figures most influential in terms of maintaining the traditions of the Thurso was David Sinclair (grandfather of Eddie McCarthy, the current river superintendent), who worked on the river for 54 years, forty of them as superintendent, until the mid-1970s. He was particularly proud to have gillied for HM the Queen Mother – although he had the dubious distinction of having gaffed one of her fish twice! (He gaffed the salmon in the Sauce Pool and threw it high up onto the bank, whereupon it managed to extricate itself and drop back down into the water, so that a rather embarrassed superintendent had to repeat the procedure.) On another occasion the Queen Mother was fishing on Loch Beg when a salmon leapt into the boat – she insisted that the fish was returned to the water.

Over the past century total rod catches have been fairly consistent, although in the past few decades there has been much greater reliance on summer and, particularly, early autumn (September) fishing. Rod numbers have also increased. Below are the average annual catches.

	Salmon
1907–10	394
1911–20	604
1921–30	803
1931–40	577
1941–50	435*
1951–60	796
1961–70	1,371
1971–80	867
1981–90	839
1991–2000	783
2001–03	504

* Excluding 1945, which was not fished.

The 1927 season was exceptional, with 2,241, of which 1,414 were taken by the end of May. More recently 1981 produced 1,838, including 715 in nine frenetic

Loch Beg (the river's Beat 12), a vast holding pool towards the top of the river,
covered by boat as well as the bank

days in September, when a heavy and sustained run of fish coincided with high
water.

The vast peat beds adjoining the upper beats used to be a considerable asset,
as they would steadily release water into the system (in many areas it was not
possible to stray from the riverbank without sinking into the peat). But the great
drought of 1976 had a radical impact: it dried out great areas of bog, and
somehow they never recovered all their sponge-like qualities. As a consequence,
water levels drop far more quickly than previously. The situation has been exacerbated by the widespread afforestation of the catchment above Loch More.

Until the 1960s the spring catch always exceeded that of the autumn. Then, in
the mid-1960s, there was a great influx of autumn fish, and it is thought that they
pushed the springers off the redds. At any rate, the spring runs have never recovered to their former abundance. The fact that rod catches as a whole have held up
well is obviously due in no small part to the great area of spawning water above
Loch More, where human presence is negligible, and which has always been
essentially a sanctuary; that it has remained so is an undeniable advantage of
single ownership. Natural spawning in the main river was for many decades
supplemented by the use of egg boxes; this was still commonplace in the 1950s
and only petered out because monitoring the boxes was so labour-intensive. The

hatchery is now used exclusively for the benefit of the river, with fish stripped on the bank, and the resulting fry (between 150,000 and 300,000) planted out in the headwaters. Recent electro-fishing surveys have shown that the system's juvenile stocks are as good as anywhere else in Scotland.

The estuary nets, which tend to operate from 1 June each year, have long been a highly contentious issue. In the post-war years they could harvest 6,000 fish per annum. Net catches have declined considerably in recent years, but the operation is still something of a public-relations disaster, not least because it takes place within the town. Whether or not there is a surplus of grilse to be cropped, for the visiting angler who is fishing the beats in drought conditions, the sight of large numbers of fish being hauled in by the nets, almost inevitably provokes an attitude of deep resentment. One irascible angler, Major Hugh Cook, developed such a deep resentment for the nets in the mid-1960s that one July day he hired a boat and took it round and round the bay, breaking up the shoals of grilse and salmon so that the coble never had a chance. There is little doubt that the river would attract more summer tenants if the nets were removed.

The Thurso is a challenging river, and it is difficult to comprehend how the great Francis Francis, writing in 1867, reached the conclusion that it is 'easy to fish' and 'a capital river to enter a green hand on'; his visits must have coincided with unusually benign weather. In contrast, Grimble related that one novice, who

The Old Woman's Pool

by local repute 'could not throw a fly as far as a good Yankee could spit', arrived with six rods and within three days had to wire for another dozen 'by return'! Fishing the slower pools of the lower Thurso in a strong adverse wind requires considerable skill and power. 'Backing up' (or 'winding over', as it was called in the nineteenth century) is employed to great effect in the spring. The angler casts straight across, before taking two steps upstream to get a loop in the line and then edging backwards, whilst handlining, with the speed of retrieve dependent on conditions. The old Thurso gillies had a slightly different technique. They cast out at an angle of 45 degrees; then, instead of stepping upstream, they would walk directly back from the bank (handlining at the same time), ending up five yards from the bank, with five yards of line still in the water, to lift off, before they walked forward false-casting to start the process again.

The image of the Thurso is of a slow, featureless river. Really this is misleading; although there are many deep, canal-like stretches (inevitable, given an average fall between Loch More and the sea of 13 feet per mile), much of the water, especially from Beat 8 upwards, is really Highland in character with short pools, fast runs and a dramatic gorge. Here Eddie McCarthy recalls that it once took over three hours to land a fish of just 6 lb for the late Lord Thurso. It was hooked in the Sauce Pool and ready to net in a matter of minutes, when the dropper fell out and the tail fly then hooked itself in the fish's belly, which

The Upper Mill Stream on Beat 8

prompted it to take off downstream. Following it was tortuously difficult, necessitating climbing up and down rock faces and round trees, and the fish was eventually brought to the bank in the Upper Bridge Pool.

When he was 15, Eddie McCarthy had another difficult experience when he gillied one day for a doctor and his wife. She hooked a very heavy salmon and, as the saying goes, 'it played her'. After close to two hours the strain was telling on the lady, and she pleaded with Eddie to take the rod. At first he refused, but finally relented. Five minutes later the hooks came away, and the doctor gave Eddie a severe dressing down, blaming him in no uncertain terms for the loss. Twenty-five years later the doctor was passing through the area and called into the Ulbster Arms for a meal. He asked the barman if 'that Eddie McCarthy' still worked on the river. When the barman pointed out Eddie in the far corner, the doctor exclaimed with vitriolic bitterness: 'That's the little bastard who lost my wife the biggest fish she ever had'!

The record Thurso salmon weighed in at 47 lb; gillie John Sinclair caught this leviathan in the early 1920s in the Lower Bridge Pool below Loch More (evidently his angler that day resented this success, because for years after he claimed the fish as his own). A fine carved replica of the salmon hangs in the reception of the Ulbster Arms. Gillie Willie Finlayson landed the next heaviest fish, at 44 lb, around the same period in the Cruives Eye Pool.

One particularly unusual and commendable aspect of the Thurso is that it offers free fishing to local children. Some twenty years ago, when beat boundaries were being rationalized, it was decided to retain three-quarters of mile of both banks by Halkirk solely for the use of youngsters. The children were asked to come up with a name for their beat; appropriately they called it 'No-man's-land'.

FORSS

Based on a glance at a map, it would be reasonable to assume that the Forss has much in common with the Thurso. They enter the Pentland Firth just five miles apart, and they flow through similar moorland and agricultural terrain. Otherwise they differ markedly, though. The Forss has a far smaller catchment (at 58 square miles, little more than a third of that of the Thurso), and thus is far more susceptible to drought – dwindling to virtually nothing at times. In addition, spring fishing on the Forss is all concentrated in the lower river below the Falls (a mile above the mouth), which are an effective temperature barrier.

The Forss rises at over 500 ft in Loch Torr na Ceardaich, just east of the Sutherland border. The upper reaches are known as Cncloisgte Water,

Cnocglass Water (receiving the tributary from Loch Chaluim) and Torran Water (all on Dorrery Estate, and all good spawning territory). After reaching the mile long Loch Shurrery, the Forss meanders twelve miles to the sea at Crosskirk Bay.

Up to the early twentieth century the lower Forss was part of the Sinclair family's portfolio of property. This included Forss House, an early nineteenth-century mansion house beautifully situated close to the Falls. The estate was sold in 1919 to Major Radcliffe (a fanatical angler), and his family retained it until 1971. Between then and 1977 it was owned by John Farrell, and there were two further owners before it was acquired by Salar Properties in 1984. This company launched a successful timeshare scheme for the fishings (the lower three miles of the river) and sold off Forss House, which subsequently became a hotel.

In the mid-nineteenth century Sandside House and Estate, including the river from Stempster Bridge (the upper limit of the lower Forss) to the Point of Achalone, was the seat of Captain MacDonald. In around 1876 he sold to Thomas Pilkington the glass magnate. At some point the Pilkingtons bought the Achvarasdal Estate, which included the salmon rights from the Point of Achalone up to the Forsiescye Burn. Between the latter and Loch Shurrery was the Shurrery Water, which was also held by the Pilkingtons. This was the situation until 1930, when Sandside Estate (with the salmon rights from the Point of Achalone to Stempster Bridge) was sold to the Taylor family; the Shurrery Estate was retained and sold to Sir Robert Black in 1951. In 1958, on the death of Colonel Brian Taylor, Sir Robert Black purchased the rights owned by Sandside Estate.

In the late 1940s the Murray Threipland family bought the Achvarasdal Estate. In 1952 they leased their fishing rights to Sir Robert Black, and this arrangement continued when the Murray Threiplands later sold the estate to Willie Ogg. Up until 2003 the Black family, owners of Shurrery, either owned or leased most of the water from Loch Shurrery down to Stempster Bridge. In late 2003 Sir David and Lady Maureen Black sold Shurrery to Peter Hovig. Above the loch is Dorrery Estate – originally owned by the Crown Estate, subsequently by the Munro family and Donald Carmichael; it is now largely the property of the RSPB.

Andrew Young (1857) noted the good sea-trout fishing and the summer grilse runs, but was uncharacteristically off the mark in his statement that the Forss 'can scarcely be noticed as a salmon river'. For a system of its size, it has always had a reasonable spring run. Grimble cited March and April as the best months: two rods were reported to have had 160 fish in six spring weeks. Calderwood was sceptical of this figure, though, and, referring to the early 1900s, gave an average spring catch of 20 to 30 and an annual average for the whole river of 'about 100'.

During much of the Radcliffe era the Forss House beat averaged over 150 fish per annum, with a substantial proportion taken in the spring. After 1963 (169 fish) the following ten years saw something of a decline with an average of 52. In recent years, with a notable swing towards summer and autumn catches, annual average catches of salmon/grilse were:

1985–89	103
1990–99	79
2000–02	54

For their fishings between Shebster Bridge and Loch Shurrery the Black family's annual averages were:

1958–59	37
1960–69	22
1970–79	5
1980–89	13
1990–99	8
2000–02	4

The upper river is really a matter of feast or famine. In the late 1950s a young lady on her first-ever day's fishing had six fish in a day (it was years before she caught another). On the other hand, without water the upper river is essentially unfishable, and blank years are not uncommon. It is also important to emphasize that during this period these fishings were never let, on the basis that for most of the time to do so would be to take money under false pretences.

In 1956 Loch Shurrery was dammed to provide a water supply for Dounreay Atomic Energy Station. The dam incorporates an elaborate fish pass, although there is some disagreement as to its efficacy. Whilst there is a compensation-flow regime, perhaps the main negative impact of the dam is that it compromises the intensity and extent of natural spates.

Crosskirk Bay was always a highly productive netting location, and during the nineteenth century and much of the twentieth, catches of several thousand a year were often achieved. Calderwood expressed concern that at the seaward neck it was almost narrow enough for bag nets from either side to meet – effectively barring fish from entering. In 1903 a dispute over the exact limits of the estuary had to be settled by the erection of iron posts. The intensity of netting increased dramatically and controversially in the 1970s, and this drew the attention of the statutory salmon authorities and the police. The nets were finally taken off in 1985.

During the 1980s six springers a day was not that unusual an occurrence. In the canal-like pools of the lower river, especially the Sea and the Hut, wind is vital, and in a strong northerly wind fishing *up-river*, pioneered by Rab Murray, has proved to be very successful. The Falls hold fish back in the early months, but they are by no means insurmountable by April. The drop is broken by a series of ledges, and, once spring fish go over, they tend to make straight for the loch.

The record salmon for the Forss was landed on 14 August 1954 in the Corner Pool, where a pair of similar size were lying. A carving of the 42 lb fish, caught by David Coupar, hangs in Forss House Hotel.

HALLADALE

Legend has it that the Halladale was named after Halladha, a son of the first Earl of Orkney, who perished in a late fifteenth-century battle in the strath and was buried on the spot. Whether he was pillaging or trying to prevent pillage is unclear – this was an era of almost ceaseless feuding in Scotland's far north. And for the most of the last 150 years, the River Halladale has itself been systematically pillaged.

The system drains 108 square miles and is some 22 miles long, with angling restricted to the lower 12 miles. Its headwaters run off the northern slopes of the Knockfin Heights, just west of the top of the Thurso catchment. There is very little holding water until soon after its confluence with the Forsinain Burn, where the river enters a gorge section. Below the gorge the Halladale receives its main tributary, the Dyke Water, from the south-west. It then has a course of eight miles to its mouth by Bighouse Lodge. Bighouse Estate was the ancient seat of the MacKays and was acquired by the Sutherland family in 1830.

The Lodge, completed in 1765, dominates the estuary. The historical importance of salmon netting to the Estate is underlined by the large net store adjacent to the river, the icehouse and the Lodge's salmon-shaped windvane. The river mouth, sheltered from the sea by extensive sand-dunes, was an ideal netting location – fish were very easily spotted and, once in the estuary, were essentially trapped, unless there was really high water to lift them over the sand bar. In periods of prolonged dry weather fish had virtually no chance of actually getting through into the river.

During the early days of organized angling on the Halladale there was a reasonable balance between the nets and the rods. Andrew Young (1857) called it a 'fine little river' with 'first-rate sport', as 'a great number of salmon run up'; he went so far as to make favourable comparisons with the much larger Naver.

Glen a Gobhair Pool on the Lodge Beat (upper river)

Between 1861 and 1873 the nets were operated by Sutherland Estates; there were no bag nets, and the sweep net worked from April until 10 August. Rod tenant Mr R. Robertson wrote later that 'angling was then worth paying for': thus, in 1862 one rod had 106 fish in August and September. Relations deteriorated when a lease of the coastal netting rights was granted in 1873 to William Dunbar, who introduced bag nets and attempted to redefine the estuary by placing them inside the estuary limit set out in the 1864 Byelaw: a line drawn 'due west across Melvich Bay from the most projecting point of Salmon Rocks on the east shore'. Archibald Young (Commissioner of Salmon Fisheries) in his 1878 report confirmed that two nets were fishing inside the estuary limits.

The subsequent netting tenant, Alexander Speedie, was even more of a liability. The terms of his lease permitted ten bag nets between the Caithness boundary and Armadale, but he fished at least 16, of which seven were in Melvich Bay, including one inside the estuary limit. This brazen breach was allowed to persist from the mid-1880s to 1905. In exasperation Mr Robertson wrote to the Estate factor: 'Mr Speedie cares nothing as to boundaries, it is fish he wants and it does not matter how they are got'. Speedie also had the sweep netting rights; fish that made it into the river were driven back downstream by 'stoning' into a net set from side to side in the shallow stream by the icehouse. Speedie's methods were nothing if not 'exhaustive'.

The fact that the Estate tolerated Speedie's behaviour reflected the monetary reality. He was paying £200 per annum for the rights in Melvich Bay and the river mouth. In contrast, the rents to the Estate from angling amounted to just £30 (compared to £600 from rents on the Naver), split between three parties; there was some sub-letting. Rod catches were in the order of 50 salmon per annum. In 1910 the Estate, which by then had taken the net fishings back in hand, drew up a set of 'angling rules', incorporating six rotational beats for the six rods: two for Forsinard Lodge, one for Forsinard Hotel, one for the Bighouse tenant, one for local landowner Mr Pilkington of Sandside Estate and one for Melvich Hotel. Between 1904 and 1918 annual rod catches averaged 47 salmon and grilse. To put things into perspective, from 1911 to 1916 the bag nets averaged 428 salmon and 1,640 grilse, and the sweep net averaged 321 salmon and 665 grilse.

In 1919 the Duke of Sutherland sold Bighouse, including the lower ten miles of river fishings as well as the sweep net rights and the bag net rights in Melvich Bay, to a Mr MacAndrew. During this era there was at least some prolific sea-trout fishing on the lower river, with fish in the 3 lb class which managed to slip through the nets; there are very few sea-trout left now. Within a decade or so Bighouse was sold on to a Colonel Hartley, who showed some interest in developing the angling potential. He completed half a dozen pool improvements, employing railway lines and 40-gallon drums filled with concrete, and also built earth dams at Loch nam Breac (which a century earlier had been altered to discharge into the Strathy) on the west side and two linked dams at Loch Sainn and Loch Saird on the east side, to allow for a limited water storage capacity to give some relief in drought conditions.

The estate remained with the Hartley family (of confiture fame), until the mid-1960s when it was sold to the MacFarlanes (the biscuit manufacturers). They retained it until 1979, when Mr Honig bought it; he began an asset-stripping programme. The netting rights were sold to a partnership including local netsman Ian Paterson. Evidently they had considerable success, as in 1982 and 1984 the rods caught no grilse whatsoever, whilst the sweep net achieved figures of 2,473 and 3,024 respectively. Between 1980 and 1984 the net averaged 2,963 salmon and grilse a year, compared to just 85 for the rods. In early 1983 Mr Honig launched a timeshare scheme for the lower river, selling 15 rod-weeks (out of a total of 130), before his death later that year.

Forsinard Estate, with the upper twelve miles of the river, was also sold by the Duke of Sutherland in 1919. Two years later the Prince of Wales visited Forsinard Lodge for stalking. A vital requirement for his stay was a bedroom with a fireplace, and, as none of the existing bedrooms contained such a luxury, a wooden extension (complete with fireplace) was very hastily erected; this most temporary addition is still an integral part of the lodge, along with the heads of stags shot by the Prince.

In the ensuing sixty years Forsinard, where grouse and deer tended to be the main sporting quarries, passed through a number of owners, who had little interest in the river – not least because fish were scarce and holding water on the upper river was almost non-existent (most of the time it was literally little more than a burn). A notable exception was a Conservative MP and colonel of cartoon-like appearance, who owned Forsinard for a period in the post-war years. According to Lord Hardinge of Penshurst (*An Incompleat Angler*, 1976), this 'most imposing character' would during the spring months wait in the south for a phone call from his gillie, alerting him as soon as very heavy rain started, after which he would be on the first sleeper train north. On arrival he would head straight for 'those beautiful miniature rocky gorges', now heavily swollen, from which he would extract six or so springers in quick succession. Just three such fleeting visits each spring used to produce admirable catch figures ('a sound basis for letting'); tenants, who were not aware of the circumstances of his catches, were often less than amused.

In 1979 Forsinard was acquired by a misguidedly optimistic entrepreneur, who began extensive land-reclamation projects – all total failures. These works caused problems to the river for several years, particularly flash floods. In 1982 Fountain Forestry purchased the Estate. This company's *raison d'être* was planting and managing forestry on behalf of distant wealthy clients, for whom there were major (now discredited) tax incentives.

The following year Fountain also bought Bighouse, and for the first time since 1919 the whole river was under single ownership, with the exception of the netting rights at the mouth. No doubt with a view to selling the river in the medium term, Fountain started a programme of improvements, including the reburbishment of the three dams, the enhancement of one deep pool on the upper river (providing protection for springers) and the excavation of a channel upstream of the sweep netting location to allow grilse, in particular, access into the river during low water. However, on the negative side, very extensive forestry planting began on the west side of the upper watershed, leading to progressively worse flash floods, silting of the redds and in all probability acid run-off affecting fry and parr.

In 1985 Fountain managed to buy the sweep netting rights. Ian Paterson (one of the netting partners) was keen to sell. He was never a great advocate of the sweep, as he realized, with considerable foresight, that its continued unrelenting operation could 'wipe out stocks' in a location such as the mouth of the Halladale. (Indeed the previous year the rod catch had amounted to just 28 salmon and no grilse, the second lowest figure since the start of official records in 1952.) The sweep net was finally closed in 1987, after two years of comparatively minimal effort. Then Fountain itself was split up, and in due course much of the land at

The Forsil Pool in heavy spate

Forsinard was sold to the RSPB, whilst the river and sweep net rights were purchased by Jonathan Bulmer in 1989.

At last the Halladale and the all-important estuary were in the hands of a sympathetic and determined single owner, whose prime objective was improved angling. In many ways it is remarkable that the fish had survived what amounted to over '100 years of severe caning', as one observer put it. Their survival is testimony to the great productivity of the nursery areas. The other redeeming factor was that the sweep nets had mainly targeted the grilse; for decades the depressingly limited annual rod catches had largely consisted of salmon.

Mr Bulmer appointed Pete Keddie as his river superintendent. Pete proved to be thoroughly dedicated to the task, as well as a very skilled pool constructor – with the able assistance of local contractor Jonny MacKay. Armed with the necessary resources, they began a schedule of pool improvements and habitat enhancement; the transformation of the river to its current appearance was under way.

However, one serious complication looked set to undermine these efforts. Forestry planting continued unabated in the upper areas of the river, maintaining and increasing the threats of faster run-off, increased acidity and silt during spates. Jonathan Bulmer fought a protracted legal battle to restrict planting, and he succeeded in changing planting guidelines to reduce the adverse effects. In late 1996 he sold his Halladale interests to a small consortium of individuals known as the Partnership. They have continued, and indeed accelerated, the restoration programme, focusing especially on the provision of deeper pools on all beats, to counteract distress to fish caused by hot weather and low water, and further habitat improvements. Sadly Pete Keddie died prematurely in 1998, but he was in effect the architect of subsequent pool work until 2000. A great deal of habitat restoration work was carried out and still continues.

The measures taken in recent years have clearly been beneficial. The following figures for average annual catches of salmon and grilse are illuminating, particularly in the light of the cessation of sweep netting in 1986 (two bag nets still operate in Melvich Bay for a restricted period during the grilse runs):

	Rods	Sweep net
1952–60	156	2,211
1961–70	145	3,790
1971–80	123	3,997
1981–86	102	2,351
1987–90	273	
1991–2000	279	
2001–04	348	

The recent consistency in catches has obviously been achieved against a backdrop of greater marine mortality, although the remarkable figure for 2004 (628, or over 200 more than the previous all-time record) suggests that the problems at sea are by no means permanent. Management of the system has focused on maximizing the number of smolts, and a small hatchery is used to boost juvenile numbers in the headwaters, particularly burns inaccessible to adult fish. The maturing and felling of the conifer plantations should have a positive effect – they are unlikely to be replanted. In addition, the RSPB have instigated a programme of blocking up man-made hill drains on their property, which should reduce flash floods, and they also have plans to remove some of the plantations that they inherited.

Whilst the amount of holding water has increased greatly in the last decade, without the benefit of a major loch, the Halladale will always be a spate river. There is limited capacity to supplement natural spates. A full-blown spate, which in the 1950s would provide a good fishing level for a week or so, now runs off in just three days. It is worth noting, though, that, even in a prolonged drought, the lower two miles of the river will still produce fish. This section was cut into a canal in 1831, as part of an ambitious land-reclamation scheme; the centre of the embankments included a vertical shaft of sand and gravel 'to protect them from the inroads of moles'. Whilst not the most attractive stretch of water, it is highly reliable for backing-up in spring and also for wake-fly fishing in summer, so long as there is a reasonable wind.

Grimble cited March and April as the best months for salmon, but nowadays the Halladale is not fished hard before late April, which makes it difficult to gauge the state of spring numbers. There is certainly an early run. On 21 February 2000 Mike Mackenzie was the only rod out on the river, and he landed three springers, none of them sea-liced. The record salmon (30 lb) was a February fish, taken on the 16th in 1923 in 'McBeatle's [sic] Pool, No 3 Beat, with rod by Donald Fraser, water bailiff'; a fine cast of it hangs in the Melvich Hotel. In the late spring of 2000 local children found a heavy fresh-run fish in the Akran Burn by the lower river; it had beached itself after becoming stranded when the level in the burn dropped, and was later estimated at between 25 lb and 26 lb. The average weight of Halladale springers (11 lb) is quite disproportionate to the size of river they run and every year fish in the 17 lb to 20 lb class are caught.

The largest salmon taken on rod and line in recent years (a summer fish of just under 24 lb) was landed in the mid-1990s in the Smigel Burn Pool by a heavily pregnant Lady Marcia Bulmer, a most proficient angler, who distinguished herself by often fishing the river with an infant on her back.

Run Out – one of the most productive pools

STRATHY

It is perhaps pertinent that Lewis's *Topographical Dictionary of Scotland* (1846), in its entry for the Parish of Farr, accords the River Strathy a similar status as the Borgie: both are stated to have a 'plentiful supply of salmon'. Since then the Borgie has become an angling river of some renown, whilst the Strathy has languished in comparative obscurity. The reason has a good deal to do with its immediate marine situation rather than the river itself.

The Strathy drains a long strip of moorland terrain, bordered by the Halladale to the east, the upper Helmsdale catchment to the south and the Naver to the west. The headwaters flow off a range of hills over 1,000 ft high, notably Cnoc nan Tri Chlach. The Strathy itself runs north from Loch Strathy, absorbing numerous tributaries, and after a course of some 14 miles, some of it past extensive older conifer plantations, discharges into Strathy Bay.

The Sutherland family bought Armadale and Strathy in 1813 as part of their strategic expansion programme (Bowside Lodge on the Strathy is understood to have become one of their favourite retreats). However, the Duke of Sutherland sold the Estate at the close of the nineteenth century to William Ewing Gilmour of Rosehall, who subsequently disposed of Strathy to the Board of Agriculture in 1920. They retained it until 1982, when the Secretary of State conveyed the Estate, excluding the sporting rights on the lower river and the lucrative netting rights in Strathy Bay, to Fountain Forestry; in 1998 Fountain's corporate successors sold it to the Bowside Partnership. The rights on the lower river are now leased to Fountain International and Bowside Partnership.

By the early nineteenth century the mouth of the river, which crosses a sandy beach, was a significant sweep-netting location – not least because access to the river is often difficult, at times impossible, except in high-water conditions. This was clearly an issue, as in 1829 George Black of Montrose, who did several reports for the Marquess of Stafford on the best netting locations, recommended that a channel be dug to allow fish access for spawning. By 1857 Andrew Young reported that a good number of fish were netted at the mouth of the Strathy but was ambivalent about its rod-fishing potential, on the one hand deeming it 'too small to be considered an angling stream' whilst, on the other, remarking that 'after the river is flooded for some time, grilses and sea-trout find their way up and are caught with the fly'. Neither Grimble nor Calderwood made mention of the river.

By the latter part of the nineteenth century the west side of Strathy Bay, leading out to Strathy Point, was firmly established as one of the best, if not the best, stations for bag netting in the north. Fish destined for both north-coast and east-coast rivers migrate round the headland from the west and then hug the shoreline in Strathy Bay. By the early 1870s two bag nets were being fished. Alexander Speedie leased the coastal rights from the Caithness march to Armadale from the mid-1880s until the early 1900s, and he employed six bag nets in Strathy Bay. His annual rent in 1885 for the Bay and the right to fish the mouth of the river with net and coble was £150.

Intensive netting of the Bay has continued ever since. These nets (now often referred to as 'Strathy Point') have long been capable of taking 10,000 salmon/grilse annually on a regular basis. Their post-war heyday was between 1964 and 1974. The official figures for catches by all methods for this period in the Halladale and Strathy District show an annual average of 13,232, of which probably at least 80 per cent were taken in the Strathy nets. To put this figure in context, the average total catch in the same period for all Districts between Cape Wrath and the Kyle of Sutherland – including all the far north's most important rivers – was 45,479. The Strathy nets are still capable of taking 5,000 or more fish per annum with ease.

Given the extent of the netting operations, therefore, the incentive to improve the river's stocks and, indeed, to develop its potential as a rod fishery has been limited. The Strathy nets are of course a mixed-stock interceptory fishery – and it should be stressed that only a small proportion of the fish caught in these nets are of Strathy origin. However, in all but spate conditions Strathy fish have limited access to the river and, while they wait to run, they are highly vulnerable. Since 1982 this problem has been exacerbated by the separation of the management of interests between the river and the nets. The latter are now owned by the Scottish Executive, which inherited them from the Department of Agriculture. The Strathy netting rights are currently leased out until 2007 for £15,000 per annum, but the Executive has given an undertaking that it will not renew the lease thereafter.

The removal of the nets would allow the river's angling potential to be more fully realized. Records for the river are sparse. In the 1970s rod catches were in the order of 20 to 30 per annum, and from 1989 to 1998 the river was very lightly fished, as Fountain concentrated on the shooting and stalking. However, in 2000 almost 100 fish were landed over just three spates.

With a more consistent angling effort (which inevitably is unlikely to be achieved before the netting ceases), and with a fair incidence of spates, the river should produce an average of at least 75 per annum. The Strathy is entirely spate dependent, although a new self-cleansing channel has allowed some access into the system from the Bay at lower water levels. The spring run remains an unknown quantity.

In contrast to their predecessors, the current owners view the river as a priority. Their policy has not been to create or dramatically alter pools, but rather to allow nature to take its course with sympathetic habitat enhancement. In the 1930s there was considerable work on pool improvements, but very little of this survived for long. The upper river is now split into two rotating beats. Local public access to the lower river is actively encouraged.

NAVER

The Naver, draining 186 square miles, has the largest catchment of all rivers north of the Kyle of Sutherland. The watershed includes some of central Sutherland's most imposing terrain, including Ben Klibreck (at 3,157 feet the county's second highest peak), much of the Ben Armine range, and the northern slopes of Ben Hee. From the last flow the westerly headwaters of the River Mudale, which meanders east, augmented by several significant spawning tributaries including the Meadie Burn, to its mouth in Loch Naver by Altnaharra. This end of the loch also absorbs the River Vagastie from the south. Loch Naver, an impressive sheet of water six miles long and dominated by the towering Klibreck, discharges into the River Naver itself. Just below the loch, the river receives the waters of the River Mallart, a high moorland stream emanating from remote Loch Choire. It then flows north for some 18 miles, past several deserted townships, to its estuary in Torrisdale Bay.

In the early nineteenth century the mouth of the Naver was Sutherland Estates' primary netting location on the north coast, between 1821 and 1824 landing an annual average of 1,024 salmon and 3,335 grilse. The estuary nets usually commenced operations in February. With the growth of bag netting, inevitably the sweep net became less productive – landing, for instance, 211 salmon and 1,412 grilse in 1866 and an annual average of 399 salmon and 1,912 grilse in 1876/7. Archibald Young (Commissioner of Salmon Fisheries) noted in his 1878 Report that the bag nets (operated by Dunbar) were ignoring the rules and fishing within the estuary limits – defined under the 1865 Byelaw as within a line drawn from Chaishaidhe Point in the west to Aird in Casleich Point in the east. Incidentally, Young called the Naver 'the earliest, the longest and probably the best of the salmon rivers in the county of Sutherland'.

This was always a very early system and Archibald's namesake, Andrew Young, writing two decades earlier, bemoaned the impact of the Home Drummond Act of 1828, which delayed the start of salmon seasons throughout Scotland. Before that, he recalled, 'many excellent salmon' had been caught in the Naver in December, and he complained that the Act 'has deprived the Naver of two months of its most valuable fishing time'.

The Lower Dunvedin Pool (Beat 5) in August

The value of angling rents on the Naver grew steadily to £600 per annum by 1878 (remaining at this level until the early 1900s), and increasingly the tenants worked with the Estate to improve the rod fishings. The 'Angling Rules' for the river were formalized in 1886, and many of them are still in place today. The Naver was divided into six rotational beats (two each for Skelpick, Rhifail and Dalvina, later Syre) with one rod per beat; Skelpick had an additional private static beat above the tidal water. Anglers were restricted to fly only, and it was stipulated that 'no keeper or ghillie be allowed to fish except in his Master's presence'. In 1901 two of the tenants, Richard Alison-Johnson (Skelpick) and William Danckwerts (whose family rented Syre from 1853 to 1914), took a three-year lease on the Naver and Borgie nets for £250 per annum. They operated the nets from May to the end of July, taking 301 salmon and 486 grilse from the Naver and a rather more lucrative 175 salmon and 1,550 grilse from the neighbouring Borgie in their first season, grossing £1,089 with a profit of £483. They made a similar profit in 1902. The estuary nets reverted to the Estate in 1904, and that year the mouth of the Naver was more rigorously swept (in fact the catch was a comparatively modest 233 salmon and 1,001 grilse), something that caused much anger amongst the angling tenants, who landed just 204 (their worst season for 30 years).

In 1890 a fish ladder was built around the Mallart Falls, and by 1892 the tenants were complaining that the spring angling had declined as a result.

Their main concern was to retard the ascent of spring fish, and with this in mind they sought permission in 1896 to restore the cruive below Loch Naver. Soon afterwards they installed a wooden structure (removable gates allowed the free passage of fish each weekend) to prevent fish reaching the loch. However within a year it was destroyed by a spate; then it was rebuilt, before being breached again. Incidentally, just upstream of this, at the outflow from the loch, there are the remnants of another obstruction, built at the same time, whose purpose was to hold back massive blocks of ice, to prevent them damaging the structure below.

Another matter that was given much thought around the turn of the century was the possibility of improving the summer angling through the judicious use of dams. The tenants met the Duke of Sutherland in 1905, and they reviewed plans to dam Loch Choire (estimated cost £600) and Loch Meadie (raising it 10 ft at a cost of £1,200); the former was reckoned to be impractical and the latter prohibitively expensive. Damming Loch Naver was not an option at this time, because, in contrast to the situation with the Badanloch dam on the Helmsdale, the rights of the tenants above such a dam had to be considered. This possibility was re-examined in the late 1990s, but this time the main stumbling block was the Altnaharra sedge, a plant rare in Scotland but said to carpet much of Siberia (the road up Loch Naver would also have had to be raised for a short distance), and the conservationists won the day.

Rod catches in the late nineteenth and early twentieth centuries were not exceptional by later standards, although it must be remembered that angling pressure was minimal, with just seven rods (one per beat) covering 18 miles. In the 1860s Mr Akroyd (later a familiar figure on the Helmsdale) is reputed to have 'frequently had 20 spring fish in a day to his own rod'. The average annual rod catch between 1895 and 1898 was 456, and between 1903 and 1917 it was 401. There was limited angling after the spring and typically at least 75 per cent of the catch was taken by the end of May. The estuary nets during this period generally accounted for between 1,000 and 2,000 fish.

In 1914 sale particulars were prepared for the Strathnaver estates, but the outbreak of war delayed matters, and they were eventually auctioned in London in 1919. Syre, Rhifail and Skelpick (100,000 acres in total) and the whole of the River Naver were bought unseen by Walter H. Midwood for the sum of £100,000. Included in the sale were all the netting rights from 'the march near Kirtomy Point westward to Ceann More at the east side of Skerray Bay', with a provision that no netting be carried within certain limits of the mouth of the Borgie. The purchaser soon developed a great affinity with the river, and a few years later he had the distinction of catching 24 spring fish in less than six hours.

In 1925 Walter Midwood was persuaded that the whole of the Naver's stock (at least the spring runs) could be netted out from Loch Naver; fearful of this possibility, he was 'hoodwinked' into buying the loch for £7,000. All the same, it was by no means a complete waste of money, as the loch, particularly the Altnaharra end, had a long-standing reputation as a salmon fishery. Catches of several springers to a boat in a day were achievable. Mr C. Akroyd once landed 'six clean fish on opening day' (12 January), and in the late nineteenth century one rod took 52 in seven weeks; the favoured lure was always a trolled phantom minnow.

By the time of his death in 1938 Walter Midwood still retained four beats of the river (Skelpick estate had been sold with two beats and the private water); he left two beats and Loch Naver to his son Ralph, and two beats to his other son Eric. In 1945 Eric Midwood sold his beats to the Kimball family, who had owned Altnaharra estate since 1927, for £45,000. The current Lord Kimball was a pivotal figure on the Naver during his time as chairman of the River Board from the late 1950s until 1990, when Altnaharra was sold. He was a stickler for detail, and the river was run in single-minded, almost military, fashion. Every effort was made to protect spring stocks and to allow nature to take its course, with the upper catchment above the loch treated very much as a spawning/nursery sanctuary.

Ralph Midwood was another impressive, old-school character; salmon, and indeed grouse, fascinated him. In a most innovative attempt to boost the numbers of springers, in 1959 he built a tank on Ceann-na-Coille Island between Beat 1 and Beat 2 to retain April rod-caught fish for autumn stripping. Later, in order to reduce handling, he placed a trap in mid-channel, from which, using the river's natural flow, fish were encouraged to swim up a channel into the tank. There were problems with disease, which were largely rectified, and this project produced 50,000 fry a year, until it was abandoned in 1966 because there seemed to be no marked increase in early fish runs. On Ralph Midwood's death in 1970, Syre passed to his sons, William and David, who sold it in 1988.

The Naver is still controlled by three estates. Syre (owned by the Lord Iliffe, Michael Stone and Philip Gwyn) has three beats. Altnaharra (owned by the Gray family) has two beats, and Skelpick (owned by the Hon. George Lopez) has one, together with the Private Water.

It is probably fair to say that the heyday for the Naver stretched from after the Great War until the late 1980s, when, as elsewhere, the spring runs began a marked decline. Over this 70-year period the rod catch averaged over 1,200 per annum. Catches were often prodigious. In 1964 the two Altnaharra house rods (one man and one woman) landed 604. Skelpick's record year was 1970, with a total of 702 for their rotational beat and the Private beat. As late as the 1970s catches of 50 springers per beat in May were quite common. Until very recently much greater numbers of grilse have compensated numerically for the fall in the

Spring on the Crooked Stream Pool (Beat 6)

spring catch. At the start of the new millennium, though, the Naver had some particularly sparse years. Recent annual averages for the system as a whole are as follows:

	Salmon/grilse
1990–94	1,214
1995–99	867
2000–03	816

There is some evidence of a three- or four-year cycle; thus the average for the years 1990, 1993, 1997 and 2000 was 1,432.

Netting the estuary, which, because of the high vantage point on the Bettyhill side, afforded spectators a clear view as fish were encircled, ceased in the mid-1980s. In the previous two decades the nets only operated during the grilse runs and for one tide a day, taking some 3,000 a year. All Bettyhill pensioners and all houses in Strathnaver used to be given a fish each year by the Board. In the late 1980s an interesting experiment was carried out: 300 fish were netted in the bay, and then tagged and released. Whilst most tags were recovered in the river, a

Summer evening light at Skelpick Bridge Pool (Beat 6)

number showed up much further afield, which suggests that a proportion of the Naver net catch was actually destined for elsewhere, even though the nets were very much within the estuary.

One factor that helped to maintain rod-catch levels for decades in the range of 1,200 to 1,400 fish per annum was the relaxation of some of the river's more idiosyncratic regulations. In 1916 a rule was introduced allowing a second rod on each beat, but it was only to be fished by a lady. This was not always strictly adhered to. In the late 1950s certain very distinguished tenants, who stayed at Klibreck Lodge, dressed their menfolk up as females in order to circumvent the rule, and one proprietor, aware of this chicanery, would drive up and down the strath, attempting to expose the culprits. There was one unfortunate and embarrassing incident, when he accosted a lady fisher, who always wore men's clothing on the river.

In the mid-1960s the 'lady's rod' rule was relaxed by permitting the second rod to be fished by anyone up to the age of 18, but only during the school holidays. Finally in 1990 all restrictions on the second rod were removed, except that the lady's rod rule continued for the period 15 April to 15 May until the end of the 2004 season, when the constraint on this brief interlude was also lifted. Some associated with the Naver still regret the passing of the 'lady's rod', and indeed many anglers of both sexes were very much in favour of this positive discrimination. The other regulation that has been discontinued is the limit on fishing hours. There used to be a strict eight-hour day, ending at 6 p.m., but in the early 1990s this was extended, with angling sanctioned from 6 a.m. to midnight.

Until the 1980s the Naver was to a great extent snow-fed for much of the spring, from Ben Armine, Ben Klibreck and Ben Hee, and low water temperatures helped to discourage fish from running straight through the river. With the demise of traditional winters, and hence the reserves of snow in the high corries, water temperatures have tended to be several degrees higher in the spring than used to be the case, and this may well have contributed to the decline of spring catches.

The spring run is destined for Loch Naver, while 75 per cent of the grilse are estimated to head for the Mallart. Of all the system's tributaries this is by far the most important fishery, often producing over 100 fish a year. The bottom two miles or so, including two impressive sets of salmon ladders, are leased jointly by Syre and Klibreck estates from Sutherland Estates. The five miles above are held by Loch Choire Estate. Catches here have been hugely improved since the 1980s by the use of dry flies, as pioneered by Derek Knowles (*Salmon on a Dry Fly*, 1987) and Albert Grant. Loch Choire itself has a reputation for being very dour.

Traditionally, May was the month that the Naver's heavy fish ran, and indeed the nets used to take some 'monstrous' May salmon. Rod-caught specimens of over 30 lb were not uncommon; in the 1920s one angler is said to have caught a salmon of 38 lb above Dalvina Bridge in the morning, and then one of 37 lb below it that afternoon.

During World War II, the river was extensively poached to supplement rations. A resident, who in peacetime was a 'wonderful old gillie', set out one day with his net and travelled several miles from his house before he could find a holding pool that was not already being worked. In Dal Harrald (Beat 1) he netted and landed a portmanteau fish. He never discovered its weight (it exceeded the 42-lb capacity of the available scales, and fearful of the consequences, he could not tell anyone of the episode); many years later, shortly before his death, he finally confessed.

BORGIE

Rising in the hills just north of Altnaharra, the Borgie's headwaters pass through Loch Coulside (originally Cuil-na-Sith) and then, augmented by the run-off from Ben Loyal (the Queen of mountains), through a linked chain of three lochs: Loyal (the largest, four miles long), Craggie and Slaim. The outlet from the last is the start of the Borgie itself, which drops steadily from 370 feet over nine miles to Torrisdale Bay, where its mouth is a mile west of the Naver. The whole system is some 21 miles long, but it has a comparatively narrow watershed, and in fact it only drains some 62 square miles.

The Borgie tends to run gin-clear, in stark contrast to most north Highland rivers, for the lochs perform an efficient filtering function. Given the clarity, it is no accident that the system supports great numbers of freshwater mussels. The one exception to this clarity is the Phuil Burn tributary, which joins the main river downstream of the falls (two miles below Loch Slaim); it runs very brown with metallic sediment, due in all probability to the run-off from either a seam of ore, or slag remaining from an ancient smelting industry. There is a major seam of ore to the east of Loch Loyal, and the loch was an important centre for iron smelting in medieval times and possibly earlier.

Despite its limited stature, the Borgie has long been recognized as a significant salmon 'stream'. It is the most westerly of the genuinely early north Highland rivers, and it used to yield substantial numbers of fish. According to the New Statistical Account of Scotland (1845), 'an average 2,000 salmon are caught yearly'. By the late 1880s Alexander Speedie was paying an annual rent of £80 for the estuary netting rights.

According to the 1878 report of Archibald Young (Commissioner of Salmon Fisheries), a wire grating was positioned between Loch Slaim and Loch Craggie 'with the intention of confining the salmon to Loch Slaim'. He recommended that this obstacle be removed. He also suggested that the Falls be eased by blasting the right bank, but no such plan was ever executed – presumably because it would have compromised angling below this temperature barrier in the early months.

Grimble drew particular attention to the Borgie's spring angling, noting February and March as the 'chief months for salmon'. He quoted an annual average take of 70 salmon and grilse, although he suggested that it had been more prolific previously, as in 1889–91 six fish a day to one rod had been 'common', whilst 'now three fish a day is excellent'. Rod catches were compromised because the bag nets 'throughout the whole season *entirely* disregard the law as to the weekly close time'. Sutherland Estate records confirm an average annual rod catch between 1899 and 1901 of 49.

There was also a significant estuary netting operation, which between 1904 and 1913 averaged 241 salmon and 872 grilse. During this period the rod catch was usually between 50 and 75 – virtually all taken in the spring – in 1905 the entire catch consisted of springers: 9 in January/February, 36 in March, 11 in April and 13 in May. At this time the river was let as part of the Borgie shootings, and it seems that it was hardly fished after May.

In 1916 the Duke of Sutherland gifted the Borgie Estate (12,000 acres) to the nation for the benefit of returning sailors and soldiers. In 1918 he sold the river to

Herbert Barnett. Under the sale agreement the Duke surrendered his netting rights along a total of some four miles of coastline, west and east of the river's estuary. In due course ownership of the Borgie passed to the brewers, Mann, Crossman and Paulin, who sold it to the Kimball family in 1935.

In the following eight years angling was generally restricted to two rods, and it was rare for anyone to wet a line after June. The current Lord Kimball – who in 1938, at the age of nine, caught his first salmon in the Shepherd's Pool – recalls that during April the Borgie would be 'stuffed' with fish, and up to five in a day was common. Their best season was 1938 with 143 in the book, of which 129 were taken between March and May, but inevitably, in the war years the river was lightly fished. In the spring of 1943 the forestry adjoining the Borgie, planted after 1918 with conifers that never thrived, was largely destroyed when heather burning got out of control; the flames kept leaping the river in dramatic fashion.

In 1943 the Kimballs sold the Borgie to Major Bill Blackett. It is fair to say that he really developed the river as a fishery, with rods exploiting the grilse as well as the spring runs. In 1948 he built a hatchery with a capacity of 500,000 ova, and vast numbers of fry were poured into the system. He also introduced a programme of pool creation. The lack of holding pools had always been an issue, and some work had been done to rectify this around 1900 (a great flood in August 1883 had scoured and 'shallowed' the river). Blackett's efforts received a considerable

The Falls Pool, two miles below Loch Slaim

setback in July 1956, when a similarly devastating spate washed out all the weirs downstream of the falls, and it took ten years to reinstate the damage. By 1980 there were some 50 pools, compared to '20 casts' in the late nineteenth century; there are now close to 70.

In 1959 Blackett negotiated an agreement with Sutherland Estates allowing him to build a small dam, incorporating three sluice gates, at the top of the river; this enabled Loch Slaim's level to be raised by three feet and that of Loch Craggie and Loch Loyal by two feet. The additional stored water was used to maintain levels during the late spring run in May, and to supplement flows in July and August. In recent years the sluices have been opened not only to extend the natural pattern of spates, but also all year round, when necessary, to maintain habitat for fry and parr.

Blackett established four beats (one above and three below the Falls) and two short private stretches, accommodating up to nine rods. He was himself a very keen angler, and he had an ongoing battle with his water bailiff Donnie Davidson over which of them could land more fish on the Borgie. By the end of the 1971 season Blackett had accumulated 855 salmon/grilse, whereas his employee had caught 750.

In 1977 the Blacketts sold the river to Lord Normanby. He introduced a fly-only policy, ending a tradition of occasional worming dating from the previous century. In the Kimball era the worm was permitted in the afternoon, but later its use escalated; thus on 25 September 1968 – the record year, with 535 in the book – 25 fish (all presumably very coloured) were taken on the Garden fly from just one pool (Shepherd's). The current owner, Fred Drummond, bought the river in 1987.

Average annual catches of salmon and grilse since 1961 are as follows:

1961–70	322
1971–80	201
1981–90	163
1991–2000	193
2001–04	217

The figure for 1981–90 is influenced by periods of reduced rod pressure, and two years of very low water. Whilst severe droughts also affected catches in 2002 and 2003, there was a remarkable improvement in 2004 with a total of 411, the highest figure since 1970.

As elsewhere, catches have been maintained by increased grilse catches, although the Borgie remains a significant spring fishery, with catches as early as January. The total to the end of May now varies between 25 and 65.

In recent years river superintendent Jim Stewart has reviewed the percentage of fry planted out in the headwaters. Today a maximum of 200,000 fry are reared annually, and half of them are used to restock the bottom four miles of river. The intention is to hold returning summer fish in the river – spring fish do not usually surmount the Falls temperature barrier until late April. It is also thought that fry introduced into the upper tributaries suffer high losses as smolts, when passing through the chain of lochs and running the gauntlet of predatory trout (a problem that Grimble identified). Incidentally, whilst in the nineteenth century anglers did fish the lochs with some success, they now have a rather dour reputation for salmon.

Over the decades the Borgie has produced its fair share of heavy salmon. A fine cast of a 32-lb springer, taken in the Upper Breck Pool on 16 March 1918, hangs in the Tongue Hotel, and Colonel Heyworth-Savage landed a 31-lb salmon in May 1936. Donnie Davidson had one of 33 lb, hooked on a small fly and 6-lb nylon in the Wash Pool at the top of the estuary. It made upstream to the Bridge Pool, where it 'sulked', refusing to move. Stalemate continued for a very long time, and eventually an onlooker was instructed to throw stones close to the fish; ultimately the fish took off downstream. Finally 'hours' after it was first hooked (exactly how long, history no longer relates), the salmon was gaffed in the estuary by torchlight with the hook dangling by a mere thread. And when obtaining fish for the hatchery in October 2000, Jim Stewart netted a 27-lb cock fish, which would have weighed several pounds more when fresh-run. In July 2004 an angler released a fresh-run hen salmon, 43 in. long and 10 in. deep, and estimated at 34 lb.

Colonel Lawrence Kimball caught the record Borgie salmon in April 1942. He hooked the 42-lb springer in the Rocky Pool; it was eventually gaffed in the tail of the Still Pool. At the time the Colonel was commander of the anti-aircraft-gun batteries guarding Aberdeen's Dyce Airport, and he donated the fish to the officers' mess; apparently they were extremely keen to acquire it, for they sent a lorry on a special 400-mile round trip to collect it – despite the wartime fuel shortage!

HOPE

Few salmon systems have been the subject of such confused historical commentary as the Hope. In the nineteenth century it was very much viewed as a grilse fishery. Indeed Grimble wrote in 1899 that there were 'no clean fish before the middle of June'. Ten years later Calderwood was rather more astute, suspecting that the lack of fish before June reflected a lack of angling effort. In fact Hope Lodge's records for the late 1880s and 1890s indicate that tenants did not fish the River Hope or Loch Hope before midsummer.

During the twentieth century it became accepted wisdom that the western-most of the spring systems on the north coast was the Borgie. True, the latter produces early salmon (from January), but, at least until recently, the Hope always had a strong and consistent late spring run. In fact, given the numbers, it would be a travesty not to call it a spring system.

The headwaters of the Hope system (which drains some 80 square miles) flow off the high slopes of Saval Beg, Meallan Liath and Ben Hee. Three streams combine near Gobernuisbach Lodge (part of Reay Forest) to form the Strathmore River, which tracks north for six miles to Loch Hope. This is narrow and long (six more miles) and is dominated dramatically at its northern end by massive Ben Hope. Via the short River Hope (a little over a mile), the loch discharges to the sea near the mouth of Loch Eriboll.

In 1918 the Duke of Sutherland sold Hope Estate to Captain James Milburn in a private sale – although the particulars were prepared, the property was never on the open market. In 1925 the Captain's wife died at Hope Lodge, and subsequently he became something of a recluse at Hope, save for the occasional company of his two daughters. In 1951 he sold the estate to Captain Foljambe,

A good sea trout nears the net on Loch Hope's Middle Bay

who in 1983 gave the property to his nephew. Michael Foljambe then, in 1995 and 1996, split it in two and gave the north-east section comprising some 13,000 acres to the Melness crofters and the rest of the estate, including the River Hope and Loch Hope, to his cousins, Hugh, Edward and Sam Boileau, the present owners.

Sutherland Estates netted the Hope estuary for most of the nineteenth century (between 1833 and 1843 the nets averaged 190 salmon and 2,243 grilse per annum) in a a significant operation that is attested by the fine ice house that remains intact to this day. From the early 1840s bag nets were operating as well as the sweep net. The 1864 Bylaw defined the limits of the Hope/Polla estuary as a 'straight line from Gina Point on the west through the outer end of Sgeir a Bhuic island and continued to the east shore'; this effectively stopped the use of bag nets near the mouth of the Hope. In 1866 the sweep nets took 152 salmon and 1,555 grilse, while in 1877 the take was 100 salmon and 917 grilse. (It is worth noting that by the 1860s operations often began as early as February.) Sutherland Estates ceased netting in 1887; there is no evidence of Captain Milburn engaging in netting, and the rights have certainly not been exercised since 1952.

Rod-catch figures for the latter part of Sutherland Estates' ownership suggest that angling was generally not pursued with much consistency. In this era the sporting tenant of Hope Estate had fishing on four miles of the Strathmore, three boats on the loch and exclusive rights on the River Hope. Clearly, as the average annual salmon/grilse rod catch figures for Hope Estate confirm, this all changed dramatically with the arrival of Captain Milburn.

1896–1900	14
1901–10	27
1911–20	27
1921–30	221
1931–40	122
1941–50	178
1951–60	237
1961–70	269
1971–80	152
1981–90	131
1991–2000	79
2001–03	76

Up to 1918, the figures include a few fish from the Strathmore.

Playing a grilse in the White Stone Pool

Usually at least 85 per cent of the salmon/grilse catch has been taken on the river, as opposed to the loch. Indeed the river, the lower section of which is tidal, can be a remarkably productive short stretch of water, particularly considering it is essentially a three-rod beat. In good flows there is little that will not hold fish, and there are several well-placed croys, mainly built by Captain Milburn. It is a strikingly rapid and wide river, and in several places a cast of forty yards or more will not be extreme (Grimble was being quite realistic when he recommended an 18-ft rod in times of spate).

The system has seen marked cyclical swings in grilse numbers. In the 1920s grilse often made up 50 per cent or more of the rod catch, but by the 1970s one-sea-winter fish represented less than 10 per cent of the annual catch – in 1979 just one per cent. Since then the rise in grilse numbers has been inexorable – up to over 80 per cent by the turn of the century.

As the netsmen were also aware (Sutherland estate papers confirm that the estuary nets landed salmon in March in the 1830s and 1840s, and even in February in the 1860s), there used to be a notable spring run, although angling pressure in the early months was intermittent. Fish were taken as early as 9 March (1922), with considerable numbers in April and May. Thus in 1927 rods caught 126 springers at Hope Estate between 30 March and 30 May. Fish over 20 lb were not uncommon – five such were taken in 1919 – and at least five

The Hope estuary

salmon over 30 lb (the best two at 32 lb each) were landed between 1918 and 1932.

On Loch Hope salmon have traditionally tended to be a by-catch. Primarily the loch has always been a sea-trout fishery of outstanding quality. According to Grimble (who gave the record fish as 14 lb), in the 1880s Mr T. Rutherford used to average 1,000 lb of sea trout from the loch annually. Up to 1952 catch records were only partially reliable, as often they failed to differentiate between brown trout and the sea-going version. Since then the figures are dependable and catches have been impressively consistent. Below are Hope Estate's average annual sea-trout catches:

	River	Loch	Total
1952–60	200	516	716
1961–70	120	567	687
1971–80	178	511	689
1981–90	215	608	823
1991–2000	98	565	664
2001–03	173	661	834

In the records sea trout are defined as fish over 1 lb 8 oz (although latterly, with catch and release, some fish below this weight may be included). The average weight was always between 1 lb 12 oz and 2 lb (and this is still thought be the case – with the proviso that many weights are estimated), with a good number of bigger fish. The all-time record fish, taken from the Middle Bay beat of the loch in the 1950s by gillie Hugh Sutherland, weighed just over 17 lb. Since the demise of Loch Maree and Loch Stack in particular, Hope is now without equal on the Scottish mainland for traditional loch sea-trout fishing (either wet-fly or the dap). The quality of its fishing has hardly changed in fifty years, and the loch is, perhaps surprisingly, not overfished.

A straightforward explanation may be that the number of boats permitted on the loch, 11 in all, has remained constant over the years and is small for the size of the water. There is no mandatory catch and release policy, but Hope Estate's 'minimum returns target' of 50 per cent is consistently exceeded. The fact that there are primarily only two estates involved in the loch fishery (Hope and Strathmore), both owned by conservation-minded families which have been in occupation for over 50 years, makes the management process an unusually simple one, and this could be another contributory factor.

The Clark family sold Strathmore Estate to Colonel Douglas Moncrieff in 1938. He gave it to his daughter Mrs Heather Gow in 1961. Strathmore's recent average annual catches, for their stretch of the Strathmore River and their boat on Loch Hope, are as follows:

	Salmon/grilse	Sea trout
1970–79	11	37
1980–89	27	110
1990–99	16	96
2000–03	14	181

The best year for salmon/grilse was 1986, with 53, and the highest sea-trout total (208) was achieved in 2003. Sutherland Estate correspondence from 1904 refers to the heaviest fish off the Strathmore River as 25 lb; it also states that there is a 'run of fresh salmon in March and April but the best month is July'.

As for the consistency of catch numbers for the system as a whole, the comparatively limited amount of fish-farm activity that has taken place to date in adjacent Loch Eriboll, is surely relevant. There have been recent moves to augment this activity, and it is hoped that such folly will be successfully resisted.

The September 1978 issue of *Trout and Salmon* included an intriguing letter from Paul B. Riley. He refers to very heavy salmon and continues: 'however, a patient of mine, an ex-poacher, caught a male salmon of 109 lb in the estuary of the River Hope in a hang-net in September 1960. It was weighed at a farm near Tongue and then sent to the Continent with others. He has dealt with a great number of salmon and had thought that the record was 115 lb, so did not think much about it. Knowing the man well, I am sure this is a genuine weight and should go on record.'

POLLA

The name Polla is derived from the Old Norse (literally 'river of small pools'). It is indeed a small system with a steep, narrow catchment, wedged between the Dionard and the Hope. From Loch Staonsaid it flows down Strath Beag for over five miles to its mouth at the southern extreme of Loch Eriboll. Two sets of falls (one 60 ft high) confine migratory fish to the four miles of river downstream. Early commentators paid little heed to the Polla. Thus Calderwood, whilst acknowledging that it could provide good baskets of sea trout, declared that it was 'of little use for salmon except as a spawning stream'.

Ownership of the Polla was linked to that of the Dionard until well into the twentieth century. In 1919, at the auction of all Ewing Gilmour's properties, it was included in the tracts of land acquired by the Elliott family. For the next three decades the Polla was just fished occasionally during spates by tenants of Eriboll Estate, who made reasonable if infrequent catches, 'mainly after dinner'. In 1950/51 Sir Reginald and Lady Rootes, who had purchased Rispond Estate in 1949, bought the Polla from the Elliotts, and since then the river has been an integral part of Rispond. The latter was a holiday retreat for the Rootes family until 1986, when it was sold to the current resident owners Charles and Jane-Anne Marsham.

The hamlet of Rispond, on the west side of the entrance to Loch Eriboll and eight miles from the river itself, was an important netting station. Here a major salmon-processing complex, including boiling houses, was built in 1788. Aside from locally netted fish, Rispond received salmon from nets elsewhere in the north-west: thus, for instance, between 1837 and 1841 salmon-boiler Donald Reid handled on average over 4,000 salmon/grilse annually from the estuary nets on the Hope, Grudie, Inchard and Laxford. According to Sutherland Estate papers in the late nineteenth century, there was no netting within Loch Eriboll inside (i.e. south of) the point near Eriboll Farm. Rispond, as a centre for netting activity, has now been closed for at least 50 years. As far back as anyone can recall, there was never a sweep net at the mouth of the Polla.

The river was virtually untouched until the 1950s, when Sir Reginald Rootes began a programme of pool improvements and construction, which lasted until the early 1970s. Since then there have been no further works, save for a small dam to regulate the water supply to the commercial smolt hatchery (Sir Reginald had dabbled in restocking, including the introduction of progeny from Borgie springers). In the late 1980s and early 1990s the hatchery was employed to compensate for poor runs, but only with eggs from indigenous fish.

It is possible that the creation of pools boosted salmon catches in the 1960s. It is also conceivable (and this is pure conjecture) that the natural filling in of these pools over the intervening decades may have contributed to higher sea-trout catches. Averages annual catches from 1950 are shown below:

	Salmon	Sea trout
1950–59	15	46
1960–69	30	47
1970–79	13	18
1980–89	13	23
1990–99	21	29
2000–03	8	119

The recent fall in salmon catches reflects the lack of spates since 1999 – they are thought to occur only a quarter as often as previously. However, sea-trout numbers have certainly compensated. They average between 2 lb 8 oz and 2 lb 12 oz (and there is some evidence that Polla sea trout grow faster than fish from neighbouring systems). The record rod-caught fish weighed 10 lb, though a sea trout of 14 lb was obtained whilst netting for the hatchery.

The odd salmon can be taken in April and May (once, a springer was caught in March), but the first real run follows the first spate after mid-June. Whilst grilse predominate, the Polla has a strain of very large salmon. In the last 20 years two at 20 lb have been landed, and netting pools for scientific monitoring purposes has produced several over 25 lb. However, this is a difficult river on which to bring a heavy salmon to the bank, particularly as light tackle is generally employed.

Perhaps the key to the Polla's comparatively healthy stocks of migratory fish is the relative lack of angling pressure. In living memory it has always been the policy that the river is limited to a maximum of three rods and they only fish on the bottom mile of water. Upstream is essentially a sanctuary.

The Polla is a special little river, where in favourable conditions anything is possible: the angler may encounter a small finnock followed by a salmon in the teens of pounds within a matter of minutes. In 1990 the late Angus MacArthur cast over a lovely rise in the Washing Pool; he then spent most of the morning playing a cormorant, which in due course, after a long run, became airborne. Eventually it landed, shook its head and broke him.

DIONARD

The north-west corner of Scotland is a place of contradictions and extremes. At times it is the most desolate and inhospitable location in mainland Britain; the ferocity of the winds, as mariners attempting to negotiate Cape Wrath (and very many failed) have long testified, can be staggering. But in the midst of an intensely barren landscape is an oasis of comparative fertility, provided by the isolated outcrop of limestone around Durness, which promotes rich green pasture and trout of better than chalk-stream quality. The Kyle of Durness is the estuary to what was the most productive migratory fish system, in relation to its limited catchment, on the north coast.

The River Dionard, which drains just 35 square miles, rises on the north-east shoulder of Meall Horn (east of Arkle), and flows four miles north to Loch Dionard, and then another ten miles, dropping 350 feet, through Strath Dionard to its long estuary in the Kyle of Durness.

The Parish (as opposed to the village) of Durness was a substantial part of what was known as 'Lord Reay's country', which comprised 800 square miles, bordered by the parishes of Tongue on the east and Eddrachillis on the south-west. In 1829 this vast tract of land was sold to George Leveson-Gower, soon to become the Duke of Sutherland. In the 1830s the Kyle of Durness was a useful source of netting revenue (in 1837, for example, its nets sent 107 salmon and 1,830 grilse to the boiling station at Rispond); the best location, according to Andrew Young, was opposite Keoldale.

In the 1840s the Duke leased the salmon netting rights from east of the Kyle of Tongue to Cape Wrath, including the estuaries of the Hope and the Dionard, to Hogarth & Co of Aberdeen. Their operation was ruthlessly efficient; according to Samuel Lewis's *Topographical Dictionary of Scotland* (1846), 'the number caught annually, including grilse, averages about 11,000'. This level of exploitation was not sustainable, though, and before long the company had fished out virtually all the stocks, and asked to be relieved of the remainder of the lease. The Duke agreed, and for the time being netting was halted, whilst fish numbers recovered.

In due course netting resumed, and in the 1864 Byelaw the extent of the estuary was defined as a straight line drawn from Storr Point in the west to Famont Point in the east. Inside this line bag nets were not permitted, but the law was often ignored – as lawyer Colin Mackenzie commented to the factor Evander MacIver in May 1878, 'those rascally fishermen are so litigious and at the same time so sharp'. The same year Archibald Young (Commissioner of Salmon Fisheries) found bag nets operating within the estuary; apparently the Duke condoned this activity, even though he had no legal right to do so.

In the second half of the nineteenth century the river was let to a succession of tenants, including Reverend Meggernie, the Trevelyan family (hence the Trevelyan burn and Trevelyan's Bay on the loch) and the Austen-Leighs, masters at Eton (hence Austen-Leigh's Pool). The angling rental increased from £20 in 1863 to £85 in 1894. As elsewhere, salmon were not the prime quarry in the Dionard during this period. Lewis's *Topographical Dictionary* emphasized that the river 'affords good fishing for trout and occasionally for salmon'.

In 1900 the fourth Duke of Sutherland sold the Parish of Durness to Ewing Gilmour of Rosehall for the sum of £300,000 – the same as the first Duke had originally paid for it. In due course Ewing Gilmour took on the Elliott family as tenants of Balnakeil sheep farm, which included Gualin and most of the River Dionard. Following the death of his son in France in World War I, Ewing Gilmour disposed of Balnakeil to the Elliotts, and sold the other big sheep farm, Keoldale (including a section of the right bank of the lower river), to William Robertson. In the early 1920s Keoldale was sold to the Department of Agriculture, which retains it to this day; the farm house became the Cape Wrath Hotel, for many years the lessee of the Keoldale fishings – indeed, the hotel's reputation was founded upon exploiting the sporting possibilities of Keoldale's 27,000 acres.

In 1935 the Elliotts sold the Gualin portion of their acquisition, together with associated netting rights in the Kyle fishery, to Commander Edmund Fergusson RN of Baledmund and his wife Marjorie. The Commander came of a distinguished line of naval officers descended directly from one of Nelson's Band of Brothers. His principal contribution to the Dionard was to build a bicycle track or path up the Strath, which greatly improved access to the upper river, and in which task he was assisted by two faithful estate workers, John George Mackay of Achriesgill and Bobbie Macleod of Rhuvolt. It was amazing what was achieved by pick and shovel and wheelbarrow. The path had reached Dougal's Burn by 1948 but no further construction took place after Commander Fergusson's premature and tragic death that year.

Mrs Fergusson was co-heiress of Sir William Currie, who had amassed a large fortune from the Union Castle Steamship Co, together with an unrivalled collection of paintings by J.M.W. Turner, one or two of which grace the National

Collections today. She was short of stature and quick of temper, but it never lasted long, and she never bore a grudge. She was capable of extreme kindness and generosity to the less fortunate, and during her widowhood many people enjoyed sport on the Dionard that they could never otherwise have aspired to (as also did a few who did not deserve it!). In or about 1970 she transferred her interest in Gualin to her second son Edmund who was devoted to it and a highly skilled fisherman.

In 1975 Edmund sold the Middle Beat (which the Fergussons never held in high esteem although it was highly productive in the right conditions) to Mark Farrer to settle the financial liabilities arising out of his mother's transfer. The following year Edmund died in a motor accident, and Gualin passed to his nephew Alastair and his sister Mrs Parsons, the children of his elder brother Finlay. His executors were compelled to sell the single bank opposite the Keoldale ownership to Colonel Gordon Grieve and Sir John Higgs KCVO to secure the retention of the rest of the estate during Mrs Fergusson's lifetime. By this time she was becoming frail, and when in 1981 she failed to make the journey to Gualin at all, the whole was offered for sale. Mr Patrick Wilson purchased it and advertised it for timeshare. However ownership soon consolidated into three parties and is now vested in three families: the Allinghams, the Bladons and the Nall-Cains.

Mrs Fergusson had considerable force of personality, and the river flourished under her management. Indeed it retained its prolific stock of salmon long after the neighbouring fisheries encountered steep downturns in their stocks. She was a notoriously light sleeper, so her fishing programme was heavily influenced by her dislike of early rising and the proclivity of Bob Macleod's house cow to wander in the night, both factors dictating a mid-morning approach to the fishing. Since cloud on the hill and/or light was a very material consideration in the fishing (as well as the water height), these factors did not interfere with sport in the way that they might otherwise have done.

In the last 100 years or so there has been little consistent netting effort within ten miles of the Kyle of Durness. Grimble had complained that 'steam trawlers' were plundering the Kyle, but this is an example of why some suspect that he never visited the Dionard: the Kyle is in fact too shallow for trawlers. Even when the tide is in, much of it is only three or four feet deep. The bag netting station at Port Odhar, north-west of the neck of the Kyle, was abandoned in 1914 (this location is very exposed and over the years many lives were lost). Mrs Fergusson occasionally netted the mouth of the river, when there was a build-up of grilse during dry spells. One peculiar event occurred in 1943/44, when an adventurer from Oldshoremore purported to obtain consent from the Department of Agriculture to operate a net and coble fishery at Keoldale, and Mrs Fergusson successfully applied to the High Court in Edinburgh to enforce a covenant, which

Molteno's Pool (Beat 3, Gualin Estate)

had been taken out in 1935 at the time of their purchase, against netting in the Kyle. The miscreant then retired to keep the Hotel at Rhiconich.

Once in the system, fish were essentially safe from commercial exploitation (although there is evidence of a cruive close to the old suspension bridge). It is a river where it is difficult to work an illegal net, because of the profusion of rocks in the pools – although, inevitably, there are exceptions. In the 1940s and 1950s it was something of a tradition for a small party from Laide to walk over the hill to Dougal's Pool – always after midnight on a Saturday. They would take four or five silver fish each, before starting the long walk back.

In spate the Dionard is probably the fastest-flowing of all the smaller rivers. It provides lovely fishing up to a height of two feet above summer level; three feet is dramatic, and by four feet all the pools have disappeared. It is only really in the last fifty years that the Dionard has been rated as a salmon fishery; before that the river's reputation was mainly for sea trout, and, even then, those often took second place to grouse. Thus Dr Lloyd-Roberts, the sporting tenant before the arrival of the Fergussons, saw himself as paying for the grouse and having the river thrown in. When tenants did avail themselves of the river or loch, sea trout were usually the priority. Far more reliable salmon fishing was available else-where, but the sea-trout fishing was unsurpassed. Indeed many consider it to have been the best sea-trout system in Scotland up to about 1970.

The Gualin Estate game books give a glimpse of the sea-trout sport, although the records are unreliable, as sea trout and trout were often listed simply as 'trout' – if, that is, they were listed at all. But the runs, sustained by the excellent feeding in the Kyle, were awesome, and it is estimated that the annual influx was some 12,000 fish – in addition to at least 4,000, salmon/grilse, or possibly double in a good year. The profile of the Dionard's sea trout, and indeed the fishing in general, received a considerable boost in the 1930s, when grouse numbers declined dramatically.

In the 1950s 100 lb of sea trout to two rods off the loch in a day was quite common, including fish up to 12 lb or 13 lb; one season the average weight of sea trout from Loch Dionard was over 4 lb. The heavier fish would come in July, whereas the finnock and sea trout in the 1 lb to 2 lb class ran in September. By November the head of the loch and the burn above would be 'thick with sea trout'. Then, suddenly and mysteriously, the numbers faded – as one old-timer put it, 'like snow off a dyke'. There is still a fair run, but it is a shadow of what it was: now the average sea-trout taken on the loch is 2 lb.

With the dwindling sea-trout runs, the focus turned increasingly to salmon, and indeed it was a remarkably prolific salmon fishery up to the 1980s. The catch records for Mrs Fergusson's time are not an accurate guide to the fishery's yield. It was Bob Macleod's responsibility to keep the records, but his roles were

Upper Craggie Pool (Beat 2, Gualin Estate)

numerous, and translating all the daily notes that he took into the formal record, even during the quiet of winter, was often too much for him. Nor were all his guests entirely forthcoming about what they had caught. After all, if you declared eight fish it was open to Mrs Fergusson to conclude, with justification, that she had done her duty by you and not ask you to fish on the morrow! In all probability, properly fished and recorded, Gualin's average annual salmon catch in the 1960s and 1970s would have been in the order of 500, rather than the 200 or so declared. The runs have shrunk significantly in recent years; the last really good season was 1983, when Gualin had 337 out of a total for the river of 670. Now, in a good year, the Dionard as a whole produces close to 200 salmon/grilse and a little over 100 sea trout.

The Dionard has a small but discernible spring run. In the early 1930s the Lloyd-Roberts' two keepers would usually take the odd springer in April and several more in May, water levels permitting (Mark Farrer has witnessed springers caught in late March). The productive season is now really from the first high water after early June.

The Dionard is not known for large salmon. The heaviest caught by legal means is thought to be a fish of 26 lb landed by Edgar Dane, tenant of Gualin in the 1920s, though one late May in the 1950s a sea-liced springer of 28 lb was procured illegally in the Island Pool.

In its heyday Loch Dionard's sea trout (up to 15 lb) frequently dwarfed the salmon in a day's bag. Compared to other 'great' sea-trout lochs, Loch Dionard is comparatively small – under a mile long. This most dramatic sheet of water, dominated on one side by a cliff face over which a waterfall cascades, could hold tremendous numbers of fish – not only sea trout, which spawn either in or above the loch, but also salmon and grilse, which drop downstream into the main river to spawn (the river's tributary burns have almost no gravel). There are few holding pools on the upper river.

The ferocity of the wind at the loch can play fiendish tricks. In the 1960s Ian Hay and his angling companion were spending a night in the bothy by the loch. At the end of the evening's fishing, they left the boat securely tied. During the night the hut began to rock. Suddenly there was an 'almighty crash' and the cupboard used for storing food was flat on the floor – behind where it had been standing, the bow of the boat had come through the wall. On another occasion an angler watched the bothy blow away and crash against the cliff. In the late 1990s gillie Mac Stevens tied the boat to one side of the pier at Loch Dionard; the spare boat was on the other side of the pier. He and his party then retired to the hut for lunch. When they emerged, they discovered that the two boats, both still upright, had swapped places. There have been at least two instances of the wind literally lifting a boat and occupants clean out of the loch: in the

1970s this happened to the gillie from Gobernuisgach (which has access to the far end of the loch), and more recently a family of four was deposited on to the island at the bothy end.

It is only in the last few years that a track for vehicles has been created to the loch and the upper beats. Previously anglers from Gualin had a seven-mile hike to the loch – three miles of path, followed by four miles of bog – carrying all that was required: a major expedition, considering that a typical visit might include just one hour or so when conditions were perfect, without either too much or too little wind. The bothy afforded somewhere to spend the night. The long walk back to the lodge meant that anglers were generally modest in the number of fish they retained. One surgeon in the 1970s used to carry pairs of tights with him, which he suspended from his neck, and slipped his catch into the legs.

GRUDIE

The Grudie drains some 20 square miles of mountainous territory towards the south-east of the Cape Wrath peninsula. Several tributaries, including a wealth of good spawning grounds, combine to form the Grudie itself, which has a course of two-and-a-half miles. The pace on the upper section is fairly sedate, before it reaches a challenging fall; thereafter this little spate river tumbles down through a succession of pools to its mouth to the west of the Dionard.

The fact that the two rivers share an estuary, the Kyle of Durness, explains why early commentators were so confused. Lewis's *Topographical Dictionary* (1846) refers to 'Strath-Dinard, extending from the Kyle along the river Grudy for about 14 miles', and then, in the same paragraph, mentions the 'Dinard, which rises in Loch Dinard, and after a course of ten miles, falls into the Kyle'. Subsequently Young, Grimble and Calderwood all thought that the Dionard and the Grudie were one and the same, and their narratives all related to the former. Grudie salmon, long and narrow, are quite different to the deep strain that runs the Dionard.

Ownership of the Grudie was inextricably linked to that of the Dionard, until World War I, when Ewing Gilmour split up and sold off his Parish of Durness estate. William Robertson acquired Keoldale farm, including the sporting rights in the River Grudie. In the early 1920s he sold Keoldale to the Department of Agriculture, who planned to create additional crofts for returned servicemen from the Highland Division, a Chartist's vision that never really succeeded. It was, and indeed still is, let on a standard agricultural tenancy to the Keoldale

Stock Club. The sporting rights were excluded, and since 1928 have been let to the Cape Wrath Hotel.

The hotel's salmon fishings consisted of the lower beat of the Dionard and several small spate rivers, most notably the Grudie. Until the early 1950s the hotel's salmon waters were held in far less esteem than its trout lochs, then interest in these smaller streams increased, with guests visiting them during spates. (Apart from the Dionard, they were free of charge.) Only during major spates was fly-fishing favoured on the Grudie, and most fish were taken on the worm, which has remained the favoured method. It is estimated that legitimate anglers caught between twenty and thirty salmon/grilse per season on the Grudie during this period; average fishing effort amounted to perhaps ten or fifteen visits to the river per season. In the hotel's returns these fish tended to be included in the Dionard's catch. As the Dionard improved during the 1950s so fewer anglers sought out the less fashionable streams.

The Grudie, far off the beaten track, was often sought out by the young and energetic to avoid the Sunday fishing ban. The river is totally natural, except that the falls at the Bridge and Pot pools were eased with commercial explosives in the 1930s or 1940s. Before then, fish could only surmount these obstacles at certain specific water heights.

The runs mirror those of the Dionard: the odd springer on the spring tide in early May, followed by summer salmon and grilse in July, and a further run of very small grilse in mid-September. Most exceptionally, salmon of up to 17 lb have been taken. There are no records of any sea trout in the Grudie.

When the river was in good order, it was not unusual for a party to return with five or six salmon/grilse, but such ideal conditions would usually only occur once or twice a season. A prerequisite for such success was the assistance of one of the old gillies, who could be hired by the day up to the early 1950s. Thereafter the normal pattern was for anglers to fish unaided, picking up the occasional fish. Once a fisher and his two young sons found a large shoal of grilse stranded in a shallow pool and returned with 21; this was severely frowned upon back at the hotel. The most bizarre example of a stranded fish happened when Alec Morrison came upon a 6-lb grilse wriggling up the scree towards the top of the mountain behind Gualin, when water was running off it after heavy rain.

Fish stocks remained healthy, reflecting the low levels of exploitation and the fact that the long canal-like section of the river was something of a sanctuary. This continued until the mid-1980s, since when there has been a marked, largely unexplained decline. Catches now amount to no more than a handful per annum.

RHICONICH

The Rhiconich (or Inchard) drains a compact area, some 16 square miles, to the west of Foinaven and Arkle, and falls rapidly to its estuary in Loch Inchard south-east of Kinlochbervie. The river itself is so choked with boulders that, apart from a handful of small pools, it is virtually unfishable. At just over a mile long, the lower part is essentially little more than a conduit up to the two lochs, Loch Garbet Beg and Loch Garbet Mor above; these two, particularly the former, have an enduring reputation as an excellent fishery set against a magnificent backdrop of pink granite mountain.

The Rhiconich originally formed part of Reay Forest, acquired by Sutherland Estates in 1829. In the late nineteenth and early twentieth centuries it was leased to the tenant of the Rhiconich Hotel (in 1895 the rent was £40). In 1915 most of the system was sold with Oldshoremore Lodge to George Morrison of Ullapool. In 1922 he disposed of what became known as Rhiconich Estate to General Stronach, who in turn sold to Donald MacLeod of Kinlochbervie in 1934, and since 1943 the Estate has been the property of the Osborne family. Much of the upper part of the system, including a small section of Garbet Beg and most of Garbet Mor, is still part of the (reduced) Reay Forest Estate.

The Rhiconich system is a classic loch fishery for salmon and as such resembles many systems in the Outer Isles. Given the size of the catchment, the river has little flow in normal summer conditions, and a spate is required to lift fish up into the lochs. Once fish reach the lochs, sport can be spectacular. Thomas Stoddart (1847) recalled a prolific five hours of fishing on Garbet Beg, taking 38 sea trout (including several at 3 lb), two salmon and two grilse. Grimble, whilst somewhat confused over the extent and shape of the lochs, was also profuse in his praise: 'for those who like loch fishing, I do not know of any better sport to be had for the money in Scotland'. In the 1890s the fishing on the most productive loch, Garbet Beg, was let to two rods for £20 per month. In that era rod catches of salmon generally amounted to between 40 and 50 per year. The average from 1908 to 1915 was 51.

Records of fish delivered to the boiling house at Rispond between 1837 and 1842 show an average of 20 salmon and 277 grilse a year from the nets in Loch Inchard (a comparatively limited operation). However, during the second half of the nineteenth century the pressure of bag netting in Loch Inchard, as elsewhere in the north-west, was intense; the landlord of the hotel complained that 'the observance of the weekly close time by these nets was the exception and not the rule'. In 1915 the nets declared 95 salmon and 576 grilse, whilst the rod catch amounted to just 26. There is no record of a sweep net ever being operated at the

mouth and the netting rights within Loch Inchard have not been exercised for at
least sixty years.

Rod catches of salmon (from the river and Garbet Beg) from 1943 to 1985 were:

1943–55	50–70
1956–65	70–100
1966–75	20–30
1976–85	10–20

Up to 1969 angling was restricted to the family, concentrating on periods of
optimum conditions. From 1969 to 1985 the fishing was let with the lodge, averaging two to three days per week.

Recent average annual catches for the river and Garbet Beg are set out below:

1985–89	14
1990–94	32
1995–99	25
2000–03	17

Fishing effort increased between the mid-1980s and mid-1990s, subsequently
tailing off to a current level of two to three days per week.

In 1878 Archibald Young, the Commissioner of Salmon Fisheries, recommended to the Duke of Sutherland that a dam be placed at the outlet from Garbet
Beg to enable the creation of artificial floods, but the Duke did not pursue this. In
the early 1900s there was a proposal to dam Loch Garbet Mor for similar
purposes, but again it came to nothing. In the last half century management has
focused on habitat and redd improvement and weed control. Stocking was tried
on a small scale (a maximum of 8,000 fry per year) between 1943 and 1953, and
then again from 1985 to 1990.

The record salmon would appear to be a fish of 22 lb taken in 1914, though
local repute has it that another of 22 lb was caught on 22 April 1922. There used
to be something of a late spring run, but there is no evidence that this still exists.
A 19-lb red cock fish, landed in June 1959 by John Osborne, was in fact a
springer. The main grilse run is (water permitting) from early July, with a run of
salmon, much reduced in the last decade, in August and September. The best
catch took place in 1961, when 15 grilse/salmon were taken in just four hours in

the Narrows. Sea-trout numbers were prolific, but, as elsewhere in the north-west, they have slumped since the mid-1980s. Sea trout have a tendency to run through to Garbet Mor.

Loch Garbet Beg is an ideal salmon loch: shallow and narrow, with a profusion of bays that can be covered either from a boat or from the shore – a good wind is of course a prerequisite. Like any great salmon loch, its best lies are all named; one, the Minister's, is named after Viscount Grey of Fallodon (Foreign Secretary from 1905 to 1916), who was a frequent visitor. Illustrious guests in the 1950s included Field Marshal Lord Alanbrooke and Admiral Andrew Cunningham. On one occasion Lady Cunningham is understood to have hooked an otter; she played it for five minutes, thinking it was a salmon, before it took off up the bank.

LAXFORD

The name Laxford is derived from Old Norse *lax-fjordhr*, which translates as 'salmon fiord'. One can only presume that it was the teeming multitudes of salmon that prompted the Norse invaders over a thousand years ago to name the sea loch and river accordingly. By the end of the eighteenth century the *Statistical Account of Scotland (1791–99, Vol. 6)* noted under its Laxford entry the 'considerable quantity of fish killed, and of an excellent quality'.

Ever since the arrival of salmon angling in the north, the Laxford has been held in the highest esteem. Draining 67 square miles of some of the most dramatic west Sutherland terrain, it is, over its short course of four miles, the quintessential Highland salmon river, as anyone travelling from Laxford Bridge to Loch Stack will concur, even though the most stunning section is not visible from the road. Commentators have always been profuse in extolling its virtues. Grimble described it as the 'angler's ideal river, with rapids and deep pools following each other in quick succession'. Four decades earlier Andrew Young had classed the Laxford as the second-best river in the county between June and August, enthusing that 'salmon are almost sure to take the fly', which 'is seldom allowed to pass unnoticed'. The hooking of salmon required little skill, he felt, as 'they are so numerous'.

The lochs that feed the Laxford are of course important fisheries in their own right and have also long been revered – particularly Loch Stack. Young considered Stack to be 'far superior to any loch of its size in the north, if not in Scotland'. Calderwood's view (1909) was unqualified: it was the best sea-trout loch in the country.

Loch Stack

Whilst sea-trout numbers held up well, as elsewhere all was not well on the salmon front as the nineteenth century progressed. The estuary nets and river cruives averaged 164 salmon and 1,149 grilse between 1837 and 1842, falling to 75 salmon and 676 grilse between 1845 and 1849. By the last quarter of the century, after the marked growth in coastal netting from 1873 (exacerbated, according to Grimble, by 'crews of lawless steam trawlers' scooping great numbers of fish out of the estuary), the Laxford's salmon runs were severely depleted. Rod catches, which had been as high as 300 in a season (averaging 154 between 1853 and 1856), slumped to an average of just 55 between 1874 and 1909.

In 1882 the first Duke of Westminster (Lord Arthur Grosvenor) personally examined the nets in June and observed that they were all 'fishing illegally' during the weekly slap time. He wrote to Evander MacIver (the Duke of Sutherland's factor) urging that pressure be applied to the netting tenant (Speedie) to operate within the law: 'It is very unfair upon the river tenants that these things can be carried on with impunity'. The days of a dozen fish to two rods were gone, and the entry for the Laxford in *The Survey Gazetteer of The British Isles* (Bartholomew, 1904), stating that 'salmon are abundant', reflected its reputation rather than the current reality. Salmon were scarce on the spawning headstreams above Loch More, and at the turn of the century the head stalker counted just a dozen pairs of fish on the 300 yards of beds at the head of the main river below Stack Bridge (by Stack Lodge), when twenty years earlier a hundred pairs had been the norm.

While the first Duke of Westminster (who died in 1899) and his heirs leased the system from the Duke of Sutherland (for £100 per annum in the late 1890s), they only held the estuary netting rights (and at this time they were not exercised). But this was always going to be an unsatisfactory situation, so long as they were able to exert little control or influence over the coastal netting. From 1873 to 1897 the nets between Kinlochbervie and Lochinver (25 miles as the crow flies) averaged 60,338 lb of salmon per year (the equivalent, at 5 lb per fish, of some 12,000 grilse). Rents from these nets raised over £1,000 per annum, a not inconsiderable sum, for the Duke of Sutherland.

This awkward situation was only resolved in 1921, when the second Duke of Westminster (known as Duke Bendor) bought Reay Forest and Kylestrome estates from the Sutherland Estate; the purchase included a considerable length of adjacent coastline. At the same time he acquired the right to police the coastline from the Point of Stoer to Cape Wrath – i.e. 15 miles north and 15 miles south of the Laxford estuary. This control at last allowed a more equitable balance between nets and rods.

As an angler, the Duke's main interest was the river. Above the top pool he

The middle section of the Laxford

constructed a grid of metal bars (now converted to a footbridge) which, when all bars were in place, prevented fish over 4 lb from gaining access to the loch above. This resulted in an enormous build-up of salmon and grilse immediately below (the fish never dropped back) until bars were removed at the end of the season. Use of the grid continued until the early 1950s, when it was adapted into a fish trap, taking big sea trout and salmon; the catch was often 20 fish per day, which were sold in Bonar Bridge. The use of the trap, which may well have damaged stocks of large sea trout, was then discontinued in the late 1950s.

Duke Bendor will long be remembered as a most magnanimous benefactor in north-west Sutherland, where he made tremendous efforts to counter unemployment after World War II. By 1950 some 200 people were employed on various ventures, including a massive forestry scheme (on which £5 million was spent), the development of Kinlochbervie as a port, house building and transport firms. He also increased the permanent workforce on the estate, which remains one of the main employers for rural Sutherland.

One advantage of enormous wealth is the fact that there is little pressure to over-exploit natural resources. In this context there is no doubt that the Laxford system has benefited from benign management, and it has been run with little change for some eighty years. The river accommodates just four rods (with some

The Rock Pool

leeway above a certain water level) on a rotational basis, and fishing is limited to eight hours a day, ending at 6 p.m. For much of the time there is less than a full complement of rods. Estuary netting was phased out in the 1970s, having previously been restricted to occasional sweeps when large numbers of fish congregated during droughts.

The Laxford produces the odd springer, occasionally as early as the end of March, but there is no evidence that there was ever a significant spring run, and angling does not begin in earnest until June. Nowadays, for conservation reasons, fishing on the whole system stops at the end of September, one month before the statutory close date. For the 2002 season it was decided that no hen salmon should be killed.

The river's heyday was the post-war period, up to the mid-1960s. Gillie Willie Elliot recalls his first day on the Laxford, accompanying Sir Henry Clowes, one September in the late 1940s; his rod landed 13 salmon, the best at 22 lb. In July 1965 another angler landed 12 in a day. The table below of average annual catches from the river illustrates that they held up until the 1990s, when the impact of fish farms and other marine problems began to take their toll.

	Salmon/grilse
1957–60	289
1961–65	360
1966–70	238
1971–75	260
1976–80	243
1981–85	263
1986–90	260
1991–95	156
1996–2000	134
2001–03	91

The heaviest salmon (40 lb) off the system was landed on the river in the 1920s. In the 1930s a fish of 33 lb was caught on Loch Stack, and one of the same weight was taken in the Ridge Pool in September 1961.

Although from the nineteenth century onwards Stack was widely acknowledged as the best sea trout loch in Scotland (Calderwood cites a good annual catch as being 1,000 to 1,200 fish and an average basket as 15 lb to 25 lb), the status of sea trout within the system has always been ambivalent;

salmon have been seen as the priority, with management of the system directed accordingly. Sea trout were simply there, in seemingly inexhaustible numbers (according to Grimble, Lord Henry Grosvenor took 80 in a day from Mr Leache's Pool).

Back then the chances of a sea trout over 5 lb to 6 lb were remote. This all changed in the 1920s, when Duke Bendor brought over a strain of very large Norwegian sea trout. Apparently this had some effect, as double-figure fish soon became comparatively common – although most visitors prized a 10 lb salmon above a 10 lb sea trout. The best migratory trout on record from Loch Stack (18 lb 8 oz) was taken in the late 1940s; the heaviest from the river (17 lb) was caught in June 1965. Perhaps the most remarkable incident was the landing on Stack in one day in August 1957 of two sea trout, weighing 13 lb 4 oz and 13 lb 8 oz. Around this time on an average day each boat (one or two rods) would expect to take 30 lb of sea trout – although Willie Elliot's best day on the oars (in July 1956) yielded a basket of 17 sea trout for 80 lb 4 oz for his party. He once hooked a 5-lb sea trout that jumped into Lord (Christopher) Soames's lap, landing with what the victim later called 'a good clack in the balls!' And one June in the 1950s Willie Elliot was holding his boat on a drift some 200 yards from the shore when one of his guests had 'one hell of a fright': apparently out of nowhere a stag swam virtually under his rod-tip.

The runs at this time were astonishingly prodigious. In 1956 some 1,800 sea-trout were counted crossing a ford on the river off just one tide; a similar number ran upstream off the next. In 1953 three local hotels, including Scourie Hotel, were given access to Loch Stack for the first time, opening it up to a wider public and confirming the loch's reputation. The demand was overwhelming, and there are now six boats, compared to four in the 1930s. Up to 1953 there were two gillies per boat, and two pairs of oars – one for rowing and one for drifting; outboard motors were first permitted in 2004. But one thing hasn't changed: 6 p.m. is still the end of the fishing day. Loch Stack is roughly H-shaped, and this gives it an intimacy that lochs with an eight-mile shoreline do not normally have; this contrasts with the slightly larger Loch More (a mile further up and also historically an important fishery in its own right), which is comparatively featureless.

Loch Stack's memorably impressive backdrops of Arkle and Ben Stack are almost without parallel, and this enhanced the peerless quality of the sport that once was. This makes the demise of sea-trout fishing on the lochs all the more tragic. Although sea-trout catches had shown a slight decline since the mid-1960s, the advent of fish farms to Loch Laxford in the mid-1980s was a body blow, as the average annual figures below for Loch Stack and Loch More chart only too plainly.

	Sea trout	Salmon/grilse
1962–65	1,248	43
1966–70	825	28
1971–75	788	95
1976–80	659	85
1981–85	672	32
1986–90	338	39
1991–95	84	41
1996–2000	297	34
2001–03	146	12

The sea-trout figures for 1996–2000 should be treated with caution, as they include finnock, which were not counted previously; the figures from 2001 are restricted to sea trout of 1 lb 4 oz and above. Many more anglers now fish the loch specifically for salmon, with the occasional sea trout a bonus, and the policy now is that all sea trout caught on Loch Stack (and indeed in the rest of the system) must be released in order to maintain broodstock numbers.

Between Loch Stack and Loch More there is another smallish loch. Known as the 'Gillies' Loch', it was left by Duke Bendor in his will to the estate employees in perpetuity. Since 1952 there has been an annual angling competition for estate workers on Loch Stack, with the prize being a cup and a bottle of whisky.

There was a lamentable incident involving the demon drink in the 1950s. One season Dry Sack were offering a bottle of their sherry to anyone in Britain catching a sea trout over 8 lb, and that year 42 such fish were landed on the Laxford system. Many guests sportingly donated their bottles to their gillies, two of whom amassed quite a hoard. One night they decided to try it, and, believing that sherry was not a real man's drink, they consumed it in pints! They were desperately ill and unable to gillie for four days.

INVER

Commentators on the Assynt area from the first half of the nineteenth century made little, if any, reference to salmon in the Inver system. Its angling reputation was primarily as a trout fishery. Loch Assynt, six miles long, was characterized as 'abounding with trout', including ferox up to 20 lb and heavy sea trout. To the visiting sportsman salmon were of little interest – indeed they were primarily a commercial crop to be extracted by net and trap.

Two hundred years ago the Inver was, aside from the Laxford, the most important producer of salmon in west Sutherland. According to the *Statistical Account of Scotland (1791–1799)* at least two 'lasts' (8,736 lb) of 'cured' salmon were exported annually. Although the river drains just 68 square miles, it is well-endowed with spawning burns, for over thirty miles of tributaries, flowing either into the main river or into Loch Assynt, are accessible to adult salmon. The most important tributary, the River Loanan, runs from shallow Loch Awe to the east end of Loch Assynt.

The River Inver flows for five miles from the western end of Loch Assynt. The upper section of the river runs through two small lochs, Loch Garbh and Loch an Iasgaich, both of which are important holding pools. It then descends through wild open country, before finally tumbling down a spectacular gorge to Lochinver Bay.

By the second half of the nineteenth century the Inver was established as a salmon angling river (witness iron ladders from this period, some of which still survive, leading to the most inaccessible pools), and, as elsewhere, the rod tenants' resentment of the intensity of the bag netting operations (leased by Alexander Speedie) came to the fore. Whereas in the 1850s, according to Calderwood, 'one rod could get three to six fish in a day', between 1890 and 1900 the average *annual* rod catch slumped to just 20.

Evidently, some attention was then paid to addressing the imbalance between nets and rods, because soon after the turn of the century the bag nets at Clachtoll (the most prolific station) were required to observe a longer weekly close time. Then in 1910 Loch Assynt was dammed, in order to provide extra water for angling in high summer; the sluices were renovated in 1976, and completely refurbished in 2002.

Assynt was formerly part of the great Reay Forest, which was sold by Lord Reay in 1829 to George Leveson-Gower (later the Duke of Sutherland). The sporting rights on Assynt were let to the tenants of Tumore Lodge (subsequently Loch Assynt Lodge) and Glencanisp. In 1913 the Duke sold the Barony of Assynt (including the River Inver) to Major-General Stewart, who continued to divide the fishings between the tenants of Loch Assynt Lodge (the upper river) and Glencanisp (the lower river). In the mid-1930s William Filmer-Sankey and his wife Lady Ursula Grosvenor acquired the controlling interest, and in 1936 they split up the Estate. They sold Glencanisp, including the lower Inver, to Ronald Vestey (who passed it on to his son, Edmund, in the 1960s), and they also disposed of Inchnadamph; they retained Loch Assynt Lodge, the land around Quinag, and the upper Inver.

The Turn Pool on the upper river

The upper part of the river was sold on in the early 1960s. It was divided, with the top section (now known as the 'upper Inver' – a mile-and-a-half of water from the sluices down to the Geadaig burn) purchased by the Vesteys, and the bottom section (now known as the 'middle Inver' – over a mile of water from the Upper Grassy Pool to Brackloch) was bought by Peter Bradford and his wife (formerly Lady Douglas Hall). The middle Inver is now the property of Sir John Hall and Robin Bradford.

The amount of holding water on the lower Inver was increased substantially in the years immediately before and after World War II with particular attention paid to the 250 yards or so of unfishable shallow runs above the Pollan Pool. Several new pools were fashioned (in 1937) and a dam was constructed just above Pollan, effectively creating a lochan that became known as the Star Pool, after a legendary Highland pony of the name, an immensely powerful animal who dragged all the boulders and stones for this work. Star was mainly employed on the hill, and he had a reputation as a wild and cantankerous beast (he was thought to have been gelded too late); he was forever throwing stags off the saddle, and he even had a habit of rolling with a stag on his back. He was particularly difficult with men, though women generally had no trouble with him at all.

The original Star Pool dam was washed away by a spate in 1956, but it was then rebuilt, incorporating a footbridge. This and part of the dam were then swept away in an awesome flood in September 1965, before being reinstated yet again.

Figures from the Loch Assynt Lodge game book for the top half of the Inver from 1912 to 1959 (before it was subdivided into upper and middle), produce the following average annual catches:

	Salmon/grilse
1912–20*	17
1921–30	55
1931–40	114
1941–50	116
1951–59	201

* Excludes 1915–1918: no details.

It is worth noting that 'serious fishing' did not really begin on a consistent basis until the mid-1930s; before then angling was just part of the package for tenants. The record year was 1957 with 330.

The heyday for the Inver was the 1950s and 1960s, when an annual catch of over 400 salmon and grilse was often achieved. The runs were indeed plentiful. During this period the upper part of the system (i.e. above the Inver) could also be highly prolific. In spate conditions the most sought-after fishing for guests at Inchnadamph Hotel was the River Loanan – specifically the Sliding Pool. This 20-yard-long pool could hold colossal numbers. The use of the fly would inevitably lead to foul-hooking, so the then proprietor, the late Willie Morrison, *insisted* that anglers fished with a worm. At this time hotel guests would typically pick up some 60 salmon per year in Loch Assynt, mainly on the troll. The hotel also used to pick up the odd fish on Loch Awe, which could hold great numbers of salmon. One July in the 1970s Neil Campbell fished it with one particular salmon literally following the boat all day. Two years before that a couple had had a similar experience, but had managed to net the salmon at the end of the day; back at Inchnadamph, Willie Morrison duly entered it in the book and served it up as tourist lunches.

The decline in fish numbers began in the early 1970s, stabilizing to some extent in the 1980s and early 1990s, before another significant drop in the late 1990s, as average annual rod catches of salmon/grilse for the Inver show:

	Lower	Middle	Upper	Total
1967–70	228	*	*	
1971–75	104	105	*	
1976–80	146	129	*	
1981–85	108	87	46	241
1986–90	97	62	45	204
1991–95	95	59	38	192
1996–2000	87	44	18	149

* Not available.

Historically there were three distinct runs of salmon into the Inver. The spring run, centred on May, with the odd fish in March and April, was once significant; in one year before 1884, Grimble records that two rods had 39 springers in May. The summer run begins after the first heavy rain in June and continues to the end of July. Finally there was a late run in September. It is generally accepted that now only the summer run can be relied upon.

Inver salmon tend to be modest in size, typically averaging 9 lb. Inevitably, though, there have been exceptions. Grimble states that, in 1897 in the Red Pool, 'Lord Brownlow's butler and gardener, getting leave for a cast, had the luck to take the two biggest fish of the season, 31 lb and 26 lb'. Loch Assynt Lodge's game book records 11 salmon of 20 lb or more between 1909 and 1959, including the two heaviest off the Inver in the last century. These were landed in 1932 and 1933 by Lady Hall and Sir Douglas Hall – 28 lb 8 oz in the Deer Pool, and 29 lb in Brackloch, respectively. In 1936 a salmon of 27 lb 8 oz caught on the lower river reached up to the shoulders of the then four-year-old Edmund Vestey. On 11 October 1940 William Filmer-Sankey, accompanied by gillie John Macrae, subdued a 26-lb fish in the Deer Pool, after a three-and-a-half-hour battle.

One early evening in August in the late 1950s Edmund Vestey was returning from stalking when he met gillie Murdo Ross cycling home from the river. Murdo declared most solemnly: 'There's been a tragedy.' Mr Vestey immediately thought that his mother had suffered an accident. Murdo continued: 'Mistress Vestey has lost a fish.' It transpired that she had hooked an enormous salmon, which they had played (taking turns on the rod) for 'ten minutes under eight hours', but never saw it as it cruised at will between the Ladder and the Gravestone pools. Mrs Vestey was so fed up with the whole ordeal that she was mightily relieved when eventually it broke free.

The Inver system had an enviable reputation for large sea trout (some in

The Lower New Pool

double figures), the main run of which was in the late spring. Charlie McLaren took one of 16 lb on the lower river in the 1960s, while in 1952 Sir John Hall caught a 13-lb sea trout from the neck of Loch an Iasgaich (the same evening he had a 7-lb brown trout and a grilse). Sea-trout numbers fell from the early 1970s, with UDN thought to be a contributory factor, and since then salmon farms are likely to have exacerbated the decline. There are no farms for eight miles north and three miles south of Lochinver, but sea trout tend to forage further afield just offshore. The absence of farms close to the estuary is likely to have been of greater benefit to migrating salmon smolts, and this may well explain why the Inver (and indeed the neighbouring Kirkaig) has not suffered the same level of decline in salmon numbers as most west-coast rivers.

The gillie most closely associated with the Inver, for almost half a century (from the late 1930s to the 1980s), was John Macrae. He was broad (not tall) and immensely strong, with hands the 'size of shovels'. He had the keenest eye, and his knowledge of every pool was minute; he even knew every inch of Loch an Iasgaich, and his ability to manoeuvre the boat minutely on to the lies was uncanny. What's more, the midges never bothered him. He had a reputation as being a 'dour old bugger'. On one occasion he was with a gentleman in tweeds, who was fishing the stream at the head of Loch Garbh below the sluices. A fish was hooked and the angler seemed incapable of bringing it close to the shore.

John, frustrated by this ineptitude, launched himself into the water to get it, at which point the angler gave a sharp yank and broke the line, exclaiming, 'Oh my God, I lost the fish!' John's immediate and sullen response was, 'And I got droukit [soaked] for nothing!' An exquisite fisher, perhaps his greatest triumph was the landing on fly on 16 July 1940 of a 14-lb brown trout (the mounted trophy has a small head, so is not a ferox) from Loch Leitir Easaidh, one of the little satellite lochs by the western end of Loch Assynt.

KIRKAIG

As a salmon river, the Kirkaig is, on the face of it, a complete enigma. Whilst it drains 84 square miles, some 15 per cent of which is covered by lochs, only the last two-and-a-half miles of the system are accessible to salmon – their passage further upstream is blocked by the Falls of Kirkaig (a 60-ft vertical drop). Below this there are no negotiable tributaries or burns, so steep is the terrain, and the main stem of the river is mostly devoid of gravel. And yet, despite the dearth of spawning opportunities, the Kirkaig has for centuries been classed as one of the top three salmon rivers in west Sutherland.

In the eighteenth century Kirkaig salmon was highly prized, indeed above any other, by connoisseurs. According to the *Statistical Account of Scotland (1791–1799)* the river's salmon, 'in regard of quality and relish, are allowed not to yield to any in Great Britain, being spawned in a river whose many springs are the purest sources, and also being catched instantly as they come from the ocean'. The annual take from netting the mouth of the river was 'one and a half last' or 6,552 lb. In addition, a mile or so up the river there was a 'cruive, having two chests, to catch salmon, and to prevent their getting up to a great pond below the Fall, whence they cannot be taken by reason of great stones, roots of trees, and other obstacles carried yearly there in time of great speats [*sic*]; no fish was ever known to have surmounted the Cascade'. The last point was something of an understatement!

By the late 1840s the netting rights in the Kirkaig and Inver districts commanded a rental of £250 per annum, while in 1850 the angling rental was £50. Annual netting rental had risen to £350 by the early 1890s, compared to a rental for the angling on the Kirkaig and Inver of £215 per annum (a not inconsiderable sum, given that between 1890 and 1900 the average annual rod catches on the Kirkaig and the Inver were just 40 and 20 respectively).

Early in the nineteenth century consideration was given to either removing or circumventing the 'Cascade of Inverkirkaig', to allow access to the lochs and the vast potential spawning grounds above. The Duke of Sutherland's factor, in a review of the Assynt area in 1811, whilst chiding the lack of diligence of the local netsmen, stated that if fish were able to reach this area then 'the numbers would be greatly increased'. He had no idea of the costs of such an under-taking, but suggested that it might be justified if it meant higher annual rents from the netsmen.

In the following decades the possibility of a ladder round the Falls was raised occasionally (notably in 1878 by Archibald Young, Commissioner of Salmon Fisheries), but it was never pursued, as the cost could not be justified, and commentators continued to marvel that the river was able to sustain a healthy salmon population. Spawning is in fact concentrated in the lower mile with the odd pocket above.

In 1913 the Barony of Assynt, including the River Kirkaig, was sold by the Duke of Sutherland to Major-General John William Stewart, a 'railway contractor' based in Vancouver, who had been born in Assynt. In 1925 control of the estate was assumed by the Royal Bank of Canada, which evidently then negotiated an agreement with William Filmer-Sankey and Lady Ursula Grosvenor, as all three parties were included on the 1936 sale document to Ronald Vestey, who in turn passed it to his son Edmund in the 1960s.

Uniquely amongst northern rivers, the Kirkaig is entirely natural, and none

The Heather Pool

Late season on the Elder Stream

of the pools are man-made. Moreover, the genetic integrity of its salmon has never been compromised; attempts were made to enhance stocks between 1950 and 1980, but only by using Kirkaig salmon. On one occasion fry were planted out in the headwaters above Elphin. This experiment was not repeated, and there are doubts as to its success. Smolts descending the Falls would be extremely vulnerable, given the drop, and unlikely to survive. The other problem that would confront fry and smolts upstream of the Falls is a formidable population of ferox trout. Doubts whether stocking had much impact are reinforced because average annual catches have held up remarkably well in the period since, as the table below shows:

	Salmon	Grilse	Sea trout
1961–69	50	26	24
1970–79	62	34	18
1980–89	50	59	12
1990–99	54	97	24
2000–03	52	38	9

Netting of the Kirkaig estuary has not been carried out in living memory. The nearest bag netting station was at Clachtoll, some five miles north of the Kirkaig. This was operated by the Estate until the 1960s and in its heyday it could take 5,000 to 6,000 fish per season. More recently it was leased out, on the basis that the operator would be able to exercise some control of illegal netting; it was finally closed in the early 1990s. Edmund Vestey had the great foresight not to facilitate fish farms adjacent to the extensive coastline that he controls.

It is also clear from the figures that until the 1980s salmon, rather than grilse, dominated catches. The Kirkaig was always considered a salmon system, with a strain of peculiarly heavy fish: very short and deep, with big tails. Grimble referred to the capture of a salmon of 38 lb, and how typically one in four fish would be in the high teens. The largest verifiable rod-caught salmon weighed 44 lb – a cock fish landed on 23 March 1907 – and a fine wood-carving hangs in the Inver Lodge Hotel. Before the war, though, the father of A. K. MacLeod (gillie in the 1960s and 1970s) was reputed to have caught a salmon that was 'longer than the kitchen table'. Another truly massive fish, which according to legend tipped the scales at 56 lb, was apparently extracted by nefarious means just after the war.

The largest rod-caught salmon of the last half-century, at 39 lb, was caught in the 1950s in the Little Kirkaig Pool; it showed signs of disease, and it is thought that in its prime it would have weighed close to 50 lb. Until recently it was rare for a season to pass without a salmon of over 25 lb being taken, with fish of 30 lb not uncommon. But the challenge of landing a heavy fish on the Kirkaig is extreme. To be successful it is almost always necessary to follow a fish downstream – often impossible.

Whilst it is a late river with the main runs from July (or late June if there is enough water) and the very occasional fresh-run salmon in October, the Kirkaig, most unusually for a west-coast system, has something of a spring run (indeed the rod-caught record fish referred to above was a springer). It is difficult to gauge how numerous the run was historically (Andrew Young, 1857, mentioned early salmon in April), but at least it does appear to have survived, although inevitably the numbers are reduced. One 11 February (the statutory opening day) in the 1970s Alastair Matheson, who was often successful in March and April, was amazed to land two springers. In 1990 his son David had fish as early as 12 March.

As we have seen, the Kirkaig runs through some very rugged terrain. Grimble was not exaggerating when he declared that, 'no other river involves such hard walking'. On the upper river moving from one pool to another often necessitates climbing or scrambling for hundreds of feet up a tortuous almost perpendicular course, before embarking on a similarly unforgiving descent. The Falls Pool itself is legendary. When one looks down on it, one can well understand why the eighteenth-century commercial fishers accepted that once salmon reached this point, they were unassailable; there was just no way that they could be safely extracted. This great pool or 'black abyss', nestling beneath vertical cliffs, is in effect a sanctuary, where multitudes of fish hold station until eventually they drop back downstream for spawning. At times they leap relentlessly at the Fall in a forlorn dissipation of energy.

In the nineteenth century access for the angler to the Falls Pool was, according to Grimble, 'a really nasty one, requiring quite a gymnastic performance'. It has since been eased, but the descent still is not for the faint-hearted. The angler casts from a stance a dozen or so feet above the water. If a fish is hooked, it is imperative that it remains within the pool, for pursuit downstream is impossible; if it does run down, then disaster is inevitable in one of the two appropriately named pools below: Upper Smashie and Lower Smashie. Fish are landed in the Falls by one's gillie or companion sliding down on to a ledge, from where a gaff or a tailer may be employed. Once secured the salmon, attached to the gaff or tailer, is then passed to the angler above for dispatch. In 2001 gillie David Matheson was transferring an 18-lb salmon up above his head, when the fish lashed out with its tail, dealing him a severe, winding blow to the chest; he only just managed to hang on to the safety rope.

POLLY

The Polly drains some 20 square miles of Inverpolly Forest, mostly to the north of towering Stac Pollaidh. Over a quarter of the catchment is covered by lochs, notably the sprawling Loch Sionascaig with its long, meandering shoreline. The latter gathers the various headwaters and then flows west to Loch Uidh Tarraigean and over a 22 ft waterfall to Loch na Dail. Below this there is a lesser fall, after which the River Polly has a course of two miles to its mouth in Polly Bay. The lower section, slow and canal-like, is an important holding area in low-water conditions.

Inverpolly formed part of the Cromartie Estate's Wester Ross holdings. Sporting tenants of the Estate included Captain G. Hunt (from 1893), Hugo Martin (1899), Richard Charles Baker (from 1900) and Thomas Hardcastle (from 1907). From the end of World War I to 1958 the long-term tenant was Captain Lawson. Then, in 1958, Inverpolly was sold at auction to Commander MacKay, who retained it until 1960, when the Estate was bought by Edward Davies, whose family are the current owners.

Historically, as in the Kirkaig, migratory fish were restricted to the river, as all access to the lochs above was barred by falls. In 1878, on the advice of Archibald

Young (Commissioner of Salmon Fisheries), a small stream that circumvents the lower falls was in Grimble's words 'deepened and enlarged' to enable fish to reach Loch na Dail. Evidently this was not entirely satisfactory, as Calderwood (1909) noted that 'a further attempt at opening up has been made with some success'. This access was later compromised when, between the wars, Captain Lawson installed a small hydro-scheme at the lower falls. In 1960 the associated dam was removed, and once again fish could reach as far as the upper falls. In 1973 a 200-yard-long ladder was cut into the rock around the upper falls, allowing fish up into Sionascaig and the vast hinterland of potential spawning territory beyond.

Loch Sionascaig was impounded with a sluice in the late nineteenth century, and this proved quite a successful means of temporarily boosting water levels. Tenant Colonel Blunt commented on the 1906 season: 'We had a lot of fish up the river – thanks to artificial spates – in spite of a dry season at the time fish were on the coast'. In recent years the operators of the commercial smolt farm halfway down the river have had control of the sluice.

Grimble cited 1883 as a good year with 40–50 salmon off the river. However by the 1890s the average had fallen to 'eight to ten salmon and about as many grilse'; 1893 was particularly desperate, with just one salmon and 120 sea trout. At the turn of the century a hatchery was started, and the number of bag nets on the Coigach coast was reduced by over 50 per cent. Between 1902 and 1904 the river averaged 35 salmon/grilse and 153 sea trout, even though in 1903 and 1904 there was no fishing after July. Rod-catch records for the following half-century appear to have been lost, but recent annual averages are as follows:

	Salmon/grilse	Sea trout
1961–69	70	53
1970–79	11	15
1980–89	15	29
1990–99	45	31
2000–03	28	21

UDN had a devastating impact in the 1970s. Its effect was then compounded by the growth of local marine salmon farms from the mid-1980s. There has been a recovery in the numbers of salmon running the river since the early 1990s, although this is underplayed in the figures because during this period the prime months of July and August were fished only lightly.

The Polly is a small spate river and in low-water conditions netting operations in Polly Bay used to have a significant impact. The bay has a sandy bottom, and so could be swept very efficiently. This netting became a source of considerable animosity in the 1950s. Lord Tarbat (of Cromartie Estates) had formed a company, Coigach Salmon Fisheries Ltd, with Achiltibuie netsman William Muir to exploit the Estate's netting rights on the Coigach coast. In 1950 Lord Tarbat urged Muir to sweep Polly Bay ('you have the fullest authority'). However, the Inverpolly tenant, Captain Lawson, disputed this, and in 1951 he prevented the netsmen from sweeping the bay, which prompted Lord Tarbat to threaten to end Lawson's tenancy. The following year Lawson gave way over the sweeps, and Lord Tarbat sold his shares to William Muir, whose company still retained a long-term lease on the Estate's coastal nettings.

During the next few years the situation deteriorated. In the dry summer of 1955 Lawson complained that Muir was netting the bay twice a day, and that year his own catch in the river was down from the 'usual 20-30 to just two'. On one occasion Lawson is said to have thwarted the netsmen's access to the bay by blocking the track and brandishing a shotgun. Nonetheless, the intensive netting continued, and by 1957 the Estate was referring to it as 'excessive', noting that in one sweep in the Polly estuary 200 salmon and grilse were taken. Lord Tarbat, no doubt mindful that netting operations could jeopardize a future sale of Inverpolly, was by now applying pressure on Muir to curtail his activities, but to no avail.

Matters were finally resolved in 1960 when the new owner Edward Davies bought out Muir's rights to net the bay. The proprietors netted the bay intermittently (partly for hatchery purposes) during the grilse runs from the mid-1970s to the late 1980s. Totals included 1,560 salmon/grilse in 1982, 744 in 1984, 105 in 1985 and 443 (including a 34-lb salmon) in 1987, since when the rights have not been exercised. From 1970 to 1993 there was a fish trap on the lower river, to enable the reading of tags on returning adult salmon; when the trap was removed, fish (which were often held back by the obstacle) were more generally dispersed up the river, to the benefit of angling.

Civil engineering company R.J. MacLeod created most of the pools between the road bridge and the lower Polly loch in the late 1960s; the company owned an Ullapool hotel, and by way of payment the hotel had the fishing on that stretch for 15 years. In the mid-1970s two parallel lines of large boulders were placed across the sand below the Sea Pool to keep the flow of freshwater within defined limits and thus help salmon run in from mid-tide. This stretch includes three pools (known as the Exodus Pools), which are dredged out every spring.

There has been little stocking of the system since the early 1980s, although inevitably there is some 'leakage' from the smolt farm. The Polly has a limited spring run (with the odd fish from early April), but grilse now tend to dominate, running (water levels allowing) from mid-June to early September. The heaviest rod-caught salmon, as far as records go, is 17 lb. The Polly is primarily a salmon, rather than a sea-trout, system. UDN and the marine fish farms have depleted sea-trout stocks; the last few years have seen some improvement, though, with the odd fish now caught on Sionascaig.

KANAIRD

The Kanaird's upper catchment lies just to the north of that of the east-flowing Rappach and to the south of the Cromalt Hills. The headwaters gather in Loch a Chroisg, below which the river meanders for three miles, reaching a series of waterfalls above Langwell Lodge, and then continues its westward course for four miles to its estuary in Loch Kanaird. Just over a mile above the mouth it is joined from the north-east by its main tributary the River Runie. The latter affords fish access as far as a waterfall three miles above the junction. The Kanaird is generally held to be the better angling stream.

In the nineteenth century the system was included with the Drumrunie Forest shootings, which formed part of the Cromartie family's Wester Ross holdings.

The Bridge Pool

This was a highly desirable shooting estate that in the 1890s commanded an annual rent of £1,300. The salmon fishing was, as Calderwood put it, 'an attractive extra', and anglers often did not arrive until August. Cromartie Estate sold Drumrunie in 1935 to Commander Vyner. After World War II he divided the Estate. The eastern section, including the main farming enterprise in Strath Kanaird and the whole of the River Kanaird with the exception of the lower mile and a half, became Langwell Estate. This was bought in 1962 by Mrs Joan Kimball and left in 1964 to her daughter Mrs Fenwick, the current owner. Commander Vyner retained the lower section of the Kanaird and the Runie. Mrs Bramall then acquired these fishings in late 1985. David Bulmer bought Runie and Keanchulish Estate including the fishings, the estuary and the netting rights, in May 1999.

According to Calderwood there used to be a spring run, which was 'hardly fished for'. Between 1899 and 1908 the tenant Colonel Blunt averaged 18 salmon and 60 sea trout annually. Since 1962 the Langwell water has been mainly retained for family use, with just the odd day ticket issued, and there has been no fishing before mid-June, the start of the main runs. Before the fish farm arrived in Loch Kanaird in the mid-1980s, Langwell averaged 25 to 30 salmon/grilse annually; since then single figures have been the norm. Below are annual averages for the Lower Kanaird and the Runie since 1970 (returns for 1976, 1979 and 1981 are missing).

	Salmon/grilse	Sea trout
1970–74	47	74
1975–79	11	38
1980–84	24	96
1985–89	45	69
1990–94	22	24
1995–99	9	25
2000–03	6	65

UDN affected the river in the late 1970s. Fishing effort increased significantly in the late 1980s (including the occasional springer in March, and even one in February) before an inexorable decline in stocks set in. From the mid-1980s finnock dominated the sea-trout catch. And the Kanaird used to be a prolific mature sea-trout fishery. For several years before she bought Langwell, Mrs Kimball used to rent the lower river for two weeks in August, averaging over 50 sea trout.

Unusually for a small west Highland river, alterations to the bed and the course of the Kanaird have been extensive. Between 1865 and 1868 a massive flood prevention scheme was completed to protect the arable fields downstream of Langwell – hence the unnatural straightness of this section. In August 1972 the river left its banks by Langwell Lodge during a tremendous flood, and in the aftermath seven salmon were left stranded in a pool in the Park opposite. This episode prompted further straightening, and around the same time the falls above Langwell were blasted to allow fish access above for spawning. In the 1960s several lochs south of the Kanaird were exploited to power an electricity-generating station upstream of the main road bridge. When this is operating, the water it discharges into the river can be of considerable benefit to anglers downstream.

Commander Vyner netted the estuary until the early 1960s, but there is understood to have been no netting since. The Kanaird has been stocked intermittently since the war, and from the mid-1980s the Runie has been stocked on an annual basis with fish of west-coast origin. Kanaird fish, full-bellied, used to be easy to differentiate from the much slimmer Runie fish. As far as records show, the system has not produced any salmon over 20 lb. Grimble mentions a fish of 18 lb being caught in 1899, and the heaviest in recent years weighed 16 lb. When the runs were numerically significant (in the river's heyday the lower pools 'boiled' with fish at times), even quite sizeable salmon were vulnerable to packs of opportunistic seagulls operating by the mouth. The birds would pounce on fish as they struggled through the shallows between pools, dragging their prey ashore. One year in the early 1980s a local resident picked up six gull-caught salmon for his own consumption, the best being a fresh-run fish of 12 lb.

ULLAPOOL

The source of the Ullapool is the east side of the high mountains of Inverlael Forest. Initially, the river (known as the Douchary at this point) flows in a northerly direction, before turning west (becoming the Rhidorroch River) to Loch Achall – two miles long and comparatively shallow. From there the Ullapool River itself tumbles down 265 ft over a two-and-a-half-mile course (often between narrow cliffs) to its mouth and estuary on the northern edge of the port. The total length of the system is some 15 miles, but salmon are denied access to the Douchary by a waterfall four miles above Loch Achall.

From the 1600s the system was part of the Cromartie family's land holdings. In the second half of the nineteenth century the catchment formed part of Rhidorroch, one of the most prestigious sporting estates in the north-west. With its enviable reputation for the quality of its shooting and stalking, by the 1890s it commanded a rent of £1,100 per annum, one of the highest in the Highlands. The salmon fishing was also desirable. In fact one tenant, architect Talbot Clifton, was said to be so enamoured of the fishings that in 1889 he built Rhidorroch House (beside Loch Achall) in order to avoid the tedious journey by pony and trap down to the Ullapool River from the existing East Rhidorroch Lodge, five miles upstream.

In 1917 Mr J.B. Rose (of cordial fame) became the tenant, and in 1921 he bought the Estate from the Cromartie family. In 1957 Rhidorroch was purchased by the Scobie family, who retain it to this day.

Unusually for a small west-coast spate river, the Ullapool is a genuine spring system – and indeed an early one. The earliest recorded rod-caught salmon was at the end of February (in 1949), and March could be quite productive, whilst, according to Grimble, April and May were the best salmon months. It is no coincidence that the bag nets on the Coigach coast just to the north usually started by the second week of March. Until the last half century the river was normally only fished up to the end of July. The grilse run was almost non-existent before the 1960s (as the table below shows) – indeed the record rod catch in 1927 consisted of 267 salmon and just two grilse. Even in the last four decades the grilse run has been virtually complete by mid-July.

	Salmon	Grilse
1894–1903	20	1
1904–13	19	3
1914–23	38	0
1924–33	56	2
1934–43	27	0
1944–53	23	0
1954–63	39	6
1964–73	61	28
1974–83	42	17
1984–93	32	38
1994–2003	9	18

According to Grimble, before 1850 the Ullapool provided some of the best angling on the west coast; he quoted ten to twelve fish for one rod in a day as being 'not uncommon'. During the early 1800s there was a net-and-coble fishery at the mouth, with the produce taken by horseback over to Conon Bridge. However, the inexorable growth of coastal netting soon limited the numbers available to rods. Hogarth held the lease for the Coigach fishings for over three decades from 1846, and, as elsewhere, his exploitation levels were high. In his last season (1877) these nets between Achduart and Garvie took 745 salmon and 3,623 grilse. For the remainder of the nineteenth century the Coigach netting rights were leased to Speedie. The Coigach nets continued to be a significant fishery until the slump in wild salmon numbers (following the development of local salmon farms from the mid-1980s) rendered them unviable.

The sweep net at the mouth of the Ullapool, which took up to 300 salmon/grilse per annum in the post-war years, has not been operated since the 1970s. There was also a long tradition of occasional and irregular netting in Loch Achall, mainly in August; the numbers were fairly insignificant – generally less than 20 a year. There seems to have been discrimination as to what was retained; thus in 1897 55 salmon were netted in one sweep, with 44 returned to the water.

Alterations to the system have been minimal. For most of its length the Ullapool runs over solid rock, which does not lend itself to pool-creation. In the late nineteenth century two groynes were placed at the lower end of the loch, to hold water back and thus prolong good water levels below. In the 1950s some 5,000 fry originating from elsewhere were introduced intermittently, and from the early 1990s some 20,000 fry from Ullapool broodstock were introduced annually. There is no spawning on the Ullapool River, except in the slower section just downstream of the loch. Most of the spawning is above the loch, with springers creating their redds immediately below the falls.

Sea trout are practically non-existent in the system, because the Ness Falls, on the middle beat of the Ullapool River, are extremely difficult for them to surmount. The Ness Pool (below these falls) produced the system's record salmon of 33 lb on 20 June 1928, a three-sea-winter hen fish, which had smolted at just two years. In 1896 C. Clifton lost a very heavy salmon after playing it for almost three hours. The largest salmon known to have run the river met an ignominious end in June 1945. The 42-lb fish was found dead wedged fast between rocks at the Ness Falls.

BROOM

The Broom's headwaters flow off several high peaks, including Sgurr Mor (3,637 ft), at the southern edge of Braemore Forest. Historically the catchment amounted to 54 square miles but, as explained below, this is now much reduced. The River Broom itself is the product of two main tributaries. The Abhainn Droma runs from the south-east over the 120-ft-high Falls of Measach and through the breathtaking grandeur of Corrieshalloch Gorge. It is then joined from the south-west by the Abhainn Cuileig, originating in Loch a' Bhraoin before dropping down through Cuileig Gorge and two sets of falls. From this confluence the Broom has a course of five miles, rapid at first before assuming a gentle pace and more lowland character through farmland, to its mouth at the head of Loch Broom six miles south of Ullapool.

In 1867 Sir John Fowler bought from Davidson of Tulloch the estates of Braemore and Inverbroom, including most of the Broom system. Fowler was one of the leading architects and engineers of the age, his most notable achievement being as joint designer of the Forth Railway Bridge, the first major bridge of steel and the largest civil engineering structure anywhere in the nineteenth century. He left his mark on the Broom on a rather smaller scale, with the enduring footbridge over the Falls of Measach and Auchindrean Bridge below Braemore. He built pools on the Broom and the Cuileig, and altered the path of the lower river to reclaim land for agriculture. His guests included the artists Landseer and Millais.

Sir John died in 1898, but his family kept possession of the whole estate until the late 1930s, when they began to reduce their holdings. Foich was bought by Captain and Lady Crawford; he was an expert angler, renowned for fishing in an immaculate white jacket and Panama hat. Subsequent owners of Foich have been Jeremy Dewhurst, Colonel St George and the current proprietors the Van Beuningen family. At the same time Braemore was sold to Sir John Calder. The Fowler family retained the best to last; in 1961 Sir Lawrence Robson purchased Inverbroom, including the fishings on the Cuileig and the whole of the left bank of the Broom from the Junction down to the estuary. The Robson family's tenure of Inverbroom continued until 2003, when it was sold to Mark Lorimer. The fishings on the right bank are now divided between the Hon. Tom and Christopher Manners (from the Junction to the Garden Pool), Foich Estate and Inverlael Estate. The Church of Scotland owns the sweep-netting rights.

In the early nineteenth century the Broom was remarkably productive. Grimble quoted a letter from Mr Mackenzie, factor to Hay Mackenzie, describing the fishing in around 1820:

> Everyone fished both with rod and spear. The rivers were swarming with fish, and on the Broom, when in good trim, I could get from eight to a dozen fish a day with the rod. With the spear I have taken 60 in a day, and could have got more.

The letter blames the scarcity of fish as the nineteenth century progressed on the growth of bag nets and illegal activity by local trawlers.

Sir John Fowler, writing in 1883, echoed these sentiments:

The take of fish is gradually diminishing. Sea trout have almost disappeared. I impute this to trawling off the mouths of rivers by crews with long seine nets with a small mesh.... When prosecuted, their defence is that they are fishing for herrings, cuddies or white fish. Thirty years ago eight to ten fish a day to a rod was not uncommon on the Broom. Now from 50 to 55 are killed in a season, and about a dozen sea trout. Bag nets have likewise enormously diminished the supply of fish to this coast. The bye-laws regulating the observance of a weekly close time by bag and stake nets are only fairly well observed. The penalties should be more severe.

He argued for a weekly close time for the nets of 60 hours rather than 36.

Under the Byelaw of 1865 the estuary of the Broom was extended to include the whole of Loch Broom. Bag nets were thus excluded from this narrow sea loch but the there was no doubting the efficiency of the nets on the Coigach peninsula to the north. In the early twentieth century rod catches continued to be unreliable. Calderwood's second edition (1921) noted that the Broom's average annual catch was just 30; wild fluctuations were a feature – from a maximum of 98 to a minimum of 12. Post-war figures for the sweep nets at the mouth of the river indicate a modest operation, with average annual catches as follows:

	Salmon	Sea trout
1952–60	25	113
1961–70	71	166
1971–80	126	65
1981–87	31	3

These nets ceased in 1987; the impact of fish farming had destroyed their viability. The rights are now rented, but not exercised, by the Fishery Board.

As in other areas of the west Highlands, the collapse in both salmon and sea trout numbers in the late 1980s and 1990s tallies with the local growth of fish farming. The nearest farm is just south of Corry Point, the narrowest section of Loch Broom (less than one third of a mile wide); smolts have no alternative but to pass close to the cages as they migrate towards the open sea. In both 1996 and 1997 very large numbers of salmon smolts *returned* to the Broom just two weeks after leaving the river, infested with sea-lice; the shingle in the Broom's six tidal pools was silver with dead and dying fish. In 2004 the authorities turned down an application for another major farm at Annat Bay in Loch Broom following

overwhelming local opposition. Average annual rod catches for the Broom are
set out below:

	Salmon	Sea trout
1952–60	67	131
1961–70	95	110
1971–80	72	81
1981–90	80	89
1991–2000	27	13
2001–03	32	24

There was a discernible improvement in the number of adult fish running the river
in 2002 and 2003; thus Inverbroom, which operates a strict catch-and-release
policy, had 50 salmon and 43 sea trout in 2003.

Like the Ullapool, the Broom used to have a spring run, and occasionally fish
were caught as early as March. The spring run is now thought to be extinct, and
there are no clean salmon before June. The system was outstanding for sea trout
and renowned for heavy fish up to 12 lb, with fair numbers in the 6-lb to 8-lb class.

The Broom is of course very much a spate river, although the river no longer
sees the full benefit of rainfall over its catchment. In the 1950s parts of the upper
Droma watershed were diverted eastwards into the Conon system hydro-electric
scheme, and it is estimated that flows in the Droma below the gorge are reduced
by up to 40 per cent at certain times. In 2002 a small hydro scheme was built in the
Cuileig gorge. This is rather more benign, as no water is taken out of the catchment, and the flow of water below the generating station is hardly compromised.
According to the Wester Ross Fisheries Trust, 'The production of juvenile trout
and salmon is unlikely to be altered significantly by the Cuileig scheme'.

The waterfalls on both tributaries prevent access by migratory fish to the
headwaters. In normal conditions the passage of salmon up the Cuileig is blocked
500 yards above the junction by the falls at the Linn Pool. Occasionally, in high
flows, some fish are understood to surmount these falls and migrate for another
mile to an impassable falls. The great majority of the system's spawning areas are
in the Broom itself, particularly the lower reaches. There is very little suitable
gravel in the upper section, although it does have some first-class juvenile habitat,
and electro-fishing surveys indicate that some parr move upstream to colonize it.
The Broom is highly prone to the redds washing out – when high flows disturb or
sweep downstream unstable banks of gravel containing salmon or sea trout redds

– and the recent trend to wetter winters, with a greater frequency of serious spates, has exacerbated the problem. The Wester Ross Fisheries Trust conducted experiments in the winter of 1998/9 with artificial redds and found that 60 per cent of five salmon redds, and 80 per cent of five sea-trout redds were washed out. This suggests a significant problem, particularly in the context of low numbers of returning adult fish.

The Broom, by west Highland spate-river standards, is a big-fish system. Salmon (as opposed to grilse) average over 10 lb, something that has contributed to remarkable episodes with inexperienced anglers in recent years. By September 1963 the young Maurice Robson had been trying for three seasons to catch his first salmon. One morning the Inverbroom stalker and gillie Willie Matheson (an employee for 35 years) told him that he could try the river, but really, given the conditions, there was no hope, and so there was no point in taking a net. In the Post Office Pool a salmon lunged at his fly, missed and was hooked under the pectoral fin. The fish never lost the upper hand, and after 45 minutes the angler was wondering if he would ever be able to land it. His friend Hugh Brett, who had witnessed the whole saga, then waded into the river, got behind the fish and 'passed it like a rugby ball into a gorse bush'. The fresh-run hen salmon weighed 15 lb.

Hugh Brett had never done any fishing before but was intrigued by this experience. Early the next morning he went down to the Lower Garbhan Pool where he managed to hook a fish. A long struggle ensued, and he even considered cutting the line, so as not to be late for breakfast. However, he persevered and landed a fine 17-lb cock salmon. In late September 2000 Tommy Buchanan, who had never caught a salmon, was walking downstream past the Stump Pool, which, because of the low water, the estate stalker Alan Cameron had advised him not to bother with. As he went past he nonchalantly flicked his fly into the water and continued walking – and got the fright of his life when a fish seized the fly. After 45 minutes he managed to net (bending the handle into a right angle) a cock salmon of 21 lb with a huge kype. (At one point during the fight he thought he heard several people running towards him from behind – in fact it was just his heart pounding.)

In August 1981 Mrs Lillian Skeggs hooked a fish in the Kennel Pool at 2 p.m. Three and a half hours later, despite constant pressure, it had not moved. The angler, by this time very tired, handed the rod to Willie Matheson, and he instructed three of those witnessing the battle to get into the water behind the fish, to drive it from its position. They created such a violent commotion that the 28-lb cock salmon ('a hideously ugly creature') shot straight out of the pool and onto the bank.

The record rod-caught salmon for the Broom (33 lb) was taken in the late nineteenth century. Over the decades fish of over 20 lb have not been unusual. In 1937 two gillies came upon two otters devouring the remains of an enormous fish on a rock at the Junction Pool. They rescued the tail, which was packed in ice and sent to the National History Museum in London. There the experts calculated that the salmon had weighed in excess of 60 lb.

DUNDONNELL

The Dundonnell is unique amongst Wester Ross rivers in one important respect: the dominant upper section of the catchment has no loch. The head of the system is a wide bowl of barren ground at the southern edge of Dundonnell Forest, between the upper reaches of the Gruinard and Broom systems. Given the absence of a loch the river is prone to severe fluctuations in water levels and indeed flooding. It takes a north-westerly course for some twelve miles to its mouth in Little Loch Broom. In its middle reaches it cascades over a series of violent waterfalls, the bottom fall – which confines migratory fish to the lower three miles of the river – obscured within an extraordinary gorge. This is a quarter of a mile long, with sheer sides 100 ft or more high and often just a few feet apart; the water is hardly visible from above and only a thunderous roar betrays its presence below. Downstream of the gorge the Dundonnell is unusually pretty, thickly lined with mature broadleaf trees and in many ways reminiscent of a lush lowland river.

Held by a branch of the Mackenzie clan for generations, Dundonnell Estate (which then included the Gruinard system) was sold at auction in 1834 to discharge the accumulated debts of the fifth laird Kenneth Mackenzie who had died of obesity in 1826; years later Evander MacIver referred to him as a 'stupid, ignorant man ... who ate, drank and slept, and had a mania for breeding and feeding fowls'. The purchaser, with a bid of £22,000, was Murdo Mackenzie (no relation) of Ardross in Easter Ross. He was quick to appreciate the potential of developing the sporting side of the Estate, building a lodge at Gruinard as early as 1843 (in general, Wester Ross landowners exploited their sporting assets earlier than their counterparts further north). The new laird, a highly litigious character, scored a landmark court victory in 1842, as a result of which the lucrative but disputed netting rights from Greenstone Point to Stattic Point (i.e. the whole of Gruinard Bay) were declared the property of Dundonnell. The loser in the case, landowner Duncan Davidson, ended up with a bill for costs of £1,100 – more than a hundred times the rent he had received annually from the netsmen.

After Murdo Mackenzie's death in 1845, the Estate passed to his lawyer son

Hugh. In response to the partial failure of the potato crop in 1846, he employed several hundred men to straighten the lower section of the Dundonnell River by excavating a new channel across the flood plain. Evidently he took an interest in salmon matters, for he organized the removal of obstacles to upstream migration and developed and promoted 'an invention for directing water to mills without the use of weirs in salmon rivers'. In 1867 he let the sporting rights at Gruinard and Achneigie to Frederick William Brook Thellusson (by the late 1860s the Estate's income from sporting leases amounted to £1,450 per annum, only slightly less than the income from farms and crofts). From 1868 the Gruinard Bay netting rights were let to Hogarth & Co. Before his death in 1869 Hugh Mackenzie had begun to build a new sporting lodge, which was let from 1870.

The new laird Kenneth Mackenzie incurred very substantial legal costs in the 1870s. The Estate was soon saddled with onerous debts, exacerbated by the fact that the family's primary interests were in Australia. Soon after World War I the break-up of Dundonnell began. In 1932 Dundonnell Lodge (subsequently called Eilean Darach) and more than half the deer forest, including the lower section of the Dundonnell River and the valuable Gruinard River fishings (as well as all the netting rights), were sold to Rosalind Maitland. In 1942 Lieutenant-Colonel Sir Michael Peto bought the rest of the Estate. He sold it in 1957 to the Roger family. The three young Roger brothers, who persuaded their Aberdeenshire father to purchase the west coast estate, were colourful, at times bohemian, plutocrats with only a marginal interest in the sporting side of the Estate. They threw legendary parties in Dundonnell House and its splendid walled garden. In 1988, after the death of the last Roger brother, Sir Tim and Lady Rice (the current owners) bought the Estate.

With its limited amount of spawning the Dundonnell has never been a prolific salmon river. Calderwood's second edition of 1921 gives a rod catch of between ten and 30, and this is corroborated in the charming *Muriel Foster's Fishing Diary*, the early part of which chronicles her often season-long visits to Dundonnell between 1913 and 1925. Catch records for Dundonnell Estate, which has the two miles of fishings above Eilean Darach, are available from 1958 (except for part of the 1960s), as detailed in the annual averages below.

	Salmon	Sea trout
1958–63	15	8
1970–79	10	9
1980–89	33	24
1990–99	23	9
2000–03	8	15

Up to 1979 the fishing was organized on an *ad hoc* basis, and there is little doubt that intermittent attention was paid to completing the book. Thereafter, following the arrival of keeper/gillie Johnnie McSporran, a regime of formal lets was introduced.

Salmon farming in Little Loch Broom was on a comparatively small scale in the 1980s. However as the tonnage increased (from 260 tonnes in 1998 to consent for 2,062 tonnes at Ardessie and Stattic Point in 2004) there can be little doubt that the associated sea lice have had an impact on the number of wild smolts reaching the open sea through the narrow sea loch unscathed.

Eilean Darach, which also has access to the Gruinard system, has on the whole fished the lower Dundonnell fairly lightly, except between 1960 and 1964 (averaging 18 salmon and 35 sea trout) and between 1985 and 1989 (averaging 19 salmon and 72 sea trout). For most of the interim years their salmon catch was less than a handful.

Salmon run from June, water allowing, with the heaviest arriving first and heading straight for the holding pools of the upper river. George MacFarlane landed the record fish for the Dundonnell (25 lb) in the Gheta Bhan Pool in October 1981. After playing it for half an hour he complained that his arms were getting 'bloody sore' – to which his companion replied: 'If that's the case, try and catch smaller fish!' In June 1988 Johnnie McSporran caught a 22 lb salmon in the Gheta Bhan Pool.

The heaviest sea trout (17 lb 8 oz) was taken by Johnnie McSporran in the Kettle Pool in August 1983. The Dundonnell has been a very useful little sea-trout river, with fish in the 5 lb to 6 lb not uncommon (the system's sea trout grow at double the rate of Ewe fish). However, the runs have declined dramatically since the arrival of salmon farms and in recent years sampling of post-smolts has shown lethal levels of sea-lice infestation. There was some respite (with an improvement in both the size and number of fish) when the farms were fallowed between 2001 and 2003, but all the farms have since restocked, and the total tonnage is now three times that of 1998.

During the Roger era there was very limited stocking of the river, including, briefly, the introduction of Brora fry. Now, given poor runs and low juvenile numbers, stocking is taking place on an annual basis with up to 70,000 fry of Dundonnell origin, as part of a concerted programme to restore fish numbers. Stocking may help compensate for redd wash-out, which is becoming a significant problem as the frequency and size of spates increases (with the trend towards wetter winters), especially in rivers such as the Dundonnell, where the gravel sits on a solid rock bed. Floods have always been a major issue. The Black Bridge to Eilean Darach, built in the 1950s, has been washed away twice, and over the decades many pools have altered radically.

Whilst even in its heyday catches were never that impressive, the Dundonnell has always had a very special appeal. In the 1980s it attracted an illustrious roll-call of anglers, including one former prime minister and one former foreign secretary. Tenant Sir Charles Troughton would take fishings on other rivers (including the Oykel) to coincide with his visits; he would send his guests else-where, preferring to concentrate his efforts on the Dundonnell.

GRUINARD

In the mid-nineteenth century few salmon rivers anywhere were held in such esteem as the Gruinard. Within a short space of time however its reputation lay in tatters. Catches recovered significantly in the twentieth century, but the river has never quite reclaimed its former glory. On the positive side, the Gruinard is one of only a handful of west Highland systems where salmon and grilse numbers have not collapsed in tandem with the growth of fish farming.

The Gruinard drains some 60 square miles of Wester Ross's most breath-taking terrain. It flows for five miles from Loch na Sealga to its mouth in Gruinard Bay. This loch (four miles long) is hemmed in dramatically by the high mountains of Fisherfield Forest and Strathnasheallag Forest (including An Teallach), and in the remote hinterland above it are some ten miles of good spawning tributaries. Of particular note is the Abhainn Gleann na Muice – one of the finest spawning streams over 500 ft in Wester Ross, with good nursery habitat and riparian alder trees – which may be of great importance for producing earlier-running fish. Salmon also ascend Abhainn Loch an Nid to spawn below the impassable falls, but a lack of holding pools in this tributary may limit the survival of adult fish until spawning time.

Effectively there have only been three changes of ownership in the last two centuries. The river was originally part of Dundonnell Estate, which for several hundred years was held by the Mackenzie family. In 1816 the Estate passed to Kenneth Mackenzie who died young in 1835 with substantial debts that necessi-tated the sale of the Estate. Later in the nineteenth century the Estate was broken up, with Eilean Darach being acquired by Rosalind Maitland (*née* Craig-Sellar) in 1932. Although part of Eilean Darach was hived off in the early 1950s, her family retained the remainder (including the fishing rights on the Gruinard) until 2000, when it was sold to Gordon Crawford.

In the mid-nineteenth century the Gruinard was astonishingly prolific. According to Grimble, a dozen fish a day was 'common' before 1858, with one tenant taking 500 salmon and grilse 'to his own rod in one season'. And on 4 July

1864 General Bateson had 20 salmon/grilse in the Craig Pool without moving from one particular stone. However, angling catches deteriorated dramatically as the number of bag nets in Gruinard Bay increased. By 1908, when 13 bag nets were stationed on the southern bend of the Bay alone, the total annual catch from the river and the loch was understood to be no more than 30 salmon/grilse (the fact that during this period no detailed record of rod catches was kept is perhaps indicative of how poor the sport had become). The number of nets was limited from the 1909 season in order to allow stocks to recover.

When Rosalind Maitland acquired the river in 1932, the real attractions were the sea-trout fishing and the loch. Indeed it was some time before salmon/grilse rod catches became respectable again, although it has to be said that before the 1960s Eilean Darach's angling effort was often inconsistent – the fishings were run on a more commercial basis from 1972. Whilst Eilean Darach owns the rights to fish for migratory species on the whole river, by agreement Gruinard Estate (which owns the actual river bed) fishes one of the three rotating beats; both estates have a boat on the loch. Below are average annual catches for the two Eilean Darach beats and their fishing on the loch.

	Salmon	Grilse	Sea trout
1928–30	9	6	290
1931–38	17	5	323
1957–60	24	7	120
1961–70	58	25	229
1971–80	71	54	135
1981–90	43	83	52
1991–2000	18	56	19
2001–03	7	35	57*

Figures from 1939 to 1956 not available.
* For 2002 and 2003 only.

It is worth emphasizing that Gruinard Estate's beat (with tenants staying beside the river) is generally fished more consistently than those of Eilean Darach (whose lodge is 14 miles from the river). Thus the entire river catch between 1990 and 1999 averaged 151 salmon/grilse and 34 sea trout – in effect, Gruinard's single beat has tended in recent years to catch the same number as Eilean Darach's two beats. Latterly Eilean Darach's beats have been very lightly fished – for just eight weeks in 2002 and eighteen days in 2003.

The Turn Pool

Rosalind Maitland was a redoubtable character. In her time there was no vehicle track up the river, so Eilean Darach's cars would park up at the Iron House just upstream of the road bridge. Two ponies were kept there, one for the lunch and the other for Mrs Maitland in her advancing years; the rest of the party would walk up the rough track to the loch. She had a great affinity for fishing the loch. It was here in the 1930s that there was a major falling out between her and her nephew, who was home on leave. He was ordered to accompany her to the loch, something he was reluctant to do. Then, soon after she began fishing, Mrs Maitland hooked a large salmon. Her nephew muttered, 'Oh my god, we'll be here for hours!' (she had a reputation for taking an inordinately long time to land fish). Hearing this, she turned to gillie Willie Ross and commanded, 'Willie, row for the shore!' – so as to offload her unwilling partner. On the way she lost the fish. This unfortunate incident is said to have had a bearing on her decision to leave Eilean Darach to her niece, Molly Dunphie, rather than her nephew.

Molly Dunphie, renowned for her resplendent heavy tweeds and brogues on the river, died tragically in 1972, leaving a life interest in the estate to her husband, Colonel Peter Dunphie. He was an outstanding host with a punctilious attention to detail: there was always a bottle of champagne in the fridge ready to celebrate the catching of anyone's first salmon – and all first fish were entered in the book in red. Under him, lunch on the river was always on time. On one occasion

Landing a grilse in Rosalind's Run

though, the party gathered minus his nephew's 13-year-old son, and for the next twenty minutes at regular intervals he exclaimed, 'Where's that bloody boy!' However, all was soon forgiven when the youngster came struggling round the corner from Miss Baring's Pool with a 15-lb salmon. The Colonel fished until his mid-eighties. On one famous occasion he hooked a salmon in the Bridge Pool watched by a passing coach party; when he landed it, the whole assembled throng burst into applause – to his great satisfaction. On his death the estate reverted to several members of the next generation, and a sale was the only way of dividing the asset equitably.

The Gruinard is one of those rare west Highland systems where there is a discernible, if limited, spring run. In 1936 a springer was taken in March, and fish have been caught on a reasonably regular basis in April, although latterly the run seems to have moved to early May. It is thought that there are perhaps more springers than people realize. There is no real temperature barrier to hold fish back in the spring, for the falls below the road bridge are not a serious obstacle – they do not require a leap, and fish can simply swim up. Consequently, salmon can pass through the river in less than two days to the comparative sanctuary of the loch. The main grilse runs are from the third or fourth week of June – water allowing. Recently there has been some evidence of a late run of silver fish in September.

The Gruinard is not a recognized big-fish river. The record salmon (30 lb) was caught in September 1895 by S. Pearson Gregory in the Bridge Pool; the same week the Hon. T. Willoughby took a fish of 25 lb. The Eilean Darach fishing register includes ten or so salmon between 20 lb and 23 lb since 1934. In recent times David Gemmill landed a fish of 22 lb on 14 August 1979 in the Shepherd's Pool, former ghillie Murdo MacLeod took one of similar size in the same pool that year, and on the Gruinard beat Harry Davis had a cock salmon, also 22 lb, in September 1992 at the same location. At the end of 2002 a dead cock kelt was found by the Iron House Flats; it was estimated to have tipped the scales at close to 30 lb when fresh-run. In August 2004 Jason Russell released a salmon of over 20 lb.

The Gruinard system used to offer some of the best sea-trout fishing in the Highlands. Fish were generally in the 1 lb 8 oz to 2 lb 8 oz class, with some up to 6 lb. Very occasionally a leviathan has been encountered. The record fish, which weighed in at a remarkable 19 lb and was 'aged just over 12 years', was taken in the Iron House Flats by Mr Simpson on 5 July 1972. Sea-trout numbers collapsed from the mid-1980s, coinciding with the establishment of a fish farm in an adjacent sea loch. The latter was fallowed from 2001, and there was a minor revival in the sea-trout catch in 2002 and 2003. Mercifully the wide expanse of Gruinard Bay itself has been kept clear of fish farms, allowing salmon smolts a reasonably clear route out to sea.

Eilean Darach holds the netting rights in Gruinard Bay. The nets operated for most of the twentieth century, although not as intensively as in the nineteenth century. The main station was at Laid, where there is an ice house. There has been no netting since the mid-1980s.

Some minor pool improvement and creation work was carried out on the lower river in the mid-1990s. This was all sympathetically done, using the river's own boulders, by Colin Gibb. He put the tails back on to the Garden and Whale pools, fashioned a croy in the upper part of the Whale and built three small pools in the long run between the Whale and the Otter. Otherwise the river is almost entirely natural.

Traditionally the Gruinard has engendered tremendous loyalty from its tenants, many of whom are convinced that there is no comparable river in terms of both its setting and its great variety. Looking upstream one is aware that massive An Teallach is always there to the left but just out of sight. To the right, the head of the river is however visibly dominated by the very distinctive twin peaks of Beinn Dearg Bheag and Beinn Dearg Mor.

The variety of the Gruinard's pools is almost infinite. The long Turn Pool, especially the lie by the rock three-quarters of the way down, is virtually impossible to cover properly even with a 15-ft rod. In contrast, one can practically jump over the three Gibralter pools. The Craig is another difficult cast, where one attempts to drop one's fly under the rock face and then dance it down between some extremely awkward boulders.

The Bothy and the Bridge are often the most popular pools (they are the easiest to fish) and the most prolific. The Rockies are a cascade of delightful riffles, glides, runs and pools in a steep gorge – perhaps best avoided on calm days, given the levels of midge infestation, but in the right conditions offering highly exciting sport. The Otter is fished from rocks some 30 ft high, where spectators can lie and watch the take. Once hooked and played, the fish must then be walked 40 yards down to river level for landing.

The Gruinard has much in common with the neighbouring Little Gruinard, although it includes more above-loch spawning. The latter was recently designated as a candidate Special Area of Conservation for salmon under the EC Habitats Directive. It is regrettable that the Gruinard, which also represents core habitat for salmon, was not included within the designation to ensure that a significant section of Wester Ross was granted this special and highly beneficial conservation status.

LITTLE GRUINARD

The Little Gruinard flows out of the Fionn Loch, which is six miles long and up to three-quarters of a mile wide. Geographically inaccessible, it has long been renowned for the size of its brown trout, which run to 4 lb or 5 lb and more. Few lochs have such dramatic surroundings, particularly the southern end, which is hemmed in by the high peaks of Fisherfield and Letterewe Forests. This is a loch of great variety with numerous bays and headlands and two main satellite lochs – Dubh Loch and Lochan Beannach Beag. The Fionn Loch is replenished via an extensive network of spawning tributaries.

Its northern end is carpeted by a mass of huge glacial boulders. From here the river passes through the 'first' and 'second' salmon pools (in reality two lochans), followed by the Boat Pool – aptly named, as it cannot be covered effectively from the bank. Thereafter it flows due north for some four miles to its mouth at the southernmost point of Gruinard Bay. The Little Gruinard, which has a far steeper descent than the Gruinard, alternates between fast, rough runs peppered with pots and glides, and the occasional recognizable pool. There are also three sets of 'flats' (deep, canal-like stretches) up to 400 yards long; these are important holding pools, especially in low water. Apart from three man-made pools on the lower river, the Little Gruinard system is entirely natural.

In the late nineteenth century the river and loch were the property of Mrs Liot

Bankes, with the fishing let as part of the Little Gruinard shootings. In the 1920s the Marquess of Zetland bought Drumchork Lodge (by Aultbea on Loch Ewe), the Fionn Loch and the Little Gruinard. In 1948 the loch and the river were sold to Colonel Whitbread, who owned neighbouring Letterewe, while Drumchork Lodge was disposed of separately. The same year the Little Gruinard Estate, including the river, was sold on again to local businessman Ian MacLean. Then in 1954 James Lawrie purchased the estate, excluding the fishing rights, which he acquired the following year for £200 (apart from one rod that was held by Gruinard Estate). The estate remained with the Lawrie family until 1989, when it was sold to Paul Van Vlissingen, who incorporated it into his Letterewe Estate. Subsequently he also acquired the Gruinard Estate rod, and thus complete control of the whole system.

Evidently the river was very lightly fished in the late nineteenth and early twentieth centuries. Angling was little more than an occasional diversion to the shooting tenants, and the relative inaccessibility of most of the river was aso a factor. Below are average annual salmon catches from the mid-1950s.

	Salmon/grilse
1956–59	40
1960–64	103
1965–69	95
1970–74	79
1975–79	46
1980–81	42
1987–89	126
1990–94	77
1995–99	57
2000–03	69

Catches for 1982 to 1986 were not available.

The river was fished hard between 1962 and 1964 – in part to prove that it was a significant salmon river. At this time a massive hydro-electric scheme was proposed, taking in lochs Fada, Fionn and Maree. The head of the Little Gruinard was to be dammed, raising the level of Fionn by several feet, and its water would then be taken by tunnel through to Fada.

The hydro authorities had the audacity to declare that 'no salmon come out of Fionn'. James Lawrie was outraged and, with Colonel Whitbread (Letterewe) as well as Tournaig and Gruinard estates, he fought the proposals. Their campaign was clearly a factor (the £7-million cost was another) in the official decision to reject the scheme; this was the first time that the hydro authorities had ever had a scheme refused. The slump in catches from the mid-1970s to early 1980s reflects the knock-on effect of a very serious outbreak of UDN in 1970.

The biggest rod catch in a day is 14 fish, achieved by two rods (including Arthur Chamberlain who landed ten) in September 1971. There were at least five occasions on which Arthur Chamberlain and another rod had double figures in a day between them. On 24 August 1962 there were 13 fish caught (including ten by Arthur Chamberlain) in the Lower Flats and the Gorge; two were released simply to avoid carrying them all the way downstream. The next day the same two rods had 12 more from the same location. (There is no doubt that historically the nature of the terrain was usually a check on prolific catches when the river was in good trim. Until the 1980s only the lower section of river – approximately a mile from the top of the gorge – had a defined path alongside it, and it was not until 1992 that a vehicle track running parallel to the river half a mile to the west was developed.) During the Lawrie era two salmon of 20 lb each were caught; Mr R. Donaldson landed the heaviest (22 lb) in the Garden Pool on 31 July 2000 with a 9-ft split-cane rod and a size 12 Black Zulu. Fish in the mid-teens are not uncommon. Whilst the occasional salmon is caught in April and May, the main runs are from mid-June, water levels permitting.

The Little Gruinard has never been stocked, but in recent years electro-fishing has produced consistently good results. In 2003 the Wester Ross Fisheries Trust sampled ten sites on the system, and the results confirmed that the Little Gruinard had the highest average parr density of all the 11 rivers surveyed in the area. The river has had a 100 per cent catch and release policy since 1989; it was the first river in Scotland to adopt such a policy.

Although the Little Gruinard has never been a plentiful sea-trout river (producing no more than two dozen or so a year), the average weight used to be impressive, with fair numbers in the 3 lb to 4 lb class and a few exceptional fish bigger still. A quite extraordinary specimen was encountered sometime in the 1960s. James Lawrie hooked a very large fish in the Gorge Pool. When it was played out and he was attempting to land it (he had no gaff with him), the hooks came out. The following morning the fish was found dead by the Privy Pool half a mile downstream. It weighed 17 lb 8 oz and was assumed to be a salmon. A scale sample was sent off for analysis, and when the results came back James Lawrie was astounded to learn that it was in fact a sea trout and clearly a record for the river. By this time, though, the fish had been eaten and the opportunity to have it mounted was gone.

E W E

With the largest catchment and yet one of the shortest main stems of all the west-coast rivers north of the Great Glen, the Ewe system defies easy categorization. Draining 170 square miles of mostly mountainous terrain with peaks of over 3,000 ft, it is dominated by Loch Maree, 12 miles long and up to two miles wide (a century ago this deep loch, studded with numerous islands, was traversed by steamship). The main salmon spawning tributaries are south of the catchment and flow via the A' Ghairbhe River (which runs down from Loch Coulin and Loch Clair) and the Kinlochewe River (springers used to spawn high up the Abhainn Bruachaig) into the inland end of the loch. The other significant spawning areas are the Kernsary River system, which enters the loch just east of the River Ewe, and the main river itself. The Ewe, just two miles long, links Loch Maree to the sea, which it enters through Poolewe at the head of Loch Ewe.

For centuries the Mackenzies of Gairloch owned the whole of the Ewe system and catchment. Fragmentation began in the mid-nineteenth century, and the catchment now has seven owners, four of them holding significant fishings. Coulin Estate was originally part of Applecross, which was sold by the Mackenzies in the 1840s to the Duke of Leeds. Applecross was then split up in 1866, and the fifteenth Lord Elphinstone acquired Coulin as part of Achnashellach Estate. The latter was further subdivided in the 1870s, and Coulin was bought by Sir Ivor Guest. Later it was in the ownership of Lord Davies, and in 1943/4 it was sold to the Wills family; Captain Freddie Wills held it from 1973 to 1994, when it became the property of the present owners, the Hon. Philip Smith and family.

Kinlochewe, sold by the Mackenzies to the Marquess of Zetland in 1919, is now the property of Pat Wilson. The Ewe itself was sold in 1960 to Sir Reginald and Lady MacDonald-Buchanan, who already held the adjacent Inveran Estate.

Angling tradition on the Ewe goes back to the late 1700s (perhaps earlier than any other north-west Highland river), and at the start of the nineteenth century its reputation was without peer. Sir Humphrey Davy, in his *Salmonia* (1828), referred at length to the Ewe and could hardly have been more profuse in his praise. In the early 1800s the proprietor Sir Kenneth Mackenzie often took 20 or more salmon (up to 30 lb) to his own rod in a day from the river. The headwaters could also be prolific; Lord Elphinstone is reputed to have once landed 140 salmon in one summer from Lochs Clair and Coulin.

The decline in rod catches in the second half of the nineteenth century was

189

Loch Clair, an important headwater to the south of the catchment

relentless and extreme, with the average annual take plummeting to an estimated 40 or so salmon/grilse by the 1890s. Calderwood cites a catch of just eight one year. He believed that the removal of the cruive in 1847/1848 was a contributory factor. Before then the cruive had been located in different places at different periods. This device was not employed as a fish-trap but rather as a means of concentrating fish in the pool below, from which they could be easily netted (legend has it that these operations occasionally yielded fish of 70 lb). When it was located towards the top of the river, all the pools downstream of the obstacle tended to be well stocked to the angler's benefit, and in this situation the cruive also raised the level of the loch, which presumably kept the river in good trim for longer periods.

There can be no doubt, however, that the great growth of netting was the primary reason for the drastic fall in rod catches. According to Calderwood, in the early 1830s 'three cobles full of fish' were caught with one haul of the net in the Tidal Pool; 'sea trout were then given away to the poor'. The cruive and net-and-coble fishing (the latter was discontinued in 1846) were probably sustainable, but the inexorable growth of coastal netting put enormous pressure on the numbers running the system.

Between 1846 and 1887 the Mackenzie sea netting rights were leased by Alex Hogarth of Aberdeen. His bag net stations at Gairloch and Torridon (both

Dapping along the west shore of Loch Maree

to the south of Loch Ewe) averaged 608 salmon and 4,065 grilse for the decade ending in 1855, and 510 salmon and 2,402 grilse in the following decade. Figures for Hogarth's most prolific bag nets in Loch Ewe itself, including one opposite the mouth of the river at Inverewe, are not available. From March 1865 the Ewe's estuary was deemed under the terms of the 1862 Salmon Act to include the whole of Loch Ewe, with the exception of the neck, and henceforth this area was off-limits to bag netting – to Hogarth's great dismay. Nonetheless, there were still some ten bag nets in the narrow neck of the sea loch. Catches for the Gairloch and Torridon stations picked up between 1866 and 1875, averaging 1,016 salmon and 4,650 grilse. In the next decade, which saw the introduction in 1862 of the Saturday slap (obliging all nets to cease operating from 6 p.m. on Saturdays to 6 a.m. on Mondays), the produce of these two stations averaged 759 salmon and 3,624 grilse. In 1887 Hogarth complained to Sir Kenneth Mackenzie that his numbers had only been maintained through greater fishing effort, and he implored the laird to allow him to fish the mouth of the Ewe with net and coble. Sir Kenneth did not do so, and Hogarth relinquished his lease after the 1888 season.

By this time the damage had been done, and it took a very long time for salmon/grilse runs up the Ewe to recover. Netting continued, of course, but with added restrictions in an attempt to boost stocks. Thus in 1907 the

Gairloch fishings were let to Archibald Powrie of Abernethy for nine seasons (at £290 per annum rent), with the lease specifically excluding all right of fishing within one mile of the estuaries of the Ewe, Kerry and Badachro rivers. Critically, though, as regards the Ewe, there was still a concentration of bag nets at the entrance to Loch Ewe. Rod catches of salmon remained desperately low; according to Gairloch Estate records, between 1900 and 1914 anglers landed on the Ewe between one and 33 salmon/grilse a year (generally the total was in single figures); during this period annual catches on the Kinlochewe were no more than five. From 1915 to 1933 the rod catch for the Ewe averaged just nine, although it appears that in some years the river was hardly fished.

Recorded rod catches for salmon picked up after World War II. Pool House Hotel held a tenancy for the main river in the late 1940s and early 1950s, averaging 26 salmon and 9 grilse a year (as well as up to 400 sea trout) between 1947 and 1952. Anecdotal evidence suggests that official catches around this period failed to incorporate many fish caught legitimately on the Ewe but not entered in the game book. In the main, recorded catches improved over the next four decades and between the mid-1970s and the mid-1990s they were comparatively buoyant, as indicated in the table below of average annual rod catches for the system as a whole (per the official returns).

	Salmon/grilse
1978–80	286
1981–85	205
1986–90	231
1991–95	279
1996–2000	132
2001–03	113

The marked fall since 1996 shows no sign of being reversed. The relentless growth of fish farms in Wester Ross (the first salmon farms arrived in Loch Ewe in 1987) has surely contributed to the decline. Another probably significant factor is increased washing-out of redds, due to the greater frequency and size of spates in recent years. The Wester Ross Fisheries Trust conducted experiments with artificial redds during the winter of 1998–99; out of sixteen sites, only four survived intact. The Trust published a comprehensive study of the Ewe catchment in 2002, and its summary on the status of the salmon stock includes the following bleak analysis:

The declining abundance reflects a fall in marine survival of smolts to less than 3% in the mid 1990s. Up to 2,600 fish ran the river prior to 1995, but since 1995 only 700–900 have done so. At least 1,098 adults are required to reach the spawning target necessary to produce a maximum of 49,800 smolts. Rod catches indicate that this was probably achieved in 1978–1995, but in 1996–2001 runs have reached only 60–78% of the target. This is confirmed by juvenile surveys in 1997, 1999 and 2001.

The abundance or otherwise of salmon and grilse since the war is also inevitably reflected in the netting figures. The average annual combined catch for the Gairloch and Redpoint (the headland five miles to the south) stations between 1948 and 1967 was 630 salmon and 2,033 grilse (and 477 sea trout). By the mid-1980s Redpoint was the only remaining bag net operation in the vicinity. It did well for the next decade, averaging 240 salmon and 1,825 grilse from 1986 to 1990, and 231 salmon and 1,858 grilse from 1991 to 1995. Catches then slumped to an average of 29 salmon and 190 grilse between 1996 and 2000. In the final year just one salmon and 16 grilse were caught, prompting the station's closure. It reopened in 2003, taking advantage of higher prices and the long summer drought to land several hundred salmon/grilse – making a mockery of attempts to conserve and restore runs in rivers where stocks were already severely depleted.

The Lower Narrows on the Ewe

The Flats Pool, historically prolific for sea trout

Good sense prevailed and Redpoint did not operate in 2004. Legal netting in Loch Ewe itself has not been exercised since the 1970s.

The Ewe had a notable spring run from February onwards; as Calderwood put it, 'sometimes March fish are a little coloured'. In recent years very few springers have been seen before May, and now early fish tend to run straight through to the loch; it is almost expected that the first of the year will be caught on the Kinlochewe River. Multi-sea-winter salmon have always constituted an unusually high proportion of adult fish running the Ewe, and the evidence is that they are becoming more predominant: up to 53 per cent of catches between 1997 and 2001.

The Ewe is a heavy-fish system by west coast standards, and salmon in the 20 lb class are not uncommon. One June afternoon in the early 1990s Danny Fulton landed four salmon on the river, including fish of 22 lb and 26 lb. The acknowledged record rod-caught salmon (a fresh-run cock fish) is 50 lb, taken on fly on 16 June 1902 by Osgood Grant, the keeper for Pool House. The previous year a 40-lb salmon had been landed. In *The River Ewe*, Kenneth C. MacKenzie relates a vivid and detailed tale of a monstrous salmon caught in the McOrdie by one Iain Ordie – the exact date is unknown but assumed to be in the nineteenth century. The fish was taken on rod and line but never officially recorded, or indeed weighed. It was apparently 63 in. long, with a girth of 39 in. This compares with figures of 54 in. and 28 in. respectively for Miss Ballantine's great fish of 64 lb.

If salmon numbers are now greatly reduced, the decline of the system's sea-trout population has been nothing less than catastrophic. Before the fish farms appeared, the quality of the fish was superb and at times incomparable; thus in one afternoon/evening session in June in about 1980 Danny Fulton and Iain Kettle landed 11 sea trout for 75 lb from the River Ewe's Flats Pool. And for most of the twentieth century Loch Maree was one of the great sea-trout fisheries. Although several estates have access, the main fishing effort was always through Loch Maree Hotel, which up to the late 1980s employed nine gillies and put out nine boats during the main season. Below are the hotel's average annual sea-trout catches (no records exist for 1940 to 1944).

1925–29	1,668
1930–39	1,914
1945–49	2,180
1950–59	1,043
1960–69	958
1970–79	1,068
1980–84	1,101
1985–89	514
1990–94	196
1995–99	156
2000–03	60

Although there were fluctuations in abundance in the 1970s and early 1980s (thought to be due to the outbreak of UDN in the 1970s and its knock-on effects), the real collapse in numbers dates from the arrival of the first farms in Loch Ewe in 1987. Now the hotel employs just one gillie and any sea trout caught tend to be finnock. In its heyday the hotel only recorded fish over 1 lb, so in the 1960s and early 1970s sea trout in the book averaged between 2 lb and 3 lb. One should emphasize that fishing effort is now low, but there is no escaping the fact that sea survival is very poor, due to sea-lice infestation. Most of the remaining sea-trout population is female (with few fish over 1 lb); the majority of brown trout in the loch are now males, with many in the 2 lb to 3 lb class, and since the late 1990s they have consistently dominated catches.

The collapse in sea-trout stocks (as well as the fall in salmon numbers) is mirrored in the average annual catch records for Lochs Clair and Coulin.

	Salmon	Sea trout
1945–54	9	90
1955–64	9	78
1965–74	13	101
1975–84	13	68
1985–94	29	81
1995–2003	6	14

Grilse figures are not available until the 1980s and therefore are not included; in recent years they have not been significant.

In order to assist in the recovery of sea-trout numbers, Coulin Estate has built a hatchery and since 2002 has been releasing into the headwaters fish bred from native Coulin broodstock (some 180 female sea trout are held). In 2003 100,000 sea trout were released, as well as 30,000 salmon. Over 200,000 sea-trout fry were scheduled for release in 2004.

Outer Hebrides

LEWIS

LAXAY

The Laxay drains some 40 square miles of the principal wetlands of central Lewis. Much of the catchment consists of a seeming myriad of interconnecting lochs and lochans. These filter into Loch Trealaval – itself an extensive and confusing body of water with numerous tentacles linked by narrow channels. From the outlet at the eastern end of the loch the River Laxay flows south-east for two miles to Loch Valtos, and thence one mile to its estuary in Loch Erisort.

During the Matheson (1844–1918) and Leverhulme (1918–23) eras of ownership of Lewis the Laxay was the main east-flowing system in the vast Soval Estate, which stretched from one side of the island to the other. The most celebrated tenant for the core part of the Estate (including the Laxay) was the Reverend George Hely-Hutchinson, author (under the pseudonym Sixty-One) of *Twenty Years' Reminiscences of the Lews* (1871). He held a lease from 1852 to 1870, at times adding sport on the more peripheral areas of the Estate – for instance the Blackwater from 1862 to 1865. (Bizarrely, according to records from his Wiltshire parish, he did not visit Lewis every year during his tenancy.) Following Hely-Hutchinson, William Rochester Pape (1870–74) and Mr Parker (1875–84) held tenancies of Soval. For the next three decades (to 1914) there was a succession of yearly rentals.

In the first Leverhulme dispersal sale of 1924, Soval (excluding the western side of the Estate, which was marketed as Carloway) was sold to Lewisman John Bain. In 1926 he sold it on at a profit to Henry Grey Thornton, who was a keen angler and for the most part kept the system for his own use. However, he did also let it out for some two months of the season, and in the late 1930s his tenants were the D'Oyly Cartes. Mr Thornton's executors sold Soval in 1950 to Owen Humbert and Richard Bett; the latter's nephew Richard Kershaw is the current owner.

Hely-Hutchinson really developed the Laxay as a fishery, incorporating his trademark regime of dams. Evidently, according to Calderwood, he experienced many more teething problems on the Laxay than he had on the Blackwater. His dam to harness the waters of Loch Trealaval was swept away 'repeatedly'. There are now six dams on the system (including the outflows from Lochs Trealaval and Valtos), which are employed to facilitate the passage of salmon upstream and also to 'freshen' the fishing when required.

Calderwood considered the Laxay to be the third-best system on Lewis and the figures for the early part of the twentieth century – averaging almost 150 salmon and over 300 sea trout – bear this out. In the 1950s and 1960s salmon catches increased to some 250 per annum, but UDN affected the system in 1974, and this, together with widespread illegal coastal netting, contributed to a decline. There was also a serious freshwater poaching problem, now greatly reduced. Rod catches have recently stabilized at a consistent and respectable level; the ten-year average to 2003 was 96 salmon and 101 sea trout, and the five-year average stood at 98 salmon and 108 sea trout – all these catches have been fly only.

The Laxay used to have an important spring run, with salmon taken as early as March. In the 1930s and 1940s the keepers were often instructed to catch (on rod and line) five or six springers to order and send them south to the proprietor. This run appears to have petered out. But although springers are no longer seen, later in the season big dark fish, which may well be early runners, are much in evidence. The main runs are now from late June onwards. Most fish are taken in Loch Valtos (an ideal shallow loch with numerous bays and points) and the pools on the river near to the loch. The record salmon for the system (indeed for the whole of Lewis), weighing 33 lb, was caught in Loch Valtos in September 1933 by Richard D'Oyly Carte. The heaviest salmon of recent times (landed in the mid-1970s by the keeper on the lower river) weighed just under 20 lb. There have been several other fish approaching this weight since the 1950s – by Richard Bett (early 1960s), Mrs Heather Kershaw (Loch Valtos around 1982), Graham Riddick (1993 in the lower river) and another on the river in August 2003. The record season was 1989 with 240 salmon/grilse. Five fish in a day to a single rod is by no means uncommon.

No legal netting of the Laxay estuary has been carried out in living memory. In recent years considerable efforts have been directed at habitat improvement, including fencing off 600 yards of spawning tributaries, and particular attention has been paid to the spawning beds, which are raked over on a regular basis. Spawning takes place over a very wide area, mainly in the streams between lochs but also on the margins of the lochs themselves. Electro-fishing surveys confirm prolific quantities of juvenile salmon. Over half the salmon catch and all sea trout are now released. Sea trout runs have increased in the last few years with fair numbers in the 1 lb to 3 lb class.

A good wave on Loch Valtos

There was an extraordinary episode on Loch Valtos in August 1990. An experienced lady angler hooked a fish at 11 a.m. on a three-piece split-cane rod. It just never stopped running, taking her and the boat all over the loch. It finally tired and was beached at 5 p.m. The salmon, 12 lb and fresh-run, was fairly hooked, and its behaviour and energy can only be explained as a freak of nature.

CREED

The Creed is an unusually long river for Lewis. It it is still a spate system, although the large number of lochs in the catchment, over 20 in total, means that following rain the water level remains at a fishable height for a relatively long period. The headwaters near the old Pentland road filter into Loch an Ois. The outlet from the latter marks the start of the river itself, which meanders a mile to Loch a Chlachain and thence a further three miles through undulating peat moorland to the main Stornoway-Harris road. The final mile consists of a steep descent through the wooded grounds of the Castle to the mouth in Stornoway Bay.

For centuries the whole of Lewis was under single ownership: first that of the Mackenzies of Seaforth (1610–1844), then Sir James Matheson and his successors

Loch a Chlachain, the Creed system's main loch

(1844–1918) and Lord Leverhulme (1918–23). The last, disillusioned with his experiences and treatment on the island, offered it as a free gift to the inhabitants in two lots. The country districts declined the offer (and the various sporting estates were then disposed of, piecemeal, to private interests), but the people of Stornoway accepted it, and so took control of the Parish of Stornoway, which included the Creed system. In 1923 the Stornoway Trust was formed to manage the assets.

Most of the historical improvements to the river were carried out during the Matheson era. Sir James was clearly mindful of protecting the salmon resource, in contrast to many of his contemporaries in industrial Britain. As part of his Lewis Chemical Works, he erected a plant designed to convert peat into oil on the banks of the Creed – but he spent considerable sums to ensure that none of the effluent flowed into the river.

From 1850 to 1896 the rod fishings on the Creed were kept in hand; in August 1876 Lord Clifford landed a 19-lb salmon, which is understood to be the legal record for the system. In the 1870s and 1880s James Stretton Young leased the net fishings. The estate then operated the nets for some years up to Lady Matheson's death in 1896. That year the Creed system was let for the first time (as part of the 'Home Shootings') to Mr J. Wood. Over the next two decades the Home Shootings alternated between annual letting and being kept in hand. In its early years the

Stornoway Trust let the Creed with the Castle, but after the war tenants for the Castle were difficult to find and eventually the Castle was sold, after which the river became available for letting to the public. There was some local resentment in 1960 when the Trust entered into a 15-year lease for the river with an individual, although the lease did not run its full term.

Rod catch records for the system (including Loch a Chlachain and Loch an Ois) cover most of the last 130 years. Below are the average annual figures.

	Salmon	Sea trout
1871–74	74	177
1884–89	59	209
1890–99	55	179
1900–09	86	318
1910–19*	83	169
1920–29	97	67
1930–39	108	155
1940–49	139	259
1950–59	152	412
1960–69	200	236
1970–79	88	151
1980–89	45	147
1990–99	65	131
2000–03	72	219

* Excludes 1914–17, as no records exist.

The peak period was the 1960s, when some great catches were recorded, including 16 before lunch one day from Loch a Chlachain. At this period up to 14 watchers were engaged on the system. They had three bothies for shelter, one overlooking the Sea Pool (called MacMaster's Hut after a long-serving keeper), another known as the Arctic Hut and the bothy at Chlachain. Although most of the run consists of grilse, a few multi-sea-winter, double-figure salmon are landed each year. In 1988 Donnie Maclean had an 18-lb fish in the Falls Pool, and in 1991 Jimmy Carlin took one of 19 lb in the Bend. However, the heaviest is rumoured to be a salmon of 24 lb taken illegally from the Peat Stack Pool.

The decline in catches towards the end of the twentieth century was caused to a great extent by the proliferation of poaching, which had long been a serious problem due to the river's close proximity to the town. For a decade

The Falls Pool

from the late 1970s the Trust took the unusual step (as a partial remedy) of installing a trap at the river mouth. All running fish were caught and some of them released upstream; in 1979 over 500 fish were killed in the trap. Despite this, poaching continued unabated, and in three of the seasons between 1977 and 1995 there were four or less rod-caught salmon. Following a period of consistently poor rod catches between 1995 and 2000 (averaging 21 salmon per annum), the Stornoway Trust made a major change of policy. It had never been able to control poaching effectively (although in fairness it had many other priorities), so in early 2001 it granted the Stornoway Angling Association a 21-year lease on the fishery, and the club now has complete responsibility for managing the river.

There is little doubt that poaching effort has now at last declined. In the 1980s up to 86 nets were lifted annually from the coastline in the vicinity of Stornoway, but in recent years the number has been below 20. From 2001 to drought-dominated 2003 there was something of a transformation, with the club averaging 84 salmon and 278 sea trout. The club has introduced effective bailiffing, backed up by its considerable moral authority, plus bag limits of one salmon and two sea trout per day, and it has devoted much attention to habitat improvement and mink-trapping. All dams on the tributaries have been removed; only the dams at Loch a Chlachain and Loch an Ois (both dating from around 1900) have been

The Bothy Pool

retained – they allow for six artificial spates, each lasting 24 hours, to be produced, even with no rain in the interim. Redd counts indicate that the number of spawning pairs of salmon is increasing each year. Whilst there has been intermittent stocking in the past (notably in the early 1980s when the Trust built a hatchery in conjunction with its venture into fish farming), this is now undertaken on a regular basis.

One lasting consequence of the depredations of the poachers is the demise of the Creed's spring run. It has probably been wiped out, and in fact the club does not open the river until 1 June. The late start to the season also means that the smolts are able to reach the sea unhindered. The main salmon runs are from mid-June to August, with often a late run in September. Sea trout run from June, and lately their numbers have shown a definite upward trend. The nearest fish farm is six miles south at Grimshader; there are none to the north.

The first holding pool in the river, the Matheson Pool, is not called after the nineteenth-century entrepreneur owner, but another James Matheson who was keeper at Hamanavay in Uig and transferred to the Creed in his later years. He stayed at Creedmouth Cottage, and in 1913, at the age of 70, he came across three young men poaching the Rock Pool, as it was then called. A struggle ensued, which resulted in Matheson and two of the men ending up in the river. Matheson's son, yet another James Matheson, was also head keeper

The Sheriff's Pool, within the grounds of Stornoway Castle

for the system from 1936 until after World War II. Another pool, the Sheriff's, in the Castle grounds was named after a visiting sheriff from the mainland who was reputed to have caught two salmon at the same time on the same fly! (the fly passed through the gill of the first and was then taken by the second).

GRESS

Once rated as one of the best systems on Lewis, the Gress was chronically neglected for the best part of seventy-five years – so much so that now few outside the island are even aware of its existence. It is perhaps symptomatic of the prevailing attitude to the river during this period that virtually no catch records exist.

The source of the system is Loch Gress in the isolated hinterland of the northern end of the island – midway between Barvas and Tolsta as the crow flies. From the loch the River Gress flows southerly through gentle moorland for seven miles, absorbing many small tributaries, before reaching its mouth in Broad Bay five miles north of Stornoway.

Between the early 1800s and 1870 Gress was the site for one of two legal whisky distilleries on Lewis. Gress was let as a sporting estate from 1861, and through the Matheson and Leverhulme eras there was a succession of annual or longer tenancies. In the latter part of the century the Estate commanded a rental of £400 per annum, reflecting the excellence of its walked-up grouse shooting (averaging 500 birds a year) as well as the quality of the fishing. In the 1890s Charles Cook, angling correspondent of *The Field*, was a regular visitor; under the pseudonym John Bickerdyke he wrote *Days in Thule with Rod, Gun and Camera* (1894).

In 1923 Gress Estate, which falls within the parish of Stornoway, became the property of the Stornoway Trust (see the Creed entry above). In 1927 the Trust gave consideration to selling Gress for £2,000, but in the end decided against it. In the years before the outbreak of war the Estate alternated between short-term and seasonal lets. With watching and bailiffing much reduced (compared to the norm before the Trust's ownership), the scale of poaching on the river grew inexorably. A meeting of Trustees in 1938 heard that 'the poachers come down in bands of 20 or 30, and have even gone to the length of stoning the keeper'.

The situation deteriorated further during the war. From 1945 to 1949 the tenant for Gress was Harry Holmes, who, although he caught sea trout during his tenancy, never landed a salmon. This was because, according to his keeper Murdo MacDonald, writing decades later, 'the river had been killed off before he got

Dibbling the Rock Pool

205

The semi-tidal Black Pool

there and as a thriving salmon river it has been dead ever since'. Mr Holmes was at least able to control the seal population. He had the keeper walk in front of him along the cliffs playing the bagpipes, and the seals' curiosity would bring them into the shallows where they were simple targets for Mr Holmes' rifle (apparently he never missed).

Indiscriminate poaching continued on a grand scale. In the 1950s and 1960s nets festooned the coastline from the river mouth northwards for more than a mile, and spare nets were blatantly left to dry on garden fences. In 1949 Dr Gregg, a consultant at Lewis Hospital, took a lease on Gress lodge and the fishings and shootings, but by the 1960s the sport on the Estate was almost worthless. In 1974 he was instrumental in setting up the Gress Angling Association, whose members built and repaired pools and weirs (which had fallen into disrepair) and began restocking. However, faced with at best ambivalent local support, these activities lost momentum, the club became dormant, and the river suffered a further long period of neglect.

Eventually, following press reports of dubious 'angling' practices, the club was reactivated in March 2002 with considerable local backing, and in 2004 the Stornoway Trust granted it an 18-year lease to manage the river. (It is fair to conclude that the Trust's management of the Gress for the previous 75 years left a great deal to be desired.)

Gress AA has instigated a far-reaching programme to regenerate migratory fish runs in the system. Measures include the restoration of weirs and pools, habitat improvement, mink-trapping, delaying the opening date of the season until 1 June (to protect any early-running fish) and a catch-and-release initiative. The club's activities and thriving local membership act as a high-profile deterrent to poaching in the river and estuary. The latter is now understood to be largely under control, although there remains a problem with illegal coastal netting. The Stornoway Trust has not leased out the legal netting rights in the Steinish and Tong pools in Broad Bay (to the south of the Gress estuary) since the late 1990s.

Gress AA's catches for 2002 amounted to 38 sea trout and no salmon; those for 2003 were 200 sea trout and four salmon. Electro-fishing surveys, confirming good numbers of juveniles, have been particularly encouraging. There is of course a very long way to go to restore the Gress to its former glory, although the potential is beyond doubt. Catch figures after 1923 are almost non-existent, but some earlier records have survived. In the 1870s and early 1890s up to 100 salmon and 544 sea trout were taken annually by rods.

BLACKWATER

The Blackwater is generally considered the second-best salmon system on Lewis. Its mouth is little over a mile from that of the predominant Grimersta, but the two systems are entirely different in character. Grimersta is, of course, primarily a loch fishery, but the Blackwater, although fed by lochs, is very much a river fishery.

Two distinct groupings of lochs drain into the two main tributaries, which combine to form the Blackwater itself. From the junction the river flows three miles to its estuary in Loch Ceann Hulavig, an almost enclosed branch of Loch Roag. The upper section of the Blackwater is largely broken water with fine, easily fished pools; the middle section is more sedate, with numerous holding pools, whilst the lower section is again mostly broken water, with many productive holding pools above the large sea pool into which salmon come and go on the tides.

During Sir James Matheson's tenure of Lewis the Blackwater was part of the vast Soval Estate, a situation that lasted until the end of Lord Leverhulme's brief period of ownership. The most renowned tenant of the core part of Soval (from 1852 to 1870) was the Reverend George Hely-Hutchinson, who as 'Sixty-One', wrote *Twenty Years' Reminiscences of the Lews*. Between 1862 and 1865 he took an additional lease on the peripheral Garynahine section of the Estate, including the Blackwater system. He recalled how he had been utterly frustrated by the high level of exploitation by the bag nets in Loch Roag at times of low water. Replicating an arrangement he had seen on the Costello in Galway, he built a small dam at the outlet of Loch 'Dismal' (his name for one of the lochs) to hold back enough water that, when released, could create an artificial spate. He synchronized this capacity with spring tides to great effect, and the principle was soon emulated elsewhere on Lewis. Hely-Hutchinson described the Blackwater as 'the best rising river I ever threw line on'.

For over fifty years from 1872 the Blackwater was available to guests of the inn at Garynahine, and the most loyal angler was Major Herbert Allport, who visited every year from 1882 to 1920 for sojourns between a fortnight and four months. His most successful day (in August 1899) produced a catch of 29 salmon/grilse, and in total he accounted for almost 3,000 fish from the Blackwater.

In Lord Leverhulme's dispersal sale of 1924 Soval was divided; the Blackwater was marketed as part of Carloway estate. Surprisingly, given the quality of the fishing (and indeed the shooting), there was no interest, and in fact it was not until late in 1927 that the river and the hotel, together with 12,000 acres, were purchased by Grimersta Ltd. Since then the estate has been called Garynahine. It was run as a hotel with fishings up to 1945, when Grimersta syndicate member Vice-Admiral Drummond leased the fishings together with the hotel, which became Garynahine Lodge. This arrangement continued until

The Round Pool

1960, when Grimersta sold their investment to Captain Allan Perrins, who had a magnanimous but somewhat uncommercial approach to the river – allowing any local person to fish so long as they provided details of anything they caught.

Following the Captain's death in 1965 the estate passed to his wife, who disposed of it in 1970 to two brothers, William and Francis Thyme. They ran it on conventional lines until 1981, when they sold out to investors trading as the Garynahine Estate Company Ltd. There followed a chequered, often colourful and occasionally controversial period. In 1983 the company launched what was termed the 'ultimate timeshare' scheme. There is little doubt that they strove to improve the fishings, but the prices attached to the timeshare were unrealistic, the scheme was a failure and in the late 1980s Garynahine became the property of A. S. Edgar (Farms) Ltd. In 1993 the latter sold the estate to Christopher Buxton (the current owner), who has invested substantially in it and run it along traditional lines.

The Blackwater is a genuinely wild fishery – there has been no stocking in living memory. The remnants of what is believed to be Hely-Hutchinson's original dam are still visible at Loch Crogach, but several other dams built subsequently have been removed, and there are now no impediments to upstream migration. The lochs, which are only fished lightly, are in effect sanctuary areas. During the last decade the focus of attention has been on habitat improvement, especially

Shipton's Pool

improving access for spawning. Literally miles of small burns have been dug out where the peat has fallen in. This policy has proved remarkably successful, for electro-fishing surveys in September 2003 by the Western Isles Fisheries Trust produced the highest densities of juvenile salmon that they had ever encountered anywhere.

On the negative side the Blackwater has lost virtually all its sea trout. In the nineteenth century these fish were extraordinarily abundant; however, today sea-lice levels on sea trout in Loch Roag (one of the most intensively farmed sea lochs in Europe) are described as 'horrendous'. Recent sampling has monitored 150 or more lice per fish – a level of infestation that is invariably fatal.

In the distant past the mouth of the river was sweep-netted. The local netting rights are owned by Grimersta and were exercised irregularly in the 1980s (mainly a sweep at Carloway). Since 1987, though, there has been no commercial netting in Loch Roag.

The Blackwater has never been a spring river. The odd fish may be taken in May (on the second in 1995), but it is really a grilse fishery, with the main runs from mid-June; the average weight tends to be just over 5 lb. Catch records, which go back to the late nineteenth century, show a slump during the 1980s timeshare débâcle, since when there has been a steady recovery. Below are annual averages.

	Salmon/grilse
1891–1900	225
1901–10	220
1911–20	180
1921–30	160
1931–40	120
1941–50	115
1951–60	155
1961–70	190
1971–80	115
1981–90	40
1991–2000	80
2001–03	90*
100 year av.	141.5

* Including a very poor year in 2003, due to exceptionally dry weather.

The Blackwater is not a big-fish river. In the last decade the heaviest salmon in the Garynahine book is 13 lb. However, on 19 October 2002 an extraordinary cock

The Boat Pool, important holding water on the lower river

salmon of 19 lb was taken on worm in a burn just below the Pentland road. This was four days after the end of the season, and one would normally expect such an episode to receive no publicity, but, bizarrely, the captor entered the 'Fish of the Month' competition in a local newspaper. Even more bizarrely, he won!

GRIMERSTA

The Grimersta system is perhaps best understood from the top of Roineval, a 900-ft hill and vantage point, which offers panoramic views over much of Lewis. From here the vast Loch Langavat – at seven miles long, the largest loch in the Hebrides – stretches away south-west into the mountains of north Harris. Langavat, deeply indented with a 45-mile shoreline, is the headwater of the Grimersta; unusually it has two outlets, which flow in parallel into the first of a series of four small lochs (averaging a mile in length) with numerous satellite lochans to the sides. All this watery mass is clearly visible as one looks north from Roineval. Finally these lochs discharge into the sea lochs Ceann Hulavig and Roag beyond it, via the short river Grimersta, which is typically Highland in character, steadily dropping some 100 feet over one and a half miles.

The view north over the Grimersta system from the top of Roineval

The system's capacity for producing prodigious numbers of salmon is legendary, and before the advent of sporting estates it had been systematically exploited for many centuries. Key to this is the very sheltered location of the river mouth, completely protected from heavy seas. There is evidence of a series of massive walls (thought to date from the Norse period or perhaps earlier) in the Sea Pool, and much of this work is still intact. There is no doubt that the enclosure was designed to allow the trapping of fish on the ebb tide; the catch would then simply be netted or speared out.

During Sir James Matheson's ownership of Lewis (from 1844) the sporting rights were divided between six estates, of which Grimersta was by far the most noted for salmon angling. Details of this era are sketchy, as virtually all the relevant papers were lost in a fire at the Stornoway Records Library in 1924. Thomas Clarke held the first known lease between 1855 and 1862, and by the 1870s Grimersta was being leased to a syndicate of five at an annual rent of £150; they built and paid for the Lodge in 1871 and 1872.

After Sir James's death in 1878 his widow increased sporting rents significantly. George Pople of Perthshire was tenant from 1901 to 1914, enjoying some prodigious sport, then from 1915 to 1918 Grimersta was, like many Lewis estates, unlet. Lord Leverhulme bought the island at the end of the war, and his brief tenure culminated in an auction of properties in June 1924; the sale brochure

By MacKillop's Rock on Loch Faoghail Kirraval

referred to the fishing at Grimersta as 'unrivalled in the British Isles'. The 20,000-acre estate was knocked down to a syndicate of 13 members. This syndicate, trading as Grimersta Estate Ltd, has steadily evolved and is very much intact today; it now comprises 25 members, five of whom sit on the Board.

Grimersta's celebrated angling reputation was built upon the chain of four lochs between Langavat and the river. In the summer and autumn months these would typically hold vast numbers of fish in great shoals, allowing prodigious catches in the right conditions. The lochs are generally shallow, and the fishing (almost entirely from boats) is very much on the surface – intensely visual and highly exciting.

The system's elevated status stems from an event in 1888 that stunned the salmon angling world. One of the tenants, John Macleay, was a civil engineer by trade, and he preoccupied himself with designing and building dams and groynes to improve the fishing, many of which are still in place today. (His name is immortalized in 'Macleay's Stream', at the head of Loch Faoghail Charrasan, the second loch up from the river.)

Now, it was a desperately dry summer in 1888: there was no rain after April, and by June the river was a pathetic trickle. Run after run of fish arriving from the open sea were unable to get into the river, and as the weeks passed the build-up of grilse and salmon in the estuary grew to epic, indeed biblical, proportions:

perhaps, according to one commentator, 100,000 or more. With no end to the drought in sight, John Macleay promoted the idea that the outlet from the first loch, Loch Faoghail an Tuim, should be dammed temporarily to allow for the creation of an artificial spate. The gillies were strongly against the scheme, on the grounds that any released water would be stale, and so would not encourage fish to run – although what they had overlooked was the steep descent of the river to the sea, which meant that any rush of water would soon be highly oxygenated.

John Macleay was not to be denied, and at the end of August they managed to release some water from Langavat, by clearing an old redundant hatchway; next a rough and ready dam was put into place at the outlet of the first loch to hold back the water from above. They then waited a week as the level in the loch rose by six feet, before finally breaking the dam at the time of a high tide. During the man-made spate, which lasted 48 hours, all the waiting fish rushed up into the loch, which soon was literally heaving with salmon.

A few days later a New Zealander, A.M. Naylor, was due to fish. He was delayed, so it was midday before he was out on the loch, but by 3.30 p.m., when he called a halt, he had taken 54 salmon. Assuming his fly was attacked as soon as it hit the water, and only one fish was hooked at once, this means an average playing time for each fish of less than four minutes!

Typical Grimersta-style fishing, casting directly downwind from the stern, on
Loch Faoghail an Tuim

This achievement established the British record for the number of salmon taken in a single day, although another tenant managed 46 a few days later. Following Mr Naylor's catch (incidentally, he never bothered with salmon fishing again), Grimersta's place in angling history was assured. In the next few decades its reputation was further embellished by frequent reports of other incredibly prolific catches. Syndicate member Cecil Braithwaite detailed numerous red-letter days and weeks during the 1920s in his *Fishing Here and There* (1932); for instance, in August 1921 he and a friend had 97 salmon each in five days. This era included Grimersta's record year (1925) of 2,276, an astonishing number for what was essentially a five-rod fishery. On 24 August 1982 another remarkable catch proved once again that in the right conditions anything is possible at Grimersta: despite a late start Peter Wright, a regular rod on the system, landed 35 fish in the First Stream.

Here are Grimersta's average annual catches since the 1870s for the system below Langavat. (Other estates have access to parts of the system, particularly Langavat, and in recent years their catch has probably amounted to 200 to 300 salmon/grilse per annum.)

	Salmon/grilse
1871–79	648
1880–89	816
1890–99	713
1900–09	895
1910–19	828
1920–29	1,033
1930–39	919
1940–49	627
1950–59	816
1960–69	866
1970–79	722
1980–89	594
1990–99	351
2000–03	475

It should be noted, when considering these figures, that inevitably there have been changes to the fishery. The number of rods was gradually increased to eight by the 1980s. In addition, as part of the Estate's policy of allowing access to island residents, one of the four lochs, Loch Faoghail Charrasan, is reserved exclusively for a local angling club (it is however lightly fished and makes a very limited contribution to the figures), and Loch an Easa Ghil is shared with a local family. It must also be stressed that rod pressure at Grimersta has remained minuscule in relation to the vast amount of water available.

Furthermore, it is important to emphasize that the season's opening is now effectively delayed until June. Spring salmon fishing was an important part of the calendar (up to the early 1960s), and it was not that unusual for 100 salmon to be taken in April and May (Cecil Braithwaite detailed 143 fish, averaging over 12 lb, for these two months in 1927). There is still a limited spring run, but it is really not fished for.

Salmon runs dwindled from the mid-1970s. A prime factor was the development of fish farms in Loch Roag, which rapidly became one of the most intensively farmed sea lochs in Europe. Grimersta's nadir was reached in 1998, when catches dropped below 200. However, this century has seen a marked recovery (including a catch of 628 in 2002), marred only by 2003's long drought. The improving catches owe much to a concerted programme, on a number of fronts, to maximize the number of smolts going to sea.

Poaching has always been endemic on Lewis, and Grimersta has long been a particular target. An uneasy relationship with some in the local community stems from an episode of insensitive behaviour towards the crofters of Bernera by the sporting tenants in the 1870s. By the 1970s and 1980s poaching reached truly commercial levels – which, if sustained, threatened to strip the system of its spawning stock (netting was even carried out on the redds) – and intimidation and violence were rife. Poaching had to be tackled head-on in a determined and systematic manner. Whilst it was effective in the short term, this policy was controversial and caused considerable ill feeling. Since then, though, the situation has improved dramatically, and relations with the local community, eased by a greater transparency on the part of the Estate, are probably better now than has been the case for over a century.

Considerable efforts have been directed at habitat improvement and predator control. The Estate has its own hatchery with the focus of attention on planting out fed fry in September into underutilized areas of the catchment. Grimersta owns the local netting rights, and netting was finally discontinued in 1987 after several years of inconsistent practice. For some decades the Estate had limited catches to a maximum of 1,000 per annum, but generally the catch was kept well below this level. The record year for the nets was 1941, with a take of 3,024 salmon/grilse.

Salmon numbers are recovering, but there is little optimism over the future for sea trout. There used to be tremendous runs, and, although sea trout were not the primary target, rod catches generally exceeded 1,000 per annum in the latter part of the nineteenth century, with the amazing figure of 2,705 in 1888. There was a strong spring run of sea trout: thus 490 were caught by 16 May in 1903. Inevitably there were peaks and troughs, but stocks remained healthy until the local fish-farming industry mushroomed in the 1980s; Loch Roag (both east and west branches) is a long estuary in which sea trout are highly vulnerable to sea-lice infestation. Mature fish are now almost unknown.

Whilst Grimersta is primarily a loch system, the lochs no longer dominate catches as much as previously. The streams connecting the various lochs can be highly productive. The inflows into each loch (the 'Ford Stream', 'Macleay's Stream' and 'First Stream' – all legendary names) are favoured taking spots. The main river itself has gained prominence in the game book, especially the lower pools; now up to 40 per cent of the fish landed in a season may be from the river, even though it is only part of one of the four beats. In fact the river used to be largely ignored, except in the spring, so either fish are showing less haste to reach the lochs above, or angling effort on the river is much greater than it was. It does now include much more holding water, and it is also relevant that today the Estate caters for many more outside anglers, to whom the river is perhaps more familiar territory. Up to twenty-five years ago, Grimersta was extremely insular, with virtually all the fishing taken by syndicate members or their guests; in recent years, though, a change of policy has opened up the fishery to visiting anglers.

Grimersta may be mainly a grilse system, but the salmon run is not inconsiderable and there are certainly heavy fish amongst them. The record rod-caught

The Upper Battery Pool towards the top of the River Grimersta

Netting a grilse on the Bridge Pool

salmon is understood to be 29 lb, taken in the spring of 1927; the nets once landed one of 39 lb. In early 2003 the intact remains of a huge cock kelt were found: 42 in. long with a girth of 22 in., and its weight was estimated to have been 33 lb.

Grimersta is one those rare fisheries, with which a particular fly, that for decades has found only limited favour elsewhere, is closely associated. The Blue Elver (also known as the Elver or Ransom's Elver) is a most spectacular lure, fashioned primarily from the feathers of Kenya's vulturine guinea fowl. As its name implies, it was originally designed to imitate an immature eel. However, at Grimersta it is fished on the dropper (i.e. bouncing enticingly along the surface) as an attractor – sometimes it will hook fish but more often it will stimulate salmon into taking the tail fly. The alternative is the ubiquitous Muddler.

MORSGAIL

The Morsgail system's main headwaters drain some of west Lewis's most inaccessible terrain – east of Hamanavay, north of Kinlochresort and west of Scalaval. Numerous shallow lochs (notably Loch Cragach) and lochans amidst undulating moorland flow via the Abhainn a Loin into Loch Morsgail, an oval loch just over half a mile across at its widest. From here, the mile-long Morsgail River runs north, absorbing a major tributary from the south-east, to its estuary at the head of Little Loch Roag, a narrow arm of Loch Roag.

In 1849 Lord Matheson cleared Morsgail of sheep and cattle and created the first sporting estate on Lewis. For the next three decades it was kept in hand for his family and guests, and an imposing lodge was built on Loch Morsgail in 1852. The Estate is said to have been Lady Matheson's favourite retreat; in summer she spent hours at her seat by Lady Mary's Pool on the river. A track, encircling the loch, was made for a pony and trap. Between 1879 and 1914 the Estate alternated between lets to tenants and being kept in hand for the Mathesons, and during the Leverhulme era (1918–1923) the Estate was mainly kept in hand. At the 1924 auction Morsgail was amalgamated in one lot with Scaliscro and received no bids. At the following year's sale Morsgail was sold independently to James Adam Hunter.

In 1931 the Estate was purchased by a syndicate, which traded as Morsgail Ltd. Their tenant from the mid-1940s was Colonel Frederick Wingfield-Digby, who bought the Estate in 1950. When he died in 1952 Morsgail passed to his son Simon Wingfield-Digby, who sold it to his friend John Foster Robinson in 1955. He retained it until 1978, when a speculative investment company (owned by a consortium of Irish businessmen) acquired it. They tried unsuccessfully to resell it in 1980, and a buyer was not forthcoming until 1984: Alasdair R. Davidson.

Whilst the Estate has owned the local netting rights (including those on Little Loch Roag) since 1925, these have not been exercised. Rod-catch records for Morsgail Estate exist for most years from 1880, but often it is difficult to determine exactly which systems they relate to; however, it is reasonable to say that for most of the period from 1880 to 1978 the Morsgail system produced on average 50 salmon and up to 300 sea trout per annum. John Foster Robinson's game book exemplifies the confusion. Thus his record year for salmon (1964), with a total catch of 281, is rather misleading because 240 of these came off Langavat (the head of the Grimersta system). In fact two of his best years for salmon from the Morsgail chain were 1962 and 1969 with catches of 65 and 42 respectively. His catches of sea trout from the Morsgail chain were generally between 200 and 300 per annum.

There are no catch records for the late 1970s and early 1980s. The level of catches since then (averaging some 16 salmon and 60 sea trout) is a reflection of the lack of effective keepering in the years before the arrival of the present owner in 1984, and of the serious impact of fish-farming, which has had repercussions for the majority of migratory salmonid systems on Lewis. Morsgail is now possibly the only non-commercial fishing estate on the island, and inevitably this factor manifests itself in catches.

In recent years determined efforts have been made on a variety of fronts to restore migratory fish stocks. All sheep have been cleared from the upper catchment, and the main dam (at the outlet from Loch Morsgail) has been replaced, with the new one incorporating a fish-counter to monitor numbers of returning adults. (None of the other numerous dams constructed by John Foster Robinson are still functional, so that gives fish far easier access to the headwaters.) Between 20,000 and 30,000 eyed salmon ova of Morsgail origin are planted out annually. A strict catch-and-release policy is in place, with the system fished lightly by the owners and invited guests and locals. There are signs since the turn of the century of better sea-trout runs, with the occasional fish up to 2 lb, perhaps reflecting improved sea-lice controls in the fish farms. Sea trout up to 8 lb used to be taken.

The record salmon from the system is thought to be a fish of 16 lb landed by John Foster Robinson in Loch Morsgail in July 1968. Historically the main salmon runs have been from late June to August, with the odd fish in May and October. In the height of the runs in the 1960s and 1970s the operation of the system's dams was often akin to a military exercise. A look-out would be perched above Little Loch Roag. When an approaching shoal was spotted, he would signal, and then the various sluices would be opened in the appropriate order to draw the fish up into the river.

FHORSA

The Fhorsa drains much of the northern section of the west Lewis mountains. The headwaters are absorbed into Loch Suainaval – three miles long, narrow and very deep (at over 60 m in places, the deepest loch on the island). A quarter of a mile of river (an important spawning area) connects this loch with Loch Stacsavat. Fish are held back in the latter by a grid, which is lifted late in the year to allow fish up to Suainaval and beyond. Stacsavat is a classic salmon loch: on average half a mile wide and comparatively shallow, with numerous bays and points.

From the loch, the Fhorsa has a short course. There is a substantial falls, once a formidable obstacle but after the dislodging of rocks no longer so. The Gorge Pool, below the falls, is the river's main holding and angling pool. The estuary, including the Sea Pool, follows a long, meandering channel through Uig Sands, the lower reaches of which are now known as the Bruton Stream.

The imposing Uig Lodge, completed in 1876, is thought to be the first concrete building in Scotland, although such a description hardly does it justice. Its elevated panoramic views, from rugged mountains to the sweeping, idyllic bay lapped by the Atlantic, are surely without equal in the Outer Hebrides. It originally

Fishing the ebb tide on the Bruton Stream, overlooked by Uig Lodge

served as the lodge for the extensive Uig and Hamanavay Estate, and in the late 1800s the tenant was the Hon Grenville Gore-Langton. In 1878 the annual rent was £759, but it dropped to £600 in 1894 and £500 in 1899; evidently even this figure could not be sustained as in the early 1900s Lord Belper took a seven-year lease for £295 per annum. Before World War I the tenant was Harry Holmes, whose bag in 1913 included 64 salmon and 489 sea trout from the Fhorsa as well as the Red River and the Hamanavay. In 1914 the keeper, Roddy MacKenzie, was ordered to mothball the estate for the duration of the war. (It is worth noting that during the last hundred years Uig Lodge has had just four head keepers: the aforementioned, his son Roddy MacKenzie jnr, John MacKay, from 1949, and his son Kenny MacKay, from 1987.)

Following his acquisition of the island, Lord Leverhulme gave the Uig Estate to his niece Lady Emily as a wedding present in 1923. She was daunted by the responsibility, so at once gave it back to her uncle; he then divided it into two companies. Uig Crofters Ltd (in which she had no interest) was set up with control and ownership of most of the land; this company was sold in the 1925 dispersal. Uig Lodge, its policies and the salmon fishings in the Fhorsa, Red River and Hamanavay systems (together with all the coastal netting rights) became the assets of Uig Estates Ltd (with Lady Emily as the majority shareholder), which entered into a long lease with Colonel Wingfield Digby. In 1944 the company sold the lodge and the Fhorsa and Red River systems to James Donald Dobson of Glasgow, who soon disposed of the Red River. In 1977 R.H. Davies and Sons, trading as the Fhorsa Company Ltd, bought Uig Lodge and the Fhorsa fishings, and for the next five years the lodge was operated as a hotel. In 1982 the company sold the lodge and the Fhorsa system to Malcolm Green and Barry Green, the current owners.

Uig Lodge still owns the netting rights between Gallan Head, four miles to the north of Uig Bay, and Brenish, five miles to the south. These have not been exercised since 1944 and quite possibly earlier. The nearest salmon farms are in Loch Roag, although it is worth noting that the Fhorsa has never had a run of sea trout; the estuary does, however, contain slob trout (brown trout, generally silver in colour, that have adapted to brackish water but do not actually migrate to sea). There has been no stocking of the system except in the late 1980s, when salmon fry of Grimersta origin were introduced; the experiment was discontinued, as there was no discernible improvement in stocks.

The system is essentially natural with the exception of groynes (installed in the 1980s on the advice of Neil Graesser) on both sides of the inflow to Loch Slacsavat. The new lies created, known as Salmon Point, now account for the majority of fish caught on the loch.

Historical catch records for Uig Lodge are sketchy. In 1875, 391 salmon were caught on the estate as a whole, but this figure is likely to include netted fish. In the 1920s and 1930s it is understood (according to a descendant of the tenant) that between forty and eighty salmon a year were caught by rods in the Fhorsa, Red River and Hamanavay systems; it is probably reasonable to assume, given the proximity, that most of these were taken in the Fhorsa. In the Dobson era (1944–77) the fishing was not let and the family restricted themselves to a maximum of three rods. Their catch averaged some 50 salmon per annum in the 1950s (off the Fhorsa and the Red River), dropping to between 15 and 50 during the 1960s and early 1970s. Average annual catches since then are:

	Salmon
1978–80	100
1981–90	65
1991–2000	123
2001–03	83

There is no doubt that fishing effort has increased significantly since 1978, and particularly since 1989. Approximately half of the total catch is from the lochs (almost all from Stacsavat), with 20 per cent from the river and 30 per cent from the Bruton Stream.

The latter was discovered in early July 1978, when Colonel Clive Bruton, frustrated by the fact that no fish could run the river due to the dry conditions, went down to the estuary, where he watched and then fished. After some experimentation he caught three grilse and lost a salmon in the sea on fly and the tidal channel was named in his honour. This is one of the only marine locations in the Outer Isles where salmon are caught consistently on fly. Fish nose in with the tide, and when the tide starts to ebb they gradually retreat, because of the absence of holding water by the actual river mouth. Shoals of fish are then concentrated in a channel (some 200 yards long) on the north side of the neck of Uig Sands. For a two-hour period this channel is similar to a medium-flowing river, although dropping all the time.

The Bruton Stream is basically fished as if it were a river. However one essential difference is that the shoals of fish are not settled – they are moving all the time. In calm conditions fish are readily spotted and cast to directly, as in bonefishing. The channel fishes best in a breeze on a medium ebb tide with a good 'rip'; it will also fish on a flow tide, but this can be dangerous. Shoals can vary in size from 20 to 100 or more. It is particularly striking how close the fish will come, often leaping over a fly-line just beyond the rod tip and even onto the arms of a wading angler.

With the addition of the Stream, the Fhorsa is now fishable all summer, even when a prolonged drought prevents any fish from gaining access to fresh water. If the fish are on, then sport can be frenetic. The biggest catch has been 12 in a day off two tides.

The Fhorsa is not a large-fish system. Andrew Verney caught the heaviest on record (16 lb) in September 1997 on Loch Stacsavat. On the side of the tower at Uig Lodge is a concrete slab with the outline of a salmon in the 30 lb class – reputed to be from the Fhorsa, but the exact details have been lost.

HAMANAVAY (AND RED RIVER)

The extreme south-west of Lewis, which includes the island's only real mountains, is undeniably one of the most inaccessible locations in Scotland. Anyone unfamiliar with this area should consult a large-scale map to appreciate just how remote the Hamanavay system really is.

The history of ownership of Uig and Hamanavay Estate up to 1944 is included in the preceding entry on the Fhorsa. After their purchase that year, the Dobson family, who only wanted to retain Uig Lodge (together with the Fhorsa system and the Red River system), sold off the rest of the estate, the Hamanavay system going to Samuel Newall, a tweed-mill owner from Stornoway. After his death at Hamanavay during a fishing holiday in July 1967, John Foster Robinson of neighbouring Morsgail Estate (who already enjoyed frequent access to Hamanavay) acquired the system, and in 1978 he was succeeded by a speculative Irish syndicate. Meanwhile the Dobsons sold the Red River fishing rights to Simon Wingfield Digby; later Atlantic Sea Products purchased these rights and developed a commercial smolt hatchery just upstream of the mouth. In 1984 the current owners, the partners in Uig and Hamanavay, bought the land including the Hamanavay system; since then they have also added the Red River.

The Estate's principal salmon system is the Hamanavay. A chain of three lochs (Benisval, Cro Criosdaig and na Craobhaig each averaging a mile in length) drain undulating moorland and discharge to the west, via the Hamanavay River, to its mouth in sheltered Hamanavay Bay. The river is close to two miles long with a steep gradient. Towards the top of the river an important tributary, the Ghascleit, joins from the north; it flows two miles from Loch Dibadale, which is dramatically enclosed by precipitous hills. The other significant system is the Red River (Abhainn Caslavat), which runs north for three miles from Loch Raonasgail (in an awe-inspiring position beneath the sheer faces of Mealisval and Tahaval) and debouches at the southern tip of Uig Sands.

Until 1989 there was no vehicle track to the Hamanavay River, but there was however a keeper living at Hamanavay from 1882 (and possibly earlier) until the 1960s. Access was either on foot (a walk of at least two hours) or by boat round the coast. There is no doubt that its remoteness is why this is still essentially a virgin system, and it has always been lightly fished and never stocked. Traditionally it has been predominantly a sea trout system, although salmon numbers seem to have increased since the 1970s. Critical to the health of the system, particularly the exceptional numbers and quality of sea trout, is the fact that there are no marine salmon cages between Gallan Head and Amhuinnsuidhe Castle (over 50 miles of coastline, which includes the sea lochs Hamanavay, Tealasvay and Resort). Moreover, there has been no legal netting of the Hamanavay estuary in living memory.

The main angling loch is na Craobhaig (which has a population of char); the dramatic backdrop to this is the high mountain range of north Harris. Sidney Spencer wrote vividly of a day on the loch in July 1967:

> Abounding in rocky points and clean pebble and sand shores, it provides, I think, with its huge stock of medium-weight fish, the finest sea trout fishing I know. It is uncommon to come away with less than eight or ten adult sea trout, which may, but do not always, run up to 5 or 6 lb.

His bag on the rough day in question was four salmon and a 6-lb sea trout. The last was a record fish for the system at the time, and not dethroned until 31 August 1970, when a massive fish of 9 lb 8 oz was caught.

John Foster Robinson's game book for Morsgail (1958–77) indicates that only occasional sorties were made to Hamanavay, with an average take from Loch na Craobhaig between 1960 and 1976 of 15 salmon and 75 sea trout. After pool improvements in 1970, the river itself had more prominence in the game book, averaging 31 salmon and 22 sea trout between 1971 and 1977. Before this there had been virtually no holding water on the river, which just served as a conduit to the lochs, and it is still the case that fish will only run the river in a good spate. It is worth noting that all grills on the system (designed to hold fish back before the spawning season) were removed in the early 1980s.

Fish run the Hamanavay from June. The most prolific bag in one day in the 1990s off na Craobhaig was 52 sea trout (averaging 1 lb 8 oz) and one salmon to two rods. The record salmon is 17 lb, caught by Dennis Moss from Three Rock lie.

Loch Dibadale at the top of the tributary warrants special mention. Here the average weight of sea trout is heavier, although they are not so numerous (some salmon reach here too), the best catch being 25 sea trout averaging over 2 lb to two rods. When it rains, a cliff overlooking the loch depicts an almost perfect map of Britain and Ireland.

The Estate's second system, the Red River, is not as productive, having been in the past more vulnerable to illegal activity (a 24-lb salmon is understood to have been extracted in such circumstances in the 1980s). The system still has reasonable runs of salmon and sea trout and is now the focus of a restocking programme. Loch Raonasgail – which also contains char – needs a fair wind (although not too much, as then the wind tends to funnel and twist).

Records for the Estate as a whole since 1990 give the following average annual catches (including the odd salmon off Loch Langavat):

	Salmon	Sea trout	Finnock
1990–94	47	317	327
1995–99	63	343	306
2000–03	28	324	303

Catches, particularly salmon, were very sparse in 2001, as the Estate was between keepers and only partly let, and again in 2003 because of the prolonged drought.

The exceptional sea-trout fishing owes much to a consistent conservation policy over the last two decades; tenants are asked to release all sea trout whenever possible.

The Morsgail game book has some unusual entries relating to Hamanavay. One for August 1966 reads: 'General Smith shoots with a .22 a killer whale. 18 ft long, teeth 3 in.' Another, for 1964, is more mysterious: 'SCD and General Smith saw an object in na Craobhaig at least 24 ft long. It appeared alive and then disappeared. SCD said he would not have believed it, had he not seen it.'

HARRIS

AMHUINNSUIDHE

Few if any of Scotland's mountain ranges are so visually overpowering and formidable as that of North Harris. Viewed from the north or the south, it dominates the landscape. The grandeur of these hills is unforgettable, their sheer sides often rising straight from sea level; indeed most of the perimeter has no real coastal strip. Between the high peaks several narrow valleys and their watercourses infiltrate the massif. North-west of the Clisham (2,622 ft) is the Langadale River, the main headwater of the Grimersta system. To the west are several small salmon and sea-trout systems, collectively known as the Amhuinnsuidhe fishings.

The two most productive systems flow north and have a common estuary at Kinlochresort at the head of Loch Resort. The most renowned, the Voshimid, drains little more than ten square miles. At the top of the main stem of the river is Loch Voshimid, one of the most reliable salmon angling lochs in the outer isles. Fairly shallow and covering no more than one square mile, it can hold great numbers of salmon. Given its confined nature, almost all of the loch can be rewarding. With little spawning above the loch, the great majority of fish tend to drop back downstream in late October and November to spawn in the river below.

West of Voshimid lies the remote Ulladale system. The upper Ulladale River cascades down off bare rock, draining spectacularly steep terrain, before it levels out in the main spawning area above Loch Ulladale; the latter is dramatically overlooked at its southern end by a towering precipitous cliff. Paradoxically, though, most of the loch (which is of similar size to Voshimid) is shallow. From the loch the river takes a meandering three-mile north-easterly course through several small lochs and lochans. Its lower section, known as the River Housay, converges with the outflow of the Voshimid system by Kinlochresort.

Loch Voshimid, one of the most reliable salmon angling lochs in the Hebrides

Other systems flow south to West Loch Tarbert. The most notable is the Scourst, which lies just over the watershed south of Voshimid. Below Loch Scourst, half a mile long and tightly sandwiched between daunting hills, the Meavaig River is two miles long, has a gentle gradient and includes much suitable spawning habitat. To the west is the River Eaval system (also known as the Castle Burn). Although it drains the biggest catchment at Amhuinnsuidhe, from an angling point of view it is now a secondary system compared to the three already mentioned, although on occasion Lochan Beag (the Ladies' Loch) on the lower river has produced red-letter days. It discharges into the sea over an impressive set of falls just by Amhuinnsuidhe Castle; the concentration of fish below could at times be so thick that it appeared that one could walk over them. The system's upper waters have been dammed to feed a commercial hydro-electric scheme.

Harris, the property of the MacLeods for over three centuries, was sold in 1834 by Alexander MacLeod to the fifth Earl of Dunmore. The seventh Earl, wanting a residence with easy access to his main sporting activities, built Amhuinnsuidhe Castle in 1868. Soon afterwards he was declared bankrupt, and his banker, Sir Edward Scott, acquired the castle and the North Harris Estate in 1869. He ran the Estate in considerable style with some 30 permanent and ten seasonal staff. In 1919 his son, Sir Samuel Scott, sold North Harris to Lord Leverhulme for £20,000, although this was not to be the end of the Scott family's tenure – they leased the castle and the associated stalking and fishing rights for a nominal £1 a year rent.

After Lord Leverhulme died in 1925, Sir Samuel Scott bought back the North Harris Estate at the dispersal auction for just £2,000, and kept it until his own death in 1943. The family trustees then sold North Harris in 1944 to the Liverpool brewer Lord Brocket, and he resold it in 1946 to Sir Thomas Sopwith, the aeronautical tycoon, who also ran the Estate in lavish style. In 1961 North Harris was sold to Major Miller-Mundy and Captain Lowndes. Whilst the Scott family had occasionally let stalking, the new proprietors were the first to attempt to operate the Estate on commercial lines with sporting tenants staying at the castle; all subsequent owners have run the castle along similar lines. In 1968 Sir Hereward Wake acquired the Estate. He sold it to Gerald Panchaud in 1976; he died in 1989, and his widow Hélène retained it until 1994, when she sold to Jonathan and Lady Marcia Bulmer. Their tenure ended in 2003 with an unprecedented arrangement: the land on the 55,000-acre North Harris Estate was acquired by the publicly funded North Harris Trust, whilst the castle and the fishings were bought by Ian Scarr-Hall.

For many of the historical owners of North Harris the main sporting interest lay in the Estate's challenging stalking, and this was certainly true for the Scotts, although they did not neglect the fishings. During the nineteenth century the

A blustery day on remote Loch Ulladale

important netting rights in Loch Resort, which separates Lewis from North Harris, belonged to the proprietor of Lewis. In 1867 James Stretton Young (son of Andrew Young of Invershin, manager of the lucrative netting operations on the Kyle of Sutherland) took a lease of all the Lewis net fishings including Loch Resort. By the late 1870s Sir Edward Scott was paying £60 per annum in rent for the rights in Loch Resort, but there is no evidence that he exercised them, so it is reasonable to assume that his motive was to protect the runs into the Voshimid and Ulladale systems. By 1913 Sir Samuel Scott was paying £30 per annum for these rights. Ownership of the Loch Resort rights was included with the North Harris Estate in the 1925 sale, and there is no record of netting being exercised since.

It is thought that the Scotts never let the fishings. However, an article in *The Field* in December 1870 recounts a visit to Harris the previous August by four individuals whose sport included three days on Loch Scourst – where apparently 21 lb of sea trout to a rod in a day was easily achievable. It is also puzzling that the Watson Lyall sporting catalogue of 1881 mentions Loch Voshimid ('four salmon and 25 sea trout are a good day's take'), Loch Ulladale ('salmon average 7 lb; a fair day is 20 lb of salmon and 40 lb of sea trout') and Loch Scourst ('a good day is four salmon, averaging 7 lb, and 20 lb of sea trout'). It may also be relevant that Calderwood's coverage of North Harris was selective. He referred to a failed and costly scheme to open up access for sea trout to Loch a Mhorghain

Loch Scourst

(by the Lewis-Harris road), and a paragraph on the Eaval system by the castle notes that 'a fish pass, formed by rock blasting, was necessary to make this fishery what it is, but the gradient is comparatively easy, and the fishing in the lochs above is not only first class, but constantly reliable'.

The 1925 Leverhulme dispersal auction catalogue gave angling catches for North Harris of 129 salmon and 420 sea trout in 1923, and 226 salmon and 1,020 sea trout in 1924. It stated that the average was between these figures and, in a tantalizing attempt to whet the appetite of potential purchasers, that the totals for 1924 'have sometimes been beaten'. From the 1960s, with the advent of more commercial regimes, angling was soon established as the Estate's most marketable sporting attraction. By the Wake era, catches of 200 salmon and 800 sea trout were being quoted. Average annual catches for the last twenty years are set out below.

	Salmon	Sea trout
1983–85	255	792
1986–90	244	495
1991–95	96	228
1996–2000	105	563
2001–03	187	651

There is little doubt fish numbers declined from the mid-1980s, with fish farms in West Loch Tarbert a contributory factor. Fortunately, there is no fish-farming activity along the coastline west of the castle and as far north as Gallan Head on Lewis, so that migratory fish from the Voshimid and Ulladale systems have little if any exposure to the hazards associated with marine aquaculture. The estate's 2003 catch of 222 salmon and 836 sea trout was highly encouraging.

Voshimid is the most prolific system, and over the years it has produced many extraordinary catches. After a desperately long dry period, a heavy spate in late July 1977 lifted all the fish that had been held back in Loch Resort up into the lochs. On the afternoon of the 26th Andrew Coombs, with Kenny Morrison on the oars, launched a boat on Loch Voshimid in a howling gale. The burn from Lochan an Fheoir above was a raging torrent, and in the corner of the loch by the inflow lay a huge number of fish. Coombs seemed to contact something virtually every cast – fish appeared to be racing each other to reach his fly. The total for the week in question was 112 salmon and 65 sea trout, but in less than four hours he landed 16 salmon and 16 sea trout (and lost at least as many more). Hélène Panchaud and two other rods once had 21 in a day from Voshimid.

The other systems have their days, though, even if they are overshadowed by Voshimid. Thus Lady Marcia Bulmer once landed seven salmon in an afternoon on the Ladies' Loch. And Scourst, which was the best sea trout loch, produced the heaviest salmon (at just under 19 lb) on record. On 11 September 1987 Donald Carmichael, with Kenny Morrison as gillie, saw a head-and-tail rise in the stream at the north end. When the fish took Kenny recalls there was a 'fair old barney'. He pulled the boat away from the shore, but in the deeper water the fish just sat on the bottom. There was complete stalemate for over an hour, even though the rod was bent double. In due course Kenny decided to row for shallower water; the salmon then 'went mental', and eventually it was landed. That evening Donald Carmichael, an eminent nuclear physicist, declared, 'tonight I have a greater feeling of achievement than I ever got from a lifetime of scientific research'. The fish had spent four years in freshwater, followed by two winters at sea.

The Amhuinnsuidhe fishings are, of course, all spate systems, insofar as heavy rain is required to enable fish to reach the lochs; at times the area receives very localized precipitation, as the North Harris mountains are well known for creating their own weather. The systems are essentially loch fisheries, and the lochs all have an intimate nature, given their limited acreage. There is close contact between the angler and his quarry, particularly when dibbling a dropper on a short line. Very occasionally, in a bank-bursting spate, the rivers are fishable. In such conditions in early July 1979 Andrew Coombs followed a shoal up the river (which looked like a 'mini Spey') towards Loch Voshimid, catching six salmon and losing considerably more in a brief interlude.

LAXDALE

The Laxdale drains a narrow barren strip that cuts into and practically severs the northern end of the South Harris hills. This intimate system has five main lochs and flows north-west into the long Luskentyre Estuary, where the two-mile course of the stream across the sands can alter radically following a major spate. The lower loch, Loch Fincastle, is artificial and was constructed in the late nineteenth century by damming up the head of the estuary; saltwater reaches it only in major spring tides. Salmon were reluctant to settle in it for many years, but it subsequently became a consistent success. Above it is Loch Laxdale, extending to no more than two acres, which Hamish Stuart referred to as 'that singular tarn' and 'probably the smallest salmon and sea trout loch in the world'. Salmon go no further up the main stem than this loch, but sea trout can migrate on to three higher lochs: Sluice, Bearesta Mor and Bearesta Beg.

In 1834 Alexander MacLeod of Harris (whose family had held Harris since 1493) sold the island to the Earl of Dunmore. In 1919 Lord Leverhulme bought South Harris, and he lived at Borve from 1923. His landholdings were broken up after his death in 1925, and since then Borve Lodge Estate, including the Laxdale system, has had a succession of owners: Mr E. Fradgley (1927–33), Ministry of Agriculture (1933–37), Colonel J. Walker (1937–56), Mr and Mrs G.D. Wilkinson (1956–64), Sinclairtown Property for the Hon. G.R.J. Cormack (1964–78), Highlands and Islands Development Board (1978–85) and Blomidon Investments for Dr D.F. Horrobin and Ms S. Clarkson (from 1985).

Over the years the fishery has never been run on a strictly commercial basis and this factor has often limited fishing effort. In its dependence on drawing fish into the lochs from the bay, it is, of course, very much a spate system. Catch records go back to 1929, except for the period 1940 to 1952, and annual averages are as follows:

	Salmon	Sea trout
1929–33	16	275
1934–39	39	224
1953–57	17	139
1958–62	22	184
1963–67	42	237
1968–72	48	149
1973–77	39	133
1978–82	64	91
1983–88	51	209
1989–93	49	128
1994–98	44	101
1999–03	37	65

Although a short still-water section of river below Loch Laxdale can produce fish in a good wind, it is estimated that 99 per cent of the catch is taken on the lochs.

Depending on water levels, the main salmon runs are from mid-July, whilst sea trout arrive from the second half of June. In recent years salmon numbers have held up well. However, since the development of marine salmon farms, sea trout are much less numerous, and their average weight has declined, with double-figure fish almost unknown.

The amount of spawning territory for salmon is limited. Generally, those that take up residence in Loch Fincastle spawn in the mile of river below Loch Laxdale, and those that settle in Loch Laxdale spawn in the Geirsdale Burn, which enters

Loch Fincastle, constructed in the late nineteenth century

the loch from the north. Since 1966 the Estate has operated its hatchery annually, with few exceptions. Both salmon and sea trout are stripped on the redds, with up to 200,000 eggs obtained (though in recent years much more modest numbers have been taken), and the offspring are reintroduced into the system at the alevin stage. There has been a continuous ongoing programme of clearing the river and burns of any obstructions, repairing dams and raking out silt deposits from the available spawning gravel; in 2002 a new fish pass was constructed below Loch Laxdale to ease access. So far as anyone is aware, netting rights in the estuary have never been exercised. And poaching in the estuary (and indeed fresh water) has become almost negligible in recent years, although the system is still carefully watched.

The restricted nature of the lochs means that locating the fish is comparatively easy and so, in favourable taking conditions, prolific catches are attainable. In September 1982 two rods (Tony Scherr and Neil Martin) had 19 salmon in a day from Loch Fincastle. In July 1972 a single rod picked up 7 salmon and 11 sea trout in a day from Loch Fincastle. In 1967 one party in July landed 143 sea trout averaging 2 lb 8 oz (this was the record year for sea trout, with 273 recorded). The best salmon catch was achieved in 1982 with 161 in the book. The heaviest sea trout (13 lb) was taken in 1957, and the record salmon (16 lb) in 2002. Tony Scherr, until recently manager of the estate, has amassed the remarkable total of some 1,300 salmon and sea trout off the system over a 38-year period.

OBBE

T he Obbe system consists of some ten square miles of water, more than any other on Harris. Its headwaters accumulate in Loch Langabhat (at two-and-a-half miles long the biggest loch on the island) in the heart of the South Harris hills. The system flows west, absorbing tributaries from the north, to Loch na Moracha and Loch Steisebhat, and then to the man-made Mill Pool and its mouth in the virtually enclosed Obbe (Loch An t-Ob), which Hamish Stuart described as 'a large tidal basin of almost circular shape', on the island's south-west coast.

Like the rest of South Harris, the Obbe system was owned by the MacLeods of Harris up to 1834, followed by the Earls of Dunmore to 1919, and then Lord Leverhulme until his death in 1925. The last spent the staggering sum of £250,000 on the harbour at Obbe (subsequently named Leverburgh) in an attempt to create a major herring-fishing and -processing port; after his death these assets were sold off to a demolition company for just £5,000. In the break-up of South Harris

Loch na Moracha

234

at the end of the Leverhulme era, a consortium of shareholders acquired the Obbe system, running it on a beat arrangement. The main shareholders were Kyles Lodge (the Lomas family) and the Rodel Hotel. In the 1940s Major-General Sir Colin Gubbins also became a shareholder. Over the last three decades the great majority of the shares have been bought by the Jourdan family, which now runs the main part of the fishery.

Unfortunately most of the historical catch records for the system have been lost (many were destroyed in the Rodel Hotel fire in 1964), but it is probably fair to say that it consistently produced between 50 and 100 salmon and several hundred sea trout annually. The 1881 Watson Lyall guide mentions 'as many as five salmon and 129 sea trout in one day by two rods'. In the early 1900s catch records for the Hebridean Sporting Association (see note below) indicate about 1,100 sea trout and some 40 salmon annually from their Rodel fishings (the great majority from the Obbe system). Calderwood differs slightly by referring to 'about 1,000 to 1,200 sea trout and about 70 salmon' each season (these sea trout catches included finnock). The five-year average to 2003 was 36 salmon and 127 sea trout, with the latter averaging 2 lb 4 oz. It is worth noting that the nearest salmon farm is five miles away in Rodel Bay – hence the comparative abundance of mature sea trout.

In 1903 the Hebridean Sporting Association Ltd leased the sporting rights for much of South Harris, carrying out considerable work on some of the migratory fish systems. The Mill Pool at Leverburgh does not appear on maps before the early 1900s, which suggests that in all probability the Association built the dam on the seaward side (separating it from the Obbe) soon after 1903. It is likely that the dam at the outlet from Langabhat was built around the same time. This is still operational, and allows the creation of artificial spates; it incorporates a fish pass, but very few salmon are taken in this comparatively featureless loch.

Loch Steisebhat, shallow with many bays and headlands, is the system's primary salmon angling water, followed by Loch na Moracha. The brackish Mill Pool, which is flooded by spring tides, fishes well for sea trout from April onwards, although it has the disadvantage of being located in the middle of the village. There are no records of the estuary ever being legally netted. The tidal Obbe basin is almost entirely salt water and, according to Hamish Stuart, used to offer 'excellent fishing with the fly for salmon and sea trout' with fish taking 'freely'. He recalled an instance when an angler fishing three flies hooked three salmon at the same time; only the fish nearest the rod was eventually landed.

The policy in recent years has been to maximize natural spawning through habitat restoration, including the cleaning of the spawning burns. The amount of spawning territory is extensive. Electro-fishing surveys indicate increasing juvenile numbers. A significant contributory factor has been the determined programme to combat mink, which have been essentially eliminated from the catchment.

The salmon runs begin in late June and continue through into October. The fish are typically Hebridean in size, with very few in double figures. Calderwood referred to the record being 14 lb; the heaviest in recent years was a fish of 12 lb taken by Neil Gunn in Loch na Moracha in September 1994. The best sea trout (13 lb 8 oz) was caught by Lady Gubbins in Loch na Moracha in September 1964.

Note: According to extensive research conducted by Professor Michael Gardner, the Hebridean Sporting Association Ltd was formed in February 1903 by a group of Glasgow solicitors and businessmen and included shareholders from all over the UK. It leased the Rodel fishings (initially for 5 years) and on the east coast the Finsbay and Grosebay fishings (for 15 years) from Lord Dunmore; the leases included some 38 lochs, including brown trout lochs. The Association's accounts confirm that it improved the fishings, but without giving specific details. It is understood to have created at least three completely new lochs, enlarged several others, and built numerous small dams and sluices, most of which are still in place. With co-operation from Lord Dunmore, it also removed various obstacles to migration on the east-coast fishings. In addition, the Association undertook a good deal of landscaping of the grounds and access routes around Finsbay Lodge and the nearest lochs. In their early years catches averaged about 1,100 sea trout and 2 salmon per annum in the Finsbay/Grosebay systems.

NORTH UIST

Of all the Outer Hebrides, the cliché 'more water than land' most aptly describes Benbecula and North Uist; the former is virtually flat, while much of the latter's terrain is far more rugged – indeed it is traversed by a fair range of hills, with one exceeding 1,000 feet. North Uist is approximately 12 miles by 16 miles, and is said to include between 600 and 800 lochs.

North Uist was the property of the MacDonalds of Sleat from the early seventeenth century until 1855, when Godfrey William MacDonald sold it to Sir John Powlett Orde. In 1908 the Duke of Hamilton purchased the island from the trustees of Sir Arthur Campbell-Orde. In 1960 Hamilton and Kinneil Estates Ltd sold it to

Loch Geireann (Skealter system)

the Rt. Hon. Doon Aileen, Countess Granville. North Uist remains in the hands of the Granville family.

The main salmon system is Skealter, which consists of an extensive chain of lochs – Upper Skealter, Lower Skealter, Geireann and Ciste – with the last just a stone's throw from the outfall into the sea near Lochmaddy on the island's eastern side. The absence of a river can be an advantage, as a good tide is usually sufficient to lift fish into Ciste; in other words, angling is not completely dependant on heavy rainfall.

Skealter is a most unusual Hebridean system, because it used to have a significant spring salmon run from the first spring tide in March onwards. This run is reputed to have its origins in a programme during the early 1900s of stocking with fry from the River Beauly. Spring fish, known locally as 'greenbacks', do still exist, albeit in reduced numbers, and their average weight is some 10 lb. The record fish (32 lb), landed in 1932 in Lower Skealter by Colonel Craven, was in all probability a springer. The heaviest since then (29 lb) was taken on 17 March 1961 (St Patrick's Day) in Upper Skealter by Father J. Morrison, a Catholic priest from South Uist, who was fishing with a Protestant gillie. The celebrations that night in the bar of the Lochmaddy Hotel cost the priest £20, a not inconsiderable sum at the time, and late in the evening the gillie is understood to have told him that he intended converting to Catholicism.

The mouth of the Skealter system, which used to have a significant spring run

Fish in the 20-lb class used to be caught on a regular basis, and until recently Skealter was considered primarily a spring fishery. Thus the Rev. Joseph Adams in his *Fifty Years of Angling* (1938) noted how a single rod stopped fishing after taking nine springers in a day, and dismissed the grilse run 'as by no means comparable with what takes place in the early part of the season'.

In the 1950s the average annual salmon catch on North Uist was of the order of 100. The record year for salmon was 1993, with 240 caught, eclipsing the previous best in 1964 of 207. But then, in the mid-1990s, salmon stocks took a sudden downturn. Now salmon numbers are recovering, with the main run into Skealter, predominantly grilse, in July and August. The number of fish today bears no comparison with that of the heyday of the post-war years – when watchers at night could observe great shoals, hundreds strong, circling Ciste – but current salmon runs into the Skealter system are difficult to gauge, quite simply because angling effort in the last few years has been comparatively light, and obviously this is reflected in catches. The ten-year average (to 2003) for rod catches of salmon on North Uist stands at 58. In recent years the grids on the Skealter system have been removed to allow early access to the headwaters.

A century ago Skealter was supposedly the only system on North Uist that held salmon. This is by no means certain; some early commentators did refer to salmon in other lochs, although this should not necessarily be taken at face value,

Vallay Sea Pool

as often fish over 5 lb or so were erroneously called salmon. However, over the decades salmon have indeed colonized several other systems on the island, including Geireann Mill (where they are now more numerous than ever before), and have been successfully introduced into Grogary. It is worth noting that from the 1980s to the early 1990s the stocking, ranching and trapping of salmon was carried out on some systems.

Sea trout catches on North Uist have remained remarkably stable. A few fish are in the lochs (there are half a dozen or so sea trout lochs) by June or July, but fresh water sport is really concentrated into September and October. On Geireann Mill (a vast and productive loch) or Horisary (consistently the best sea trout water), the average angler should still pick up a brace or so of sea trout from 2 lb or 3 lb upwards per day. On North Uist the normal approach is to 'row the lochs' and fish on to the shore – in contrast to South Uist, where drifting is the preferred style.

What sets North Uist apart from other Hebridean fisheries – and indeed gives a tremendous boost to the variety of fishing on offer – is its sea-pool fishing for sea trout, something that is almost unique. Sea trout are in the sea pools from April to November, but the most reliable period is from late June onwards, with sport in the latter part of the season dependent on a lack of rainfall; from early September most of the fish will move up into fresh water, if flows from the lochs are encouraging. One curious fact about North Uist sea trout is that they are not

Crystal clear water in Malacleit Sea Pool

'loch-specific' and are quite likely to return to a different system from that in which they originated.

The island has 14 recognized sea pools, all on either the west or the north coasts. They have the appearance and indeed usually the characteristics of a river (in places some are 50 yards wide, whilst others are of more modest size), flowing at first seawards until the current reverses with the incoming tide. They fish best for the two hours before low tide and the hour afterwards, and sport in the sea pools is often fast and furious, the average weight of fish caught being 3 lb. Sea trout in the 3-lb to 5-lb class are common, and occasional salmon are also taken. The feeding at the lower end of the food chain in these pools and the surrounding waters, where for most of the year the temperature of the sea varies little from 9°C, is incredibly rich. The sea pools continue to fish well even when conditions inland are hopeless – for instance hot, bright sunshine.

The island's ten-year average for sea trout (to 2003) is 200; the emphasis is on quality rather than quantity. The best year in recent times was 1965, with 352 sea trout, followed by 1992 (320), 2000 (297) and 1993 (293).

North Uist has a discretionary catch-and-release policy which applies across all its waters, with generous guideline limits on the number of fish that may be retained. Taking too many fish has long been discouraged on the island. In the early 1980s a prospective visitor, with an apparent freezer-filling tendency, telephoned Lochmaddy Hotel and quizzed the proprietor: 'How many fish will I catch in the week?' The reply was appropriately blunt: 'I don't know – try somewhere else.'

SOUTH UIST

As a general rule the further south one goes in the Outer Hebridean chain, the sparser salmon populations become. Barra, the most southerly island of consequence, is devoid of salmon, and South Uist has very limited runs with some increase in recent decades. South Uist's loch systems are dominated by sea trout, and for anglers these have always been the island's primary attraction; the occasional salmon has usually been a welcome by-catch.

South Uist has in effect changed hands just three times in the last two centuries. In 1840 MacDonald of Clanranald sold four-fifths of the island to Colonel John Gordon of Cluny, and he left the estate to his daughter-in-law Lady Gordon Cathcart. In 1942 her executors sold it to Herman Andreae, and in 1960 it was acquired by the current owners, a syndicate of families.

Major R.A. Chrystal, in *Angling at Lochboisdale, South Uist* (covering 1882 to 1937), commented that Loch a Bharp was the only loch to contain salmon. He was perhaps wrong to be quite so categorical; Lewis's *Topographical Dictionary* (1846) referred to two systems carrying salmon, and Hamish Stuart, author and regular visitor in the 1890s and early 1900s, was evidently aware that the Howmore system also carried the odd salmon. It is fairly clear that many anglers in this era had some difficulty differentiating between grilse and large sea trout, particularly when they expected to catch the latter.

However there is no doubt that Loch a Bharp (brackish at times with its outlet to the sea in Lochboisdale at the south-east of the island) has historically had the most stable population of salmon, although catches have rarely been inspiring. According to Chrystal's analysis of the Lochboisdale Hotel fishing registers, it was unusual for more than a handful of salmon/grilse to be taken, and in the very early part of the twentieth century a catch of zero was the annual norm. Apparently salmon were more in evidence in the 1920s and 1930s, though this was hardly reflected in catches, but on 13 September 1935 Chrystal distinguished himself by landing a salmon of 23 lb, the record for the loch; a painting of this fish now hangs in Grogary Lodge.

In Chrystal's time salmon, including sporadic fish in May, were more common than grilse. Now Bharp is mainly a grilse system, with the runs beginning in late June or early July. The best season was 1985 with 47 grilse, though the ten-year average (1994 to 2003) stands at eight grilse. The Bharp system (the loch is fed by three small rivers) has been stocked intermittently since the late 1930s; in recent decades this has included ova originating from Beauly grilse, which may be a factor in the shift towards one-sea-winter fish.

Historically Kildonan, a machair loch halfway up the island's west coast, never carried salmon. However, since the 1960s a commercial salmon smolt farm has been located on the Mill Loch, a satellite of Kildonan, and it is thought that escapes from the farm kick-started a grilse run. In 1994, the record year, 77 grilse were caught, and the ten-year average to 2003 stands at 17.

As indicated above, the Howmore River system (six miles further up the west coast and including the lochs Roag, Fada, Schoolhouse and Castle) is understood always to have had a discrete salmon population. This has increased since the 1970s, with a record year in 1986 of 99 grilse and a ten-year average (1994-2003) of 45.

Despite the relative rise in salmon numbers, which has been to some extent checked since the mid-1990s, South Uist is still essentially a sea trout fishery, with an enviable reputation built up over 150 years. Chrystal's annual summaries detail most of the events and episodes that contributed to this status. These include

Playing a leaping 3-lb sea trout on Loch Roag, part of the Howmore River system

The Mill Loch on the Kildonan system, where salmon runs have developed since the 1960s

Lieutenant-Colonel Echalaz's 9 lb 4 oz sea trout from Kildonan in July 1894, and Sir James Hodson's and Dr Flett's joint catch (an unbeaten record) in eight days' fishing on Kildonan in September 1919 of 52 sea trout for 147 lb 12 oz, including one of 8 lb and 14 over 4 lb. The same Dr Flett, on 17 September 1937, caught a brace of sea trout on Loch Fada of 7 lb 12 oz and 7 lb 8 oz.

There were early moves to regulate the fishery and ensure that it was self-sustaining. The unfortunate practice of fishing for sea-trout kelts in March and April does not seem to have continued beyond the 1890s. Lochboisdale Hotel, then estate-owned and offering the only access for visiting anglers to the sea-trout lochs, burnt down in 1918. When it was rebuilt on a smaller scale, it was permitted just six sea trout rods, thus curtailing any overfishing. In 1935 a size limit of 15 inches was introduced (and that year the hotel's sea-trout catch was 321 for an average weight of 2 lb 2 oz, emphasizing the quality of the fishing rather than the quantity).

It is worth noting that there has never, as far as records go, been any commercial netting of sea trout (or indeed salmon) on the island. In the last three decades with the growth of salmon-farming, the nature of South Uist's coastline has been the saving grace of its sea-trout populations. The farms have been located in the sheltered sea lochs of the island's mountainous east coast, because the west coast, where most of the important sea-trout systems discharge to the sea, is completely unsuitable for marine cages.

The Estate's fishing returns for the past decade (including Bharp, Kildonan and Howmore) confirm that sea-trout catches are still buoyant.

	Salmon	Sea trout
1994	205	541
1995	91	326
1996	65	542
1997	47	398
1998	92	445
1999	48	481
2000	42	582
2001	40	383
2002	14	751
2003	42	539

Every year South Uist still produces two or three double-figure sea trout in the 10-lb to 14-lb class; fish of this size are now virtually unheard of elsewhere in the Highlands and Islands. The record for the island (14 lb 8 oz) was taken by John Kennedy in Loch Roag on 4 July 1992 – very early in the season for a fish of such calibre to be in fresh water.

South Uist's machair lochs have an intimate quality, and certainly in bygone days anglers often became well acquainted with particular leviathan fish, often hooked but rarely landed. In these shallow waters with extensive weed beds the odds always favoured double-figure sea trout, which were encountered time after time in the same location; thus on Lower Kildonan the angler was never more than 50 yards from the reeds, and this factor, challenging the skill of the angler to the utmost, helped to make it, in Hamish Stuart's estimation, the 'best angling loch in Scotland'. These great fish tended to be given names – for instance 'Big Willie' confounded anglers on many occasions on Lower Kildonan in 1927, although Chrystal was convinced that 'he' was misnamed, 'as it was undoubtedly a hen fish'!

APPENDIX I

Salmon netting in the nineteenth century

The historical importance of salmon to the North Highlands and Outer Hebrides, an area endowed with few easily harvested natural resources, can hardly be overstated. Salmon, with their integral ability to return to their river of origin, were always a dependable crop, available to be extracted on an annual basis either from the estuaries or the rivers themselves. The fish were easily caught with little capital expenditure; a coble, which is in essence just a substantial rowing boat, was the main requirement.

Prior to the nineteenth century virtually all the value in salmon was as a foodstuff; in Scotland's far north salmon had yet to develop as a sporting quarry. Anyone trawling through eighteenth- and nineteenth-century internal papers and correspondence from Highland estates will be struck by the frequency of references to salmon netting. This is hardly surprising given that for centuries netting was highly lucrative to those holding the rights, with the proceeds often representing a very significant percentage of estate income. Thus in 1808 21 per cent of Sutherland Estates' total revenues were derived from leasing out their netting rights on the Brora, Helmsdale and Naver (these rivers had long been their main netting locations). This fell to 8 per cent by 1815, as the Estates' interests diversified.

By the 1820s Sutherland Estates had taken the netting operations back in hand. At this time they went to very considerable lengths to ensure that natural predators did not jeopardize future runs of salmon. Thus in January 1828 Angus Leslie, the factor at Dornoch, informed his superior in London that eagles were 'killing fish on the spawning fords on the Naver' and that some had been 'shot'. The following month he reported that keepers had dispatched three kingfishers at Brora, two at Helmsdale and two (as well as an otter) at Borgie. In 1828 the Estate sold 610 kits of salmon and 1,652 kits of grilse from its northern netting enterprises, realizing a clear profit of £2,299; one of the expenses was whisky for the netsmen! This dropped to £1,806 from sales of 686 kits of salmon and 1,027 kits of grilse in 1829. (A kit was a small barrel containing 30 lb to 40 lb of parboiled salmon topped up with strong vinegar.)

Up to this point commercial exploitation of salmon in the North Highlands, either by netting (net and coble) or the use of cruives (fish traps within rivers), was although profitable still comparatively small-scale. However, within a few years, as innovations in methods of netting, preservation of fish and transport were adopted, it became a major industry. In the 1790s netsmen operating near the mouth of the Annan in Dumfries-shire had pioneered a new way of trapping fish in a net, which provoked a revolution in the Scottish salmon fishery. Amongst the sandbanks of the Solway Firth they experimented with a 'tide or floating net' whereby the 'operation of the tide secured the fish'. The network was fastened to stakes and soon the design was improved so that the entrance to the enclosure (the trap into which fish gravitate having swum along the netting leader) was closed by the action of the ebb tide. This was the origin of the stake net (employed on sandy coastlines) and its modification, the bag net (used on the same principles, but with anchors rather than stakes, on rocky coastlines). Unless damaged by storms, stake and bag nets (known as 'fixed engines') are, once set up, operational round the clock requiring no human effort aside from emptying the traps between tides.

In 1799 a stake net was employed at Seaside on the Tay estuary. It was immediately successful, taking 7,000 fish in one season. Although the legality of this method of fishing was fiercely resented and contested on a local level, it soon spread north. In 1815 stake nets adorned the coast by Golspie and by 1816 the 12 miles on the north side of the narrow Dornoch Firth, through which the Carron, Oykel, Cassley, Shin and Evelix discharge to the open sea, were similarly exploited. The owner of the south side of the Firth, MacKenzie of Ardross, successfully challenged the legitimacy of these nets in court.

The Dornoch Firth together with its long tidal extension the Kyle of Sutherland was the great netting prize in the far north. Forming as it did the boundary between Sutherland and Ross-shire, it lay at the start of the nineteenth century at the periphery of the sphere of influence of the Sutherland Estate. This all changed when in 1832 the Duke of Sutherland bought from MacKenzie of Ardross the estates of Mid Fearn and Easter Fearn (on the south side of the Firth), as well as the rights to salmon fishings belonging to him in the Shin and in the Dornoch Firth. The following year the Duke acquired the estate of Creich (on the north side of the Firth) from the Houston family. These strategic purchases gave the Duke both sides of the Firth at Creich. His factor commented: 'It gives his Grace command of the fishings. It is a good bargain and a capital arrangement. The Bonar and Balnagown fishings [further inland] are much reduced in value by it, for either in respect of the Fearns or of Creich we may sweep the whole course of the narrow part of the Firth.'

These investments paid immediate dividends for Sutherland Estates. Whilst their nets picked up 4,121 salmon and 15,584 grilse in the Dornoch Firth and the Kyle in 1833, the annual average increased to 4,387 salmon and 26,183 grilse in the following two years. The prolific and lucrative nature of this location for netting is underlined by the frequent and protracted litigation amongst the main protagonists. Thus in the early 1840s the Duke of Sutherland brought an action against Hugh Ross of Cromarty to prevent the latter from using stake nets within the Firth; this was finally resolved when the Lords of Council in Edinburgh ruled in the Duke's favour. In 1876 the Duke won a major case against Sir Charles Ross of Balnagown, following which the latter was required to remove 'obstructions' below Bonar Bridge. Incidentally the massive scale of netting operations both upstream and particularly downstream of Bonar Bridge is still clearly visible at low spring tides, when a myriad of walkways and netting channels is exposed.

Elsewhere in the north, from the 1840s onwards, the estates alternated between netting themselves and leasing out their rights to third parties. The latter included a handful or so of netting barons who saw the Highlands as an opportunity to add turnover to their operations elsewhere in Scotland, facilitated by the growth of the railway network (although many locations still required the use of ships to take the fish to market). These entrepreneurs introduced the use of ice as the main means of preserving fish until they reached market and the proliferation of icehouses (for storing ice right through the summer months) by northern estuaries dates from this period; ice had first been employed on the Tay in the late 1700s.

The netting barons were men like William Hogarth of Aberdeen and Alexander Speedie of Perth. Typically they would commit to seven-year leases of great stretches of coastline – for instance from the Caithness boundary to Cape Wrath and from Lochinver to Cape Wrath.

In 1845 Hogarth took a lease of all the estuary and coastal netting rights for the whole of the west and north coasts of Sutherland; the lease included no limits on either methods or the number of nets. Between 1845 and 1847 Hogarth's nets declared an average of 2,932 salmon and 19,000 grilse annually. However these catch levels were not sustained and by 1850 the rent was unpaid, following which the Duke of Sutherland took the rights back in hand. For several years there was minimal netting and stocks recovered. Netting intensified in the early 1870s, although the estuaries were left alone, and the Duke's catches were substantial.

In the meantime Hogarth had transferred his interests to the Isle of Lewis, leasing the netting rights through the 1850s. The Lewis fishings were then let in 1862 to Thomas Clerk and Daniel McAllister before James Stretton Young (son of Andrew Young of Invershin, author and manager of the Duke of Sutherland's netting interests in the Kyle of Sutherland) acquired the lease in 1867. Young was lessee of all the Lewis net fishings for some 40 years; he died in 1916 and his son Anderson Young continued the operations until 1925.

Back on the north mainland the leading player in the latter part of the nineteenth century was Alexander Speedie. In 1872 he leased the fishings from Strathy Point to the Caithness boundary for £350 per annum. He was briefly usurped between 1877 and 1880 by William Dunbar of Brawl Castle (on the Thurso), who paid £1,450 per annum for the coastal and estuary rights from Cape Wrath to the Caithness boundary; Dunbar had operated bag-nets to the west of Strathy since 1872. Speedie was reinstated on the north coast in 1880 although with greater restrictions, particularly with regard to the Naver, Borgie and Hope estuaries, and he continued until 1906, by which time the annual rent was £835.

On the west coast Speedie held leases (at £700 per annum) from 1878 to 1906 for the rights from Loch Roe (just north-west of Lochinver) to Cape Wrath. He was restricted to eight stations (bag-nets only) 'outside of estuaries as defined'. Between 1879 and 1898 his average annual declared catch for these stations (37 bags in total) was 1,370 salmon and 7,663 grilse. Speedie, in common with the other netting barons, did not abide by the rules. He consistently ignored the weekly close times (the weekend 'slap') from 6 p.m. on Saturdays to 6 a.m. on Mondays. In 1883 the Procurator Fiscal, supported by the Duke of Sutherland (Speedie's lessor) and the Duke of Westminster, took him to court and he was found guilty. However he continued as lessee (clearly Sutherland Estates did not wish to forgo the rental income) although within four years complaints about his cavalier attitude to the slap times resurfaced. Speedie's behaviour on the north coast was similarly brazen, as exemplified in the chapter on the Halladale.

As the century drew to a close Sutherland Estates came under increasing pressure from their sporting tenants to reign in the netsmen – not only to make them adhere to the regulations (to which they paid almost no regard) but also to reduce netting pressure generally. As early as 1871, Archibald Young (the Commissioner of Salmon Fisheries for Scotland) had given an indication of the way forward, when he wrote to the Duke's factor in Golspie: 'I am inclined to think that no fixed nets should be placed within a limit of half a mile from either side of the mouth of any of the Sutherland rivers, and that no net of any kind should be used within the rivers themselves, which should be kept entirely for angling which is yearly becoming more sought after and more valuable.'

In the end it was indeed economic reality that curtailed the previously almost unfettered activities of the netsmen. This is clear from the Estates' rental incomes. In 1885 the Tongue office of Sutherland Estates, which handled the latter's north coast interests, collected rentals of £15,332, including £755 from the nets and £4,995 from sporting (shooting and fishing) tenants. By 1900 total rentals handled by the same office were £18,019; whilst income from the nets had risen to £2,135, the income from sporting tenants of £11,844 represented the lion's share. For Sutherland Estates in their entirety half of rental income at this time was derived from sporting tenants. Even on the west coast river rents were on a par with Speedie's annual £700 payment. Minutes from the factors' meeting of 1906 noted that 'taking the fishings in house would enable angling to benefit' and from the 1907 season the west and north coast nets were brought back in hand. Shortly before the aborted 1914 dispersal sale the auctioneers Knight, Frank and Rutley advised the Duke of Sutherland's factor Colonel Morrison to close both the estuary and coastal nets as 'with His Grace's northern estates it is the fishing that is going to sell them'. The advice was not heeded but the point was made and relevant netting rights were often included in the subsequent sales of estates.

There had also been parallel developments from the 1890s whereby angling tenants, notably on the Helmsdale and the Naver, leased the netting rights which impacted most directly on their sport; such rights were either not exercised at all or carried out with much reduced effort. By 1900 the writing was even on the wall for the netting interests on the Kyle of Sutherland. That year angling rents (£1,500) from the four Kyle rivers equalled the netting rents and by 1907 a syndicate of local estate proprietors had leased almost all the local nets which they worked themselves with the aim of achieving more of a more equitable division in terms of exploitation between the nets and the rods. The economic balance of power had fundamentally altered and across most of the north netting interests were never able to regain their previously dominant position and influence.

Current angling access details

NORTH HIGHLANDS

FINDHORN

Forres Angling Association: Permits from Forres Tackle Shop, 97D High St, Forres, Moray IV36 1AA. Tel: 01309 672936. Website: www.forres-angling.net

Darnaway: Moray Estate Development Co. Tel: 01309 672213.

Logie & Relugas: Logie Estate Office. Tel: 01667 458900.

Glenferness: Estate Office. Tel: 01309 651202.

Lethen: Lethen Estate Office. Tel: 01667 452247.

Cawdor: Cawdor Estate Office. Tel: 01667 402402.

Tomatin area: Findhorn Fishing. Tel: 01808 511439. Website: www.findhorn-fishing.com

NAIRN

Nairn AA: Visitor permits from Pat Fraser, 41 High St, Nairn. Tel: 01667 453038. Website: www.nairnaa.org

Nairnside: Miss R. Rose, Nairnside House, Culloden Moor, Inverness IV2 5BT. Tel: 01463 794235.

NESS

River Oich

Aberchalder beat and part of Loch Oich: Miss Jean Ellice, Aberchalder Farm, Aberchalder Estate, Invergarry PH35 4HN. Tel: 01809 501287.

Glendoe beat (north bank): George Watson. Tel: 01320 366234.

South Bank, lower Oich: Grahams of Inverness. Tel: 01463 233178.

River Moriston

Glenmoriston Lodge Estate: Tel: 01320 351300.

Loch Ness

Boats available from Glenmoriston Lodge Estate (details above).

River Ness

Inverness AC water: Permits from Grahams of Inverness. Tel: 01463 233178.
Ness Side: Scott MacKenzie. Tel: 01463 231614.
Ness Castle: Davy Stewart. Tel: 01463 225123.
Laggan: Gordon Dawson. Tel: 01896 668904.

BEAULY

River Beauly

Beauly Angling Club (tidal water below Lovat Bridge): R. Morrison, Ironmongers, West End, Beauly. Tel: 01463 782213.
Lower river and upper river: Occasional lettings through Edward Mountain, Bidwells, Etive House, Beechwood Park, Inverness IV2 3VW. Tel: 01463 715585.

River Farrar

Culligran Estate: Frank Spencer-Nairn, Culligran Estate, Struy, Nr Beauly, Inverness-shire IV4 7JX. Tel: 01463 761285. Email: juliet@culligran.demon.co.uk

River Glass

Alison Fraser, Erchless Forest Cottage, Erchless Estate, Struy, By Beauly, IV4 7JO. Tel: 01463 761205. Email: riverglass@erchlessforest.fsnet.co.uk

CONON

River Conon

Dingwall & District AC (lower river and estuary): Sports & Model Shop, High St, Dingwall, Ross-shire IV15 9RY. Tel: 01349 862346.
Brahan beats: Occasional lets through Mr Willis-Fleming, Conon Fishings Co Ltd, c/o Savills, 12 Clerk St, Brechin, Angus DD9 6AE. Tel: 01356 628600.
Lower Fairburn: Fairburn Estate Office. Tel: 01997 433273.
Upper Conon (Loch Achonachie AC): Okain McLennan. Tel: 01381 620674.

River Blackwater

Middle beat: Eliza Leslie Melville. Tel: 01997 414242.
Upper beat (Loch Achonachie AC): Okain McLennan. Tel: 01381 620674.

ALNESS

Novar Estate Fishings: Novar Estate Office, Evanton, Ross-shire IV16 9XL. Tel: 01349 830208. Email: novarest@aol.com

Alness Angling Club: Visitor permits from J.B. Paterson, Ironmonger, 35 High St, Alness, Ross-shire IV17 0PT. Tel: 01349 882286.

CARRON

Gledfield:
Cornhill: } CKD Galbraith, Lynedoch House, Barossa Place, Perth PH1 5EP. Tel: 01738 451600.
Dounie:

Gruinards: Smith Milligan, 14 Golden Square, Aberdeen. Tel: 01224 626282.

Braelangwell: Mr D. Godman, Manor House, Compton Abdale, Glos GL54 4DR. Tel: 01242 890247.

Glencalvie: CKD Galbraith (details above)

OYKEL

Lower Oykel: No rods/tenancies available.

Upper Oykel: Oykel Bridge Hotel, By Lairg, Sutherland IV27 4HE. Tel: 01549 441218.

Assynt Estate: Inver Lodge Hotel, Lochinver, Sutherland IV27 4LU. Tel: 01571 844496. Assynt Estate Office, Lochinver, Sutherland IV27 4JY. Tel: 01571 844203.

CASSLEY

Rosehall: Donald Morrison, 10 Cassley Drive, Rosehall, Sutherland IV27 4BE. Tel: 01549 441371.

Glenrossal: Michael Hasson, Glenrossal, Rosehall, Sutherland IV27 4BG. Tel: 01549 441323. Email: info@glenrossalestate.com Website: www.glenrossal.uk.com

Duchally: Balnagown Estates, Kildary, Ross-shire IV18 0NU. Tel: 01862 843601.

SHIN

Lower river: Denton Clark & Co, 4 Vicars Lane, Chester CH1 1QU. Tel: 01244 409660. E-mail: e.clark@dentonclark.co.uk

Upper river: James Greenwood, Old Park, Park Lane, Maplehurst, West Sussex RH13 6LL. Tel: 01403 891706. Email: james@lairgestate.co.uk Website: www.lairgestate.co.uk

EVELIX

No ready access except to guests at Skibo Castle.

FLEET

Rogart Angling Club: Permits from Rogart Post Office. Tel: 01408 641200.

BRORA

Lower River, north bank and south bank: CKD Galbraith, Lynedoch House, Barossa Place, Perth PH1 5EP. Tel: 01738 451600. Email: sporting@ckdgalbraith.co.uk

Loch Brora: Permits/boats from Cunninghams Newsagents, Brora. Tel: 01408 621204.

Upper River (including lower Blackwater): Roxton Bailey Robinson. Tel: 01488 683222. (Note: very occasional vacancies – waiting list applies.)

HELMSDALE

Town Water: Permits available from Strathullie, Harbour House, Shore St, Helmsdale. Tel: 01431 821402. Also the Belgrave Arms Hotel. Tel: 01431 821242. Also River Helmsdale Fishing Tackle, Dunrobin Street. Tel: 01431 821372.

Helmsdale beats: Very occasional availability through Roxton Bailey Robinson. Tel: 01488 689701. (Please note that there is a long waiting list.)

BERRIEDALE

No ready access (membership of local angling club limited to those living within estate boundaries).

DUNBEATH

Access limited to local angling club.

WICK

Permits from Hugo Ross Fishing Tackle, 56 High St, Wick, Caithness KW1 4BP. Tel: 01955 604200. Email: hugo@hugoross.co.uk

THURSO

The Secretary, Thurso Fisheries, Thurso East, Thurso, Caithness KW14 8HP. Tel: 01847 893134.

FORSS

Little ready access. Lower river time-shared.

HALLADALE

The Estate Office, The Kennels, Forsinard, Sutherland KW13 6YT. Tel: 01641
 571271. E-mail: audrey@halladale51.freeserve.co.uk
 Website: www.strathhalladale.com

STRATHY

Vanya Hackel, Bowside Partnership, River Lodge, Near Petworth, West Sussex
 GU28 9AT. Tel: 01798 861317. Email: salmoninsutherland@dial.pipex.com
 Website: www.bowside.co.uk

NAVER

Syre (three beats): CKD Galbraith, Lynedoch House, Barossa Place, Perth PH1
 5EP. Tel: 01738 451600. Email: sporting@ckdgalbraith.co.uk
Altnaharra (two beats): Altnaharra Estate Office, West Sinclairhills Farm,
 Memsie, Fraserburgh, Aberdeenshire AB43 7AL. Tel: 01346 518001. Email:
 altnaharra@salmonfishing.freeserve.co.uk

BORGIE

Mather Jamie, Rectory Place, Loughborough, Leicestershire LE1 1UR. Tel: 01509
 233433. Email: info@riverborgie.co.uk Website: www.riverborgie.co.uk

HOPE

Hope Estate: Website: www.lochhope.co.uk Bookings for Loch Hope and
 River Hope through CKD Galbraith, Lynedoch House, Barossa Place, Perth
 PH1 5EP. Tel: 01738 451600. Email: sporting@ckdgalbraith.co.uk
Strathmore Estate (Strathmore River/Loch Hope): Mrs Heather Gow,
 Pitscandly, Forfar, Angus DD8 3NZ. Website: www.gowsport.co.uk

POLLA

Rispond Estate, Rispond, Durness, Sutherland IV27 4QE. Tel: 01971 511224.
 Email: rispond@aol.com

DIONARD

Gualin Estate: David Allingham. Tel: 01328 823233.
Lower river: Cape Wrath Hotel. Tel: 01971 511212.

GRUDIE

Cape Wrath Hotel, Durness, Sutherland. Tel: 01971 511212.

RHICONICH

Rhiconich Hotel. Tel: 01971 521224. Email: rhiconichhotel@aol.com Website: www.rhiconichhotel.co.uk

LAXFORD

River Laxford: Occasionally rods are available to tenants of Stack Lodge, let through CKD Galbraith, Lynedoch House, Barossa Place, Perth PH1 5EP. Tel: 01738 451600. Email: sporting@ckdgalbraith.co.uk

Loch Stack and Loch More: The Estate Office, Achfary, Sutherland IV27 4PQ. Tel: 01971 500221. Also through Scourie Hotel. Tel: 01971 502396.

INVER

Upper Inver and lower Inver: Available to guests of Inver Lodge Hotel, Lochinver, Sutherland IV27 4LU. Tel: 01571 844496. Website: www.inverlodge.com

KIRKAIG

Available to guests of Inver Lodge Hotel, Lochinver, Sutherland IV27 4LU. Tel: 01571 844496. Website: www.inverlodge.com

POLLY

Polly Estates Ltd, Inverpolly, Ullapool, Ross-shire IV26 2YB. Tel: 01854 622452. Email: davies@inverpolly.freeserve.co.uk

KANAIRD

Langwell Estate water: Day permits available from the Ullapool Bookshop, Quay St, Ullapool. Tel: 01854 612918.

ULLAPOOL

Rhidorroch Estate, Ullapool, Wester Ross IV26 2UB. Tel: 01854 612548. Email: rhidorroch@btinternet.com

BROOM

Inverbroom Estate: CKD Galbraith, Lynedoch House, Barossa Place, Perth PH1 5EP. Tel: 01738 451600. Email: sporting@ckdgalbraith.co.uk

DUNDONNELL

Day permits from Dundonnell Estate keeper. Tel: 01854 633335.

GRUINARD

Eilean Darach Estate: Elaine Hann, Eilean Darach Estate, Dundonnell, Wester Ross IV23 2QW. Tel: 01854 633203.

Gruinard Estate: No availability (waiting list).

LITTLE GRUINARD

Graham Wilson (Tel: 01445 731215), or write to Letterewe Estate, By Achnasheen, Ross-shire IV22 2HH.

EWE

River Ewe: Toby Metcalfe, Smiths Gore, 7 The Square, Fochabers, Moray IV32 7DG. Tel: 01343 823000. Email: toby.metcalfe@smithsgore.co.uk

Loch Maree: Loch Maree Hotel, Talladale, Achnasheen, Ross-shire IV22 2HL. Tel: 01445 760288.

Kinlochewe River: CKD Galbraith, Lynedoch House, Barossa Place, Perth. Tel: 01738 451600. Email: sporting@ckdgalbraith.co.uk

Coulin Estate: CKD Galbraith, Lynedoch House, Barossa Place, Perth. Tel: 01738 451600. Email: sporting@ckdgalbraith.co.uk

OUTER HEBRIDES

LEWIS

LAXAY

Mrs Marie Kershaw. Tel: 01606 891743.

CREED

Website: www.stornoway-angling-association.co.uk. Visitor day tickets available from Tourist Board, Cromwell St, Stornoway (01851 703088); Angus Campbell Filling Station, Cannery Road, Stornoway (01851 702127); Lochs Services, Cameron Terrace, Leurbost (01851 860288).

GRESS

Day tickets available from Gordon Diesel Services/Back Post Office, School Rd, Back. Tel: 01851 820200.

BLACKWATER

CKD Galbraith, Lynedoch House, Barossa Place, Perth PH1 5EP. Tel: 01738 451600. Email: sporting@ckdgalbraith.co.uk

GRIMERSTA

Simon Scott, Grimersta Lodge, Isle of Lewis HS2 9EJ. Tel: 01851 621358. Fax: 01851 621389. Email: grimersta@lineone.net Website: www.grimersta.com

MORSGAIL

Write to the Keeper's House, Morsgail Estate, Isle of Lewis HS2 9JH.

FHORSA

CKD Galbraith, Lynedoch House, Barossa Place, Perth PH1 5EP. Tel: 01738 451600.

HAMANAVAY

The Estate Manager/Head Keeper, 10 Ardroil, Uig, Isle of Lewis. Tel: 01851 672421.

HARRIS

AMHUINNSUIDHE

Amhuinnsuidhe Castle, Isle of Harris HS3 3AS. Tel: 01859 560200. Website: www.harriscastle.com

LAXDALE

Enquiries to Gordon Cumming, Borve Lodge Estates, Borve, Isle of Harris HS3 3HT. Tel: 01859 550202. Email: borvelodge@aol.com

OBBE

Weekly and daily permits available from the keeper. Tel: 01859 520466. Website:
   www.obbefishings.com

NORTH UIST

Estate Office, Lochmaddy, Isle of North Uist, HS6 5AA. Tel: 01876 500329. E-
   mail: Northuistestate@btinternet.com

SOUTH UIST

South Uist Estates Ltd, Estate Office, Askernish, South Uist HS8 5SY. Tel: 01878
   700301. Email: suistestates@ricsonline.org

BIBLIOGRAPHY

Adam, R.J. (ed.), *Papers on Sutherland Estate Management,* 1802–1816, Edinburgh: Constable, 2 vols, 1972.

Adams, Joseph, *Fifty Years Angling,* London: Hutchinson, 1938.

Balfour, Harold, *Folk, Fish and Fun,* Suffolk: Terence Dalton, 1978.

Braithwaite, Cecil, *Fishing Here and There,* London: Home Words Printing & Publishing, c. 1933.

Butler, Dr James, *River Ewe Fishery Management Plan 2002–2006,* Gairloch: Wester Ross Fisheries Trust, 2002.

Calderwood, William L., *The Salmon Rivers and Lochs of Scotland,* London: Edward Arnold, 1909 (revised edn 1921).

Campey, Lucille H., *After the Hector: The Pioneers of Nova Scotia and Cape Breton, 1773–1852,* Toronto: Natural Heritage, 2004.

Cavendish Bentinck, W.J.A.C.J., 6th Duke of Portland, *Fifty Years and More of Sport in Scotland,* London: Faber, 1933.

Chrystal, Major R.A., *Angling at Lochboisdale, South Uist,* London: Witherby, 1939.

Cook, Charles H. ('John Bickerdyke'), *Days in Thule with Rod, Gun & Camera,* London: 1894.

Cunningham, Peter, *River Broom Fishery Management Plan 2002–2006,* Gairloch: Wester Ross Fisheries Trust, 2003.

Davy, Humphrey, *Salmonia,* London: Murray, 1828.

Foster, Muriel, *Days on Sea, Loch & River: A Fishing Diary,* London: Michael Joseph, 1979.

Francis, Francis, *A Book on Angling,* London: Longmans, Green, 2nd edn 1867.

Franck, Richard, *Northern Memoirs,* Edinburgh: Constable, 2nd edn 1821.

Grimble, Augustus, *The Salmon Rivers of Scotland,* London: Kegan Paul, Trench, Trubner, 4 vols, 1899 (2nd edn, illustrated by Archibald Thorburn, 1902).

Hely-Hutchinson, Revd. George ('Sixty-One'), *Twenty Years' Reminiscences of the Lews,* London: H. Cox, 1871.

Henderson, Thomas, *The Findhorn: The River of Beauty,* Grant & Murray, 1932.

Iredale, David, *Dundonnell, Wester Ross,* privately published, Dundonnell, 1998.

Jones, David S. D., *A History of the Sporting Estates on the Island of Lewis,* vols

1–9, privately published by the author (Polraen, Teisbury Road, Fovant, Salisbury SP3 5JY), 2003–4.

Knowles, Derek, *Salmon on a Dry Fly*, London: H.F. & G. Witherby, 1987.

Lewis, Samuel, *Lewis's Topographical Dictionary of Scotland*, London: S. Lewis 2 vols, 1846.

MacIver of Scourie, Evander (ed. G. Henderson), *Memoirs of a Highland Gentleman*, Edinburgh: Constable, 1905.

MacKenzie, Kenneth C., *The River Ewe – Reminiscent Reflections*, Stuart R. MacKenzie (Cabarfeidh, Riverside, Poolewe, Ross-shire IV22 2LA), 2000.

McConnochie, Alexander, *Deer and Deer Forests of Scotland*, London: H.F. & G. Witherby, 1923.

McConnochie, Alexander, *The Rivers Oykell and Cassley in Sutherland and Ross*, London: H.F. & G. Witherby, 1924.

Mills, Derek, and Neil Graesser, *The Salmon Rivers of Scotland*, London: Cassell, 1981.

Radford, Alan et al., *The Economic Impact of Game and Coarse Angling in Scotland*, Glasgow Caledonian University, 2004.

Robinson, Stanley Scott, *The Law of Game, Salmon and Freshwater Fishing in Scotland*, Edinburgh: Butterworths, 1990.

Spencer, Sidney, *Salmon & Seatrout in Wild Places*, London: H.F. & G. Witherby, 1968.

St John, Charles, *Wild Sports and Natural History of the Highlands*, London: Murray, 1847.

Stoddart, Thomas, *The Angler's Companion to the Rivers and Lochs of Scotland*, Edinburgh: Blackwood, 1847.

Stuart, Hamish, *The Book of the Sea trout*, London: Secker, 1917.

Thompson, Francis, *Harris and Lewis*, Newton Abbot: David & Charles, 1968.

Thornton, Thomas, *A Sporting Tour through the Northern Part of England and a Great Part of the Highlands of Scotland*, London: Vernor & Hood, 1804.

Wigan, Michael, *The Scottish Highland Estate: Preserving an Environment*, Shrewsbury: Swan Hill, 1991.

Wigan, Michael, *Grimersta: The Story of a Great Fishery*, Grimersta Estate, Isle of Lewis, 2000.

Young, Andrew, *The Angler and Tourist's Guide to the Rivers, Lakes and Remarkable Places in the Northern Counties of Scotland*, Edinburgh: Adam and Charles Black, 1857.

INDEX

Drummond, Fred, 131
Drummond, Vice-Admiral, 208
Duchally, 60, 65
Dunbar, William, 114, 248
Dunbeath, River, 97–8
Dundonnell, River, 178–81
Dundonnell Estate, 178–9, 181
Dunmore, 7th Earl of, 227
Dunphie, Molly, 183
Dunphie, Colonel Peter, 183–4
Duntelchaig, Loch, 19
Dyke Water, 113

Easa Ghil, Loch an, 216
Easter Fearn Estate, 246
Eaval, River, 227, 230
Egerton, Sir John, 72
Eilean Darach Estate, 179, 181–3, 185
Einig, River, 53, 55, 58, 59
Elliot, Willie, 154–5
Elphinstone, Lord, 189
Eriboll, Loch, 138
Evelix, Loch, 75–6
Evelix, River, 75–6
Ewe, Loch, 189, 191–2, 195
Ewe, River, 189–96

Fada, Loch, 242
Fairburn, 36, 37, 39
Faoghail an Tuim, Loch, 214
Faoghail Charrasan, Loch, 213, 215
Faoghail Kirraval, Loch, 213
Farrar hydro-electric scheme, 31
Farrar, River, 28, 31, 33
Farrell, John, 111
Farrer, Mark, 142, 145
Fergusson, Marjorie, 141–5
ferox trout, 73, 164
Fhorsa, River, 220–3
Fiag, River, 67, 73
Field, The, 205, 229
Filmer-Sankey, William, 157, 160, 163
Fincastle, Loch, 231–3
Finlayson, Willie, 110
Fleet, Loch, 76, 77
Fleet, River, 76–8
Flett, Dr, 243
Finsbay, 236
Fionn, Loch, 186–7
Forsinain Burn, 113

Forsinard Estate
Forss, River, 110–13
Forss House Hotel, 111, 112
Fowler, Sir John, 174–5
Findhorn, River, 9–15
Forman-Hardy, Nick, 50
Forres Angling Association, 15
Foster, Giles, 30, 31
Fountain Forestry, 116, 120
Fowler, Peter, 50
Fradgley, E., 232
Franck, Richard, 28
Frithe, Abhainn na (River Free), 87

Garbet Beg, Loch, 148–50
Garbet Mor, Loch, 148–50
Garbh, Loch, 157
Gardner, Prof Michael, 236
Garry hydro-electric scheme, 22
Garry, Loch, 22, 23
Garry, River, 20–3
Garynahine, 207, 208, 210
Geireann, Loch, 237
Geireann Mill, 239
Geirsdale Burn, 232
Gibb, Colin, 185
Gillies' Loch, 156
Gilmour, William Ewing, 3, 60, 120,
    138, 141, 146
Glascleit, River, 224
Glasgow Caledonian University, 7
Glasha Burn, 49
Glass, River (Beauly tributary), 28, 31,
    33
Gleann na Muice, River, 181
Gledfield, 50, 52
Glencalvie, 47, 50
Glencanisp, 157
Glencassley, 60, 64
Glenferness, 10, 14
Glenrossal, 60, 64
Godman, Edith & Eva, 49, 51, 54
Godman family, 26
Gordon Cathcart, Lady, 241
Gordon-Cumming, Sir William, 10–11
Gordon of Cluny, Colonel John, 241
Gordonbush, 78, 80
Gorm Lochs, 60, 66
Gow, Heather, 137
Graesser, Neil, 43, 63, 66, 70, 222